The Chopra Center Cookbook

Nourishing Body and Soul

DEEPAK CHOPRA, M.D.

DAVID SIMON, M.D.

LEANNE BACKER

John Wiley & Sons, Inc.

Published by John Wiley & Sons, Inc., Hoboken, New Jersey
Published simultaneously in Canada

Design and production by Navta Associates, Inc.

For general information about our other products and services, please contact our Customer Care Department within the United States at (800) 762-2974, outside the United States at (317) 572-3993 or fax (317) 572-4002.

Wiley also publishes its books in a variety of electronic formats. Some content that appears in print may not be available in electronic books.

ISBN 0-471-26604-3

Printed in the United States of America

10 9 8 7 6 5 4 3 2 1

Contents

Preface

The most ancient and profound wisdom tradition of the world proclaims that a single undifferentiated reality—Spirit—differentiates itself into all forms and phenomena. Observer and observed, knower and known, seer and scenery are different expressions of the same underlying spirit. The science of Ayurveda takes this insight to a very deep level in which body, mind, and soul are understood as interwoven domains along the continuum of consciousness. These differentiated aspects of consciousness—which is in its essence pure existence, pure knowledge, and unbounded love—express themselves as our physical body of matter, our subtle body of energy and transformation, and our causal body of information and intelligence.

Wherever there is energy, there is information, intelligence, and transformation. Life evolves by regularly consuming and recreating itself. On our sun-drenched planet, the energy of our nearest star nurtures the lavish and extravagant growth of the ecosystem that supports the great chain of Being. Ultimately, we are all beings of light, the dust of stars circulating in the cosmos. Quantum physics tells us that at its essence all matter is trapped light. The same field of electromagnetic energy that creates thunder and lightning in the sky also generates the ideas that emanate from the synaptic networks of our brains. Human language, emotions, and thoughts are as much an expression of the pattern of swirling energy of the universe as a rock, a tree, or a human body. In other words, even our thoughts are photons of light originally trapped by the plants that grow from the earth. All life nourishes itself through this light.

Ayurveda holds that food is more than just protein, carbohydrate, and fat. It is concentrated intelligent energy of the universe. In fact, an ancient Vedic hymn boldly declares, "Food is Brahman," that is, "Food is Consciousness." When we nourish ourselves with food that is derived from the blissful marriage of Father Sun and Mother Earth, this food nurtures not only our bodies, but our minds and souls as well. The same intelligence that differentiates into seer and scenery, biological organisms and their environments, and messenger molecules and their receptors, differentiates into six types of taste receptors and the six codes of intelligence that are expressed as the flavors in food. No other biological science has this deep and profound understanding that our taste receptors are designed to access the intelligence of the universe so that we can nourish ourselves in body and soul.

Subconsciously, we recognize the relationship between food and spirit, because our language uses taste metaphors to denote emotions. We are all familiar with expressions such as sweet love, sour grapes, salt of the earth, pungent remarks, bitter resentment, and astringent humor. Ayurveda suggests that a little sweetness adds delight to life, whereas too much can be cloying. A touch of sour adds interest, but too much makes us grimace. A little salt provides endurance, but too much raises our blood pressure. Bitterness, pungency, and astringency add spice and complexity to life, but too much may cause us to feel irritable, resentful, and withdrawn. The flavors of life in the right proportion add richness to both our food and our experience.

All this might be interesting philosophy were it not for the fascinating recent scientific discoveries that the most healing foods are those that contain potent concentrations of plant chemicals that are responsible for their flavor and color. The six tastes present in food are clues to these healing phytochemicals (*phyto* is Greek for plant), which demonstrate that good food is good medicine. Although a popular myth suggests that food that is good for you cannot be pleasing to the senses, the fact is that healthy food was designed by nature over millions of years of evolutionary time to be pleasurable. With our modern emphasis on nutritionally empty, highly processed, and additive-rich foods, it is no wonder that we have epidemics of heart disease, cancer, and degenerative disorders. It is time for us to remember that nature provides us with the nutrients we need to create meals that are delicious and nutritious.

Over the years, thousands of people have come to the Chopra Center to heal themselves, to learn more about themselves, to improve their relationships, and to accelerate their spiritual evolution. Repeatedly they have told us that the meals they enjoy with us are among the most gratifying components of their experience. The food at the Chopra Center is designed to delight the senses, enliven vitality, and create joy for just being alive and having the opportunity to eat. As a result of the frequent requests of our guests we offer you the recipes of the Chopra Center for Well Being. We trust that you will experience for yourself how food can nurture not only your body, but also your soul.

Acknowledgments

This book was nurtured with the love and support of many people. Our deep appreciation goes to our dedicated Chopra Center family, including Vicki Abrams, Brent Becvar, Fran Benedict, Corrine Champigny, Janice Crawford, Nancy Ede, Jenny Ephrom, Ana Paula Fernandez, Roger Gabriel, Kristin Hutchins, Gary John, Sara Kelly, Joe Lancaster, Carolyn Rangel, Felicia Rangel, Jill Romnes, Geeta Singh, Dennis Sugioka, Maureen Sutton, and Lizzie Upitis, along with the many beloved guests and friends that have passed through our doors and shared their lives with us. Our special thanks goes to Chefs Teresa Robles, Nicolas Ruiz, and Gene Gales for their dedication to the fine culinary craft of recipe testing.

To the members of our personal families, Rita, Mallika, Sumant, Tara, Gotham, Candice, Pam, Max, Sara, Isabel, Travis, Kelley, Tom, Bea, Rick, David, and Karen, our love and appreciation flow to you for nourishing our bodies, minds, and souls.

We are sincerely grateful to our representatives at Trident Media, Robert Gottlieb and Scott Miller, for their incomparable attention to detail, and to our magnificent editorial and marketing team at John Wiley & Sons, Tom Miller, Kimberly Monroe, Kitt Allan, and Laura Cusack, for ensuring that this work accomplishes our goal of deeply nourishing the reader's body, mind, and soul.

Finally, we offer our gratitude to Annapurna, the Divine Mother, who inspires the nurturing, creative being within us all.

Deepak, David, and Leanne
The Chopra Center at La Costa Resort and Spa
Carlsbad, California

Introduction

We owe much to the fruitful meditation of
our sages, but a sane view of life is, after all,
elaborated mainly in the kitchen.

JOSEPH CONRAD

You become what you eat. This basic principle proclaims
the straightforward yet profound fact that almost every
molecule that currently resides in your body was derived from
food you put into your mouth. From the chemical-rich blood
that flows through your circulatory system to the jellylike mass
of neurons that composes your brain to the rigid calcium-
reinforced girders that make up your skeleton, your body is, in
essence, food woven around your DNA.

Did you have a piece of cantaloupe for breakfast this morning? Within hours, carbohydrate molecules of the melon will be
in your liver, waiting to supply you with energy when it is time

to shop for more fruit. The vitamin C in your cantaloupe will be a component of your antioxidant shield, protecting your lungs from carcinogens you inhale on the way to the market. Some of the beta-carotene contained in your breakfast fruit will be converted into vitamin A, shoring up the pigment cells in your retina so you can distinguish a ripe melon from one that has passed its prime.

At its most fundamental level, food is energy and information. The energy component of food is quantified by the number of calories it carries. The informational component of food is characterized by its composition of vital nutrients. The proportion of protein, carbohydrates and fats, vitamins and minerals, and the specific natural chemicals that a food source provides all describe the informational aspect of food. Digestion is the process of metabolizing the energy and information of food into the energy and information of your body. When your diet provides the right constituents and your body is capable of extracting the energy and information you need, you create a healthy, vital body.

Healthy Nutrition Should Be Easy

Next to breathing, eating is the most natural process in the world, and we believe that it should be easy and enjoyable to follow a healthy diet. Nevertheless, we see people every day who are confused about what to eat. Why has nutrition become so complicated? Partly it is because of the amazing choices that are currently available. Never before have so many people had so many food options. We enjoy choosing from dozens of different kinds of pasta, cereals, grains, and nuts. We appreciate the opportunity to sample fruits and vegetables from distant regions of the country and exotic places around the world. We welcome the access to unprecedented varieties of milk and dairy products, as well as other protein sources. And yet, with these expanded choices arise greater uncertainty. Is there a difference between frozen, canned, and fresh vegetables? Are whole grain products really better for you than refined and enriched pastas and breads? Should you be drinking nonfat, 2 percent, or whole milk? Are organic foods worth the additional cost? These are some of the questions we hear each day at the Chopra Center that reflect the sometimes overwhelming options available today.

Our access to diverse sources of information has also generated confusion. On a regular basis, new experts in nutrition offer their convincing arguments for an innovative dietary plan. One exhorts you to eat more protein and fewer carbohydrates, while another proclaims the opposite is best. One tells you to eat more animal products, another encourages you to become vegan. Recently an author has suggested that your blood type has a role to play in your nutritional choices. For every diet or nutritional plan that is aggressively promoted you can find a contradictory approach that is as vigorously advocated. It is not surprising that people are confused.

Reestablish the Mind-Body Connection

We believe that part of the problem underlying this confusion is a loss of connection between mind and body. People are so busy thinking about what to eat that they have lost the ability to hear what their body is asking for. This breakdown in communication probably began in childhood when orders to "finish everything on your plate" were obeyed even when you may not have been hungry. Most of us were taught to eat when it was time to eat and eat as much as was on our plate. Considering how many children were encouraged to disregard the signals of their body, it does not surprise us that overeating and obesity are at epidemic levels.

One consequence of the disconnection between body and mind is that many people view their appetites as the enemy. They fear that if left unchecked their hunger for food will compel them to eat vast quantities. This shows the extent to which we've lost mind-body integration, for a strong appetite is one of the most important signs of good health. When consciously listened to, it can tell you when and what to eat in order for you to remain vital and free from illness.

People have as much emotional attachment to their diet as they do to their politics and religion. We define ourselves by what we eat, and this is not entirely inappropriate, for our body is made of food. We just don't believe that healthy nutrition has to be so complicated. If you are straining to follow a diet that is supposed to be good for you, the stress probably outweighs the benefits. Eating is biological alchemy that transforms vegetables and grains into muscles and bones. Celebrate the Magic!

Eat food that is good for you and you will enliven renewal in body and mind. The question is, what food is good for you? To answer this question we draw upon two primary sources: Ayurveda and modern nutritional science. Ayurveda (pronounced *ah-your-vay-duh*), the most ancient healing system on earth, dates back to India five thousand years ago. The word Ayurveda has two Sanskrit roots: *ayus,* meaning life, and *vid,* meaning wisdom. Ayurveda, then, is a science of life wisdom, which can guide us in making the healthiest possible choices.

We also draw upon the latest information from modern science, which illustrates that healthy food can nurture and renew us in body and soul. *The Chopra Center Cookbook* is about teaching you how to eat in healthy ways so that both your need for nutrition and your need for enjoyment are satisfied. The recipes are simple and delicious. They are nutritionally balanced and consistent with both modern nutritional science and the most ancient healing system on the planet. We have seen the benefits of this program both personally and professionally. Enjoy and share the information contained within these pages. Together we can live long and healthy lives.

The Wisdom of Food

In cooking, as in all arts, simplicity is
the sign of perfection.

Curnonsky

This book is a practical guide to help you prepare delicious, healthy meals that nourish your body and soul. The principles of our program have their roots in both modern nutritional science and the world's most ancient health system, *Ayurveda*. Ayurveda is a Sanskrit word that can be translated as the "wisdom of life," or "the science of longevity." It offers a holistic approach to living that is based upon a fundamental principle: your choices are metabolized into your body.

Make healthy choices and you will have a healthy body. To the extent that you can choose, elect the option that is most likely to nourish you, and avoid choices that are toxic or depleting. One of the most direct choices you make on a daily basis is what to put into your mouth. We encourage you to choose to eat healthy, delicious foods so you can create a healthy, vital body. Pay attention to these seven simple precepts and your diet will help you create greater mental and physical well-being.

1. Eat a wide variety of foods during the day.
2. Listen to your body's signals of hunger and satiety.
3. Use food to fill the emptiness in your stomach, not your heart.
4. If the meal isn't delicious, it isn't nourishing you.
5. Favor foods that are natural and vital.
6. Use herbs and spices liberally as both flavor and health enhancers.
7. Eat with awareness.

Let's explore each point in more detail.

1. *Eat a wide variety of foods during the day.* Most anthropologists date the origin of modern human beings to about 150,000 to 200,000 years ago. Up until about 10,000 years ago, we spent most of our days hunting and gathering food. During the course of a day, we sampled dozens if not hundreds of food sources. In addition to any animal protein we could snare, we ate a diverse range of roots, leaves, fruits, nuts, berries, beans, mushrooms, and seeds. Some primates in the wild today have been observed to nibble on more than two hundred different kinds of plants each day.

The average Western diet is much more limited in variety, and as a result we miss out on the extensive natural pharmacy that is available. Unfortunately, burgers, fries, and a diet Coke do not allow us to take advantage of the nourishing properties that a delicious, widely varied diet offers. Each day, nutritional scientists are discovering new health-promoting chemicals that are available to us through food. Think variety when it comes to your diet, and be sure to include the six tastes described later in this chapter.

2. *Listen to your body's signals of hunger and satiety.* Jonathan Swift once said, "My stomach serves me instead of a clock." Your appetite is your ally. Listen to it. You probably don't go to the gas station when your fuel tank is half full. Don't sit down at the meal table if your stomach is half full. Consider your appetite as a fuel gauge from 0 (completely empty) to 10 (stuffed). Do not eat until you are at a level 2 (very hungry) or 3 (definitely hungry). Eat until you reach a level 7 (satisfied). Do not go beyond this to a level 8 (rather full), 9 (uncomfortably full), or 10 (stuffed). Once you have reached your satisfaction level of 7, wait until you are back down to a level 2 or 3 before you eat again.

Appetite	10	stuffed
Gauge	9	uncomfortably full
Eat at level 2	8	rather full
or 3. Stop at	7	satisfied
level 7.	6	almost satisfied
	5	no hunger awareness
	4	could eat
	3	definitely hungry
	2	very hungry
	1	hunger pains
	0	completely empty

3. *Use food to fill the emptiness in your stomach, not your heart.* We learn to associate comfort with food at an early age. When you were upset as an infant, the chances are your mother offered you a bottle or her breast to calm you. As adults we sometimes seek food for its soothing, rather than nutritional, properties. If you do this on a regular basis, you are almost certainly not listening to your appetite. This often results in poor digestion, disturbed sleep, and weight gain. Use food to feed your body. Develop conscious communication skills to fill your heart.

4. *If the meal isn't delicious, it isn't nourishing you.* Enjoy your meals. Delicious food is nourishing to your body, mind, and

soul. If you are struggling with a diet that you believe is good for you, but do not find at all appetizing, it will not ultimately be nourishing and you will not be able to stay with it for long. In this book we will convince you that you do not have to sacrifice delicious meals for good health.

5. *Favor foods that are natural and vital.* According to most traditional health systems, food carries a vital force in addition to carbohydrates, proteins, fats, fiber, vitamins, and minerals. This life force is known as *prana* in Ayurveda and *chi* in Traditional Chinese medicine. Freshly picked green beans from your garden are abundant in prana; beans that have been sitting in your pantry for six months are lacking in prana. To the extent possible, favor fruits and vegetables that are locally grown, freshly harvested, and prepared as soon as possible after picking. Not only are they more delicious, but you are sending your body the message that it is receiving the highest quality health-promoting nutrients.

The longer that a food has been sitting on a shelf since its harvesting, the more likely it is to be affected by oxidation. Free radicals initiate the decomposition of a fruit or vegetable immediately after it is disconnected from its source. A sliced apple or banana that has been sitting around for an hour begins turning brown because free radical molecules floating in the air deplete it of its natural antioxidants. Rancid food is this process taken to the extreme. We therefore encourage you to favor fresh foods as much as possible and to the extent that is practical reduce your intake of frozen foods, leftovers, highly processed, microwaved, and canned foods.

Reduce	Favor
Frozen	Recently harvested, when possible
Leftover	Freshly prepared
Highly processed	All natural ingredients
Microwavable	Conventionally prepared
Canned	Fresh, when possible

As more information becomes available on the harmful effects of pesticides on our personal and environmental health, we encourage you to favor organic fruits, vegetables, and dairy products as much as you can. Reduce your consumption of processed and highly refined foods. Favor fresh as opposed to canned or frozen, recognizing that there are some foods, such as garbanzo beans, tomato sauce, diced tomatoes, salsas, and condiments that are just too difficult to regularly prepare fresh. Whenever you can, avoid leftovers or reheated foods. We are not encouraging you to become overly zealous about this point. Simply have the intention to eat foods that are as freshly prepared as possible.

6. *Use herbs and spices liberally as both flavor and health enhancers.* We encourage you to take advantage of nature's edible gifts to make your meals delicious and nutritious. Become familiar with the culinary and health-promoting effects of herbs and spices and use them generously. Even the simplest quickly prepared meal can be transformed into a culinary delight through the appropriate use of seasonings. We will share with you what we consider the essential ingredients to create the nutritional alchemy that will bring pleasure to your senses and well-being to your body.

7. *Eat with awareness.* A principle of Ayurveda is: How you eat is as important as what you eat. If you gobble down your meal while driving or watching television, it will not be as nourishing or life supporting as when you eat with awareness. Savor your food through all five senses. Try to minimize the chaos in your environment while you are eating. Even if you only have fifteen minutes for lunch, hold the phone calls and allow yourself to appreciate the miracle of food.

Occasionally eat a meal alone and notice the sounds, sensations, sights, tastes, and smells that are available to you. If you are following the previous principles, your meal will not only be sumptuous to the taste, but will also look and smell delicious. A healthy meal nourishes all the senses, and when you pay attention to all five senses, your food will be more nourishing.

The Six Tastes

A simple and practical approach to ensuring healthy nutritional variety is to pay attention to the tastes of your food. According to Ayurveda, everything edible can be classified according to one or more of six basic tastes: sweet, sour, salty, pungent, bitter, and astringent. If you sample foods that correspond to each of these tastes throughout the day, your meals will provide a wide assortment of health-promoting nutrients. Let's look at these six tastes one by one.

Sweet. Sweet is the taste of carbohydrates, proteins, and fats. Foods that carry the sweet taste increase your body bulk. Breads, grains, nuts, pasta, most fruits, starchy vegetables, dairy, oils, and all animal products are considered sweet. Sweet foods supply the majority of what we consume in a day.

In every category of taste, there are foods that are highly nutritious and others that should be eaten more sparingly. Favor fresh fruits and vegetables, whole grains, cereals, breads, and nuts. In addition to supplying your energy needs, they are good sources of fiber. If you are not ready to go vegetarian, reduce your intake of red meats, favoring cold-water fish and egg whites. Minimize your intake of highly refined sugar and wheat products. Favor low-fat dairy, polyunsaturated and monounsaturated oils while minimizing cholesterol-rich products and foods containing partially hydrogenated oils.

Sour. Any food that is mildly acidic is experienced as sour. Citric acid, lactic acid, ascorbic acid, and butyric acid are just a few of the acidic chemicals that contribute to the sour taste of foods. As with the sweet taste, there are sour foods that are more nutritious than others.

Favor oranges, grapefruits, strawberries, blueberries, raspberries, and tomatoes while reducing your intake of pickled foods, green olives, alcohol, and vinegar. Small helpings of low-fat yogurt and buttermilk can aid in digestion. Although aged sour cheeses can be delicious, use them judiciously, as they are usually high in cholesterol and difficult to digest.

Salty. Salt is the flavor of ion-producing minerals on the tongue. The principal salt of our diet is sodium chloride, which comes from mines or naturally salty bodies of water. The salty taste is also carried in soy sauce and many other sauces, seaweed, fish, and salted meats. In the right dose, salt adds flavor and stimulates digestion. Too much salt can contribute to high blood pressure and fluid retention.

Pungent. We often use the term "hot" to describe the pungent flavor. The spiciness of pepper, ginger, and other pungent sources comes from essential oils that interact with chemical receptors on the tongue. Most pungent foods contain natural antioxidants and infection-fighting chemicals. Due in part to their antispoiling properties, pungent spices have been highly prized for millennia. A shortcut to the land of spices was a major incentive for the fifteenth-century journey of Columbus. Pungent flavors stimulate digestion and help mobilize stagnant secretions. Recent studies have suggested components of garlic and onions, also pungent foods, may help lower cholesterol levels and blood pressure.

Commonly available pungent foods include: chili peppers, cayenne, black pepper, fresh and dry ginger, horseradish, onions, garlic, leeks, mustard, cloves, cinnamon, peppermint, thyme, cumin, cardamom, basil, oregano, and rosemary. Adding spices and herbs to your life will serve both your palate and your health.

Bitter. Bitter is the taste of most green and yellow vegetables. Some green leafy vegetables such as endive and kale are particularly bitter. The bitterness is due to natural plant chemicals known as phytochemicals, which have detoxifying, disease-preventing, and healing properties that improve our chances for long, healthy lives. Broccoli and cauliflower, for example, are rich in the phytochemicals known as isothiocyanates, which have been shown to help fight cancer and heart disease. Asparagus, green peppers, and cabbage are rich in flavonoids, which help resist genetic injury, fight infections, and may even reduce your risk for memory loss. The bottom line: Eat your vegetables—they are good for you.

Astringent. The last of the six tastes is more of an effect than any actual flavor. Astringent foods have a drying, compacting, and puckering influence on your body. Beans, legumes, and peas are considered to fall within the astringent category, and provide excellent sources of vegetable protein, complex carbohydrates, and fiber to your diet. Several fruits are astringent, such as cranberries, pomegranates, persimmons, and tart apples. Green tea is also astringent and has been found to be a rich source of natural cancer-preventing chemicals. Astringent foods are an essential component of any diet that promotes renewal.

Weight Loss and Wellness

Many people struggling to shed unwanted pounds seek quick and effortless solutions, often bouncing from one weight loss diet to another. Unfortunately, quick fix diets seldom produce lasting benefits and may not be nutritionally balanced. At the Chopra Center for Well Being, we believe that attaining and maintaining an ideal weight is most easily achieved by following a consciousness-based approach. The principles outlined earlier, combined with a regular fitness program, will enable you to lose about one pound per week until you reach your optimal weight.

Honoring your appetite and eating with awareness will reawaken a healthy connection between your mind and body. When listened to, your body will tell you when it is hungry and when it is satisfied. Pay attention to the messages it is sending— it is trying to tell you what it needs to be healthy and fit. Ensure that all six tastes are available at every meal and you will satisfy the cravings that can sabotage your efforts to lose weight.

Please avoid crash diets. Although you may see quick results, study after study has demonstrated that the benefits cannot be sustained. Start a nutritional and lifestyle program today that will serve you throughout your entire life. Do not try to lose weight through diet alone. Exercise your body to enhance your cardiovascular system and convert fat into muscle. You will feel better about your body and about yourself. We encourage you to shift your goal from achieving a specific number on your bathroom scale to attaining an optimal level of physical and emotional well-being. The Chopra Center 30-Day Nutritional Plan will support you in achieving this goal.

Wine and Well-Being:
A Word on Alcohol

The fermentation of fruits and grains into alcoholic beverages dates to antiquity. Egyptian references to an intoxicating beverage derived from fruits stored in warm places can be identified over four thousand years ago. Around 1500 B.C., Middle Easterners created the first malt beverage from fermented grains. Wine, beer, and distilled alcoholic drinks have long played a role in cultures around the world, offering the potential for both pleasure and suffering. Although overindulgence in alcohol-containing beverages can contribute to emotional and physical distress, an occasional offering to Dionysus, the god of grapes and ecstasy, can be part of a healthy lifestyle.

Studies have shown that there are natural health-promoting chemicals in wine that may have a protective effect against heart disease and cancer. These natural disease-fighting substances, which have been shown to have potent antioxidant properties, go by such names as polyphenols, flavonoids, and resveratrol. These compounds are most concentrated in the skins of grapes. Because the production of red (but not white) wine involves prolonged contact of the juice with the grape skins, red wine has the highest concentration of these health-enhancing chemicals.

If you are so inclined, enjoy an occasional glass of wine as part of a delicious meal in the company of friends and loved ones. From a taste perspective, wine contains predominantly sour and astringent flavors, with traces of bitter and sweet; therefore, it can complement and contribute to a balanced meal. This is not the case for distilled alcohol.

With over 40 percent of North Americans affected by a family member with alcoholism, it is important to remember that alcohol has potentially adverse effects on almost every system and cell in the body and can contribute to serious illnesses affecting the nervous system, liver, and digestive tract. It is also a source of essentially empty calories with each gram of alcohol contributing about 7 calories—almost as much as a gram of fat, which has 9. A pint of beer or eight ounces of wine carry about 200 calories, while an ounce of distilled liquor has about 80 calories; therefore, alcohol is not a useful component of a weight-loss program. Our bottom line is to consider an occasional glass of wine as another source of flavors and phytochemicals that can be part of a healthy nutritional program.

The Art of Cooking,
The Art of Eating

One cannot think well, love well, sleep well,
if one has not dined well.

VIRGINIA WOOLF

The true cook is the perfect blend, the only perfect
blend of artist and philosopher. He knows his worth:
he holds in his palm the happiness of mankind.

NORMAN DOUGLAS

Nutritious food is a celebration of life, capable of enlivening your vitality and engaging all your senses. Unfortunately, because of the hectic pace of modern life, eating is more often an exercise in refueling than a celebration. Like many, you may prepare your typical dinner by microwaving a pre-made or frozen meal, heating up a can of soup, or stopping off for fast food on the way home from work. Your dining time may be spent in front of the television, catching up on your mail, or in a heated discussion with your teenage children. It is no surprise that over one-third of adults are regularly troubled by indigestion and heartburn and over half of the North American population is overweight.

The environment in which you eat can be an important component of the nourishment you receive from your meal. We encourage you to consider that the sounds, sights, sensations, and smells you ingest while eating are as important as the flavors and nutrients you put in your mouth. If you are watching the evening news while eating dinner, you are consuming those turbulent sounds and images along with your salad. If you are arguing with your family, you are metabolizing anger and frustration together with your pasta. When you fall into habits that don't support the celebration of life, you lose the opportunity to enhance your well-being and enliven renewal.

Ask yourself, "Am I being nourished by all my senses when I sit down to eat?" If you are eating while watching television, on the run, in your car, or in front of your computer, the chances are you can improve your sensory nourishment. Make a commitment to get back in touch with the delights of dining, and you will see benefits in your health, your vitality, and your relationships.

Preparing and eating delicious food can be an art form. It provides a daily opportunity to express your creativity. Have the intention to be more conscious as you plan your meals, shop for ingredients, cook your dishes, and finally enjoy the delicious product of your efforts. Your body, mind, and soul will relish the experience.

Create a Nurturing Environment

Your kitchen and dining area are great places to create living space that reflects your personal tastes, integrates the healing energy of nature, and brings beauty and richness into your life. Pay attention to colors, sounds, and textures that enliven your senses. Consider eating in your formal dining room on a regular basis, rather than saving it only for those rare holiday dinners. Use your special dishes occasionally for a family meal, savoring the sumptuousness of food served on beautiful plates. Light candles and play beautiful music during your meals. Make a pact with your family to engage only in lighthearted conversations while eating, saving the heavy discussions for later.

Even when you are eating alone, make your dining experience special. You can be your own delightful dining companion.

Become an artist in the kitchen. Begin by renewing your relationship with Mother Earth. Take a walk outside and connect with the energy around you. Appreciate the beauty of the plants, flowers, land, and natural bodies of water that compose your environment. The energy of the earth becomes the energy of your body through your intake of fresh fruits, vegetables, and whole grains. Favor foods that are in season, and to the extent possible, locally grown.

Artists thrive on inspiration. Develop a collection of inspiring cookbooks. Arrange your kitchen to be beautiful, alive, and inviting. Plant an herb garden in your home or apartment—you can create an amazing botanical bounty in pots. Take a walk through your local food store and pay attention to the vibrant colors, fragrances, and textures of the fruits and vegetables available to you. Appreciate the luscious red peppers, yellow squashes, and white mushrooms. Savor the aroma of ripe strawberries and fresh asparagus. Enjoy the cobbled texture of corn on the cob, the smoothness of tomatoes, the velvety softness of peaches. Listen to the sounds of the people moving about you. Feel their energy and excitement.

If you feel intimidated by the food market because you have not previously considered yourself an inspired cook or chef, try this simple experiment: Go into your grocery store and select one item from the produce department. We suggest you begin with broccoli, cauliflower, or zucchini. During the week, try cooking your chosen vegetable in every conceivable way. Sauté it, steam it, blanch it, marinate it for a salad, make it into a soup or casserole, cut it into bite-size pieces to eat with a dip. Don't worry if a given attempt isn't very successful. Have fun experimenting and enjoy the process. In a very short time, you will begin to build your confidence and your ability to cook creatively. Envision yourself as a culinary artist. Tap into your creative ability to produce beautiful and delicious food.

Involve your family. Children have the wonderful ability to make a routine task fun. The kitchen may end up a mess, but the time spent together will be well worth it. Be passionate about food and encourage your family to share your enthusiasm. Celebrate the planning process, the cooking process, and the eating experience. The food you eat carries the wisdom of the earth, the intelligence of the farmer, and the love of the cook. Every nurturing meal is a celebration of the seasons, cycles, and rhythms of nature. Delicious, lovingly prepared food renews, revitalizes, and nurtures your body, your mind, and your spirit.

The Basics of
Nourishment

I like a cook who smiles out loud
when he tastes his own work.
Let God worry about your modesty,
I want to see your enthusiasm.

ROBERT FARRAR CAPON

Every delicious meal is created from wholesome ingredients. When your pantry is stocked with high-quality staples, you have the foundation for delectable, nutritious meals. The longer something has been sitting on your shelf, the less likely it is to contribute to an appetizing and healthy meal. Begin the process of cooking and eating with awareness by detoxifying your kitchen. Clean out those supplies you will never use: rid your pantry of old cake mixes, ancient spices, dented cans, stale grains, and anything else that may be past its prime. Make the commitment to bring only the purest, most natural, and most wholesome foods into your home. Stock your pantry with quality ingredients to ensure that your meals are delicious and provide optimal nourishment for your body. Your body is made from the food you eat. Purchase and consume the highest-quality food to create the highest-quality body.

Pantry List

The following items can be found in natural food stores and most regular grocery stores. Mainstream food markets are beginning to carry more natural and organic foods. As increasing numbers of people purchase natural and organic items, the market for these products will grow and they will become more widely available. If you live in an area where a natural food store is not available, encourage your local grocery store manager to stock food products that are healthy and organic. Give the manager a list of a few items that you will buy, and then buy them as they become available.

Stock up on essential items for the pantry, but also plan on purchasing food on a regular basis to have the freshest possible foods on hand. If you live in an area where a particular food staple is not readily accessible, you'll need to plan ahead. Try not to keep food items too long. The Ayurvedic approach to health values freshness and encourages limiting canned, packaged, or frozen foods. If you are eating meat, poultry, or fish, use fresh, not frozen products whenever possible. Remember—fresh is best!

Herbs and Spices

Purchase your spices in small quantities. Buy what you will use. If available, buy spices from the bulk bin, which are usually less expensive. Check with your source to ensure that they are as fresh as possible.

HERBS AND SPICES TO KEEP ON HAND

Indian Spices	Herbs	Sweet Spices	Odds and Ends
asafetida (Hing)*	basil	allspice	black pepper
mustard seeds	thyme	nutmeg	sea salt
cardamom seeds	oregano	cinnamon	Chinese five spice
coriander	Italian herb mix	cloves	chili powder
cumin	sage	fennel seeds	red chili flakes
turmeric	tarragon	garam masala*	ginger
fenugreek seeds			curry powder

*Found in health food stores, Indian, Asian, and Middle-Eastern markets (check the Internet for sources if you have none of these where you live).

Grains, Nuts, and Seeds

Buy organic whole grains, nuts, and seeds whenever possible in quantities of one or two pounds at a time, and favor raw nuts and seeds. Because of their high oil content, nuts and seeds can spoil easily. When possible, buy them from the bulk bin and check for freshness. If you don't use them up right away, store nuts and seeds in recycled glass jars with tight-fitting lids or in plastic resealable bags in the refrigerator. Store grains in recycled glass jars with tight-fitting lids as well. Label all jars and bags and include any cooking instructions printed on the packaging.

Maintain a stock of the following grains, nuts, and seeds:

> rolled oats
> basmati rice
> quinoa
> millet
> multigrain cereal

dried pasta—spaghetti, penne, lasagna

couscous—white for pilaf and whole wheat for
breakfast cereal

pearl barley

whole wheat flour

whole wheat pastry flour

flax seeds

sesame seeds

sunflower seeds

pine nuts

walnuts

pecans

almonds, whole and sliced

Beans and Other Legumes

Buy beans and legumes in quantities of one or two pounds at a
time. Also keep on hand some canned or jarred cooked beans
for speedy meal preparation. You will find fresh dried beans and
lentils in bulk bins or packaged in plastic bags on the grocery
shelf. You may be able to find organic beans, both dried and
canned, in health food stores. Store the beans and legumes in
recycled glass jars with tight-fitting lids. Label them and include
any cooking instructions printed on the packaging. We consider the following to be staple beans and legumes:

red lentils

brown lentils

mung beans

garbanzos

split peas—green and yellow

white beans—Great Northern or navy

black beans

pinto beans

Condiments and Baking Supplies

Look for condiments that have pure ingredients. There is a vast variety of curry sauces, pasta sauces, salsas, salad dressings, and marinades available. Favor items with vinegar or lemon juice, which are natural preservatives. Many salsas, sauces, and salad dressings can be made from scratch, but it is convenient to have quality prepared condiments available at home when you need them.

Keep on hand small quantities of basic baking supplies. Packages of flour, baking powder, and thickeners often end up sitting on shelves for years. Buy in quantities that you will use over weeks or months to ensure the highest-quality breads and baked goods.

Keep these basic condiments and pantry items on hand:

> maple syrup
> Bragg Liquid Aminos (A nonfermented soy sauce found in health food stores. Use like soy sauce.)
> tamari soy sauce
> balsamic vinegar
> rice vinegar
> apple cider vinegar
> extra virgin olive oil
> sesame oil
> ghee, homemade or purchased (see page 38)
> vegetable oil spray for oiling pans
> Dijon mustard
> salsa
> vinaigrette salad dressing
> lemon juice (fresh-squeezed)
> apple juice
> raw organic honey
> kombu seaweed

tomato paste

coconut milk, low-fat

vanilla and plain soymilk or rice milk, low-fat

silken tofu, low-fat, firm or extra firm

We recommend the following basic baking supplies:

turbinado sugar

raw sugar

golden raisins

dried cranberries

currants

baking powder

baking soda

canola oil, cold-pressed

arrowroot

cornstarch

vanilla extract

Organic Foods

Whenever possible, use organic fruits and vegetables, freshly harvested from a local source. In many areas, you will find wonderful farmers' markets where you can purchase fresh vegetables and fruits. If you can't find organic, choose the freshest produce you can. By using freshly harvested and naturally ripened fruits and vegetables, you will be ensuring the intake of valuable vitamins, nutrients, and life-supporting energy in your diet. As part of a nutritional program diet, we recommend five to nine servings of fresh fruits and vegetables each day. This is easily accomplished by favoring a mostly vegetarian diet (see next page).

There are many different varieties of organic grain products. Reduce your use of refined flours and bleached grains whenever possible, favoring products such as basmati rice, quinoa, millet, kasha, rolled oats, and brown rice. Purchase quality whole wheat flour products, including bread flour, pastry flour, and unbleached white wheat flour. Spelt, an ancient grain similar to wheat, is a good alternative to wheat products. Try turbinado sugar, an unbleached cane sugar, and maple syrup as sweeteners.

To Be or Not to Be Vegetarian

The choice to avoid or to eat animal products is a highly individual one. Culture, upbringing, personal health issues, environmental concerns, as well as religious and spiritual beliefs all contribute to a person's dietary preferences. Our basic recommendation is to eat with awareness and follow your heart. While the Ayurvedic approach to diet does not require strict adherence to a vegetarian diet, we encourage vegetarianism as the optimal nutritional plan for health and vitality. There is abundant scientific evidence that a vegetarian or mostly vegetarian diet plays an important role in reducing your risks for heart disease and cancer. For health, environmental, and ethical reasons, reducing your intake of animal products makes sense.

We recognize that if you are accustomed to eating meat on a daily basis, you will not be inclined to stop abruptly. We suggest you initially try substituting one or two vegetarian meals a week and see how you feel. If you consume animal products, choose those that are raised as humanely as possible and are free from hormones and antibiotics. Also, consider changing the way you consume meat. Rather than devouring a large piece of meat along with a few vegetables, try eating a small helping with a larger quantity of vegetables. Favor fish and free-range fowl while reducing your intake of red meat.

Although most of the recipes in this book are vegetarian, if you choose, you can add small portions of chicken or fish to many of the dishes. Always try to eat with awareness, gratitude, respect, and delight. These are the most important qualities to awaken renewal of the body and soul.

The Chopra Center 30-Day Nutritional Plan for Renewal

A health-promoting nutritional plan is both balanced and delicious. It should be rich in essential nutrients and have the appropriate proportions of carbohydrates, proteins, and fats. It should provide a variety of flavors and textures and be easy to prepare and follow. The 30-day program we offer meets all these criteria. If you follow the program as outlined, you will attain your desired weight while consuming a diet that reduces your risks for heart disease and cancer. Over the course of a month, the Chopra Center Nutritional Plan will provide the following nutritional components:

Total fat	less than 22% of total calories
Saturated fat	less than 7% of total calories
Protein	between 15 and 20% of total calories

Although some proponents of a heart healthy diet have suggested lower intakes of total fat, the Chopra Center 30-Day Nutritional Plan is low in saturated fat and cholesterol and is much more palatable than more restrictive diets. It is also high in protein and fiber.

This nutritional plan provides a guideline for planning your weekly meals. We have included information on total calories, fat, and protein per meal and per day to help you more consciously choose the quality and quantity of the foods you eat. Depending on your needs—building muscle, losing weight, or maintaining your current body size—you will be able to mix and match each menu to create a nutritious and well-balanced diet. Most of the recipes are for four servings. If you are cooking for one or two people, cut the recipe in half. Decrease the amount of black pepper and red chili flakes when dividing a recipe. You can always add more spice to a dish. As you balance your eating habits and daily routine, you will likely find your food cravings will decrease. Use your eating awareness techniques to help gauge the amount of food you prepare for a meal. Refer to the Appetite Gauge on page 7. Ask yourself, "How hungry am I?" Prepare the quantity of food that reflects the hunger you are feeling.

Healthy desserts bring joy and delight. Get into the habit of eating small portions of dessert to satisfy your cravings for sweets without over-indulging. The Ayurvedic approach to eating is about nurturing and honoring the signals your body sends to you. Depriving yourself of the basic foods you love may cause more harm than the few extra calories you may consume. Be moderate and balanced in your eating habits.

Thinking ahead a few days can be helpful. If you want to make Rosemary White Bean Soup, for example, soak the beans overnight the night before and cook them slowly in a slow cooker while you are at work, then finish the soup when you get home.

Look for the asterisk (*) in the 30-Day Nutritional Plan. The asterisk indicates a Staple Recipe (see page 37). Review the general instructions and recipes in that chapter. All other recipes are found in the book beginning with the chapter "Breakfast and Baked Goodies" and ending with the chapter "Desserts."

All of the daily menu choices include the six tastes in each meal. Remember that six tastes—sweet, salty, sour, pungent, bitter, and astringent—should be present in each meal to create balance and harmony in the body. We also feel more satisfied after we eat a meal where the six tastes are present. As you become more aware of the six tastes in your daily meals, you will find that you can easily round out a meal by, for example, adding a squeeze of lemon to enhance the sour taste or by adding some sautéed spinach to a meal to complete the bitter taste.

Learning to make the Staple Recipes will increase the variety of food choices and enable you to add additional "tastes" in your daily meals. By doing so, you will be able to incorporate the recommended five to nine servings of fruits and vegetables and the six tastes into your diet.

The basic principles and recipes presented in this book will serve you well as you prepare meals that are sumptuous, health-promoting, and delicious.

The nutritional analysis for the 30-Day Nutritional Plan is detailed at the end of this book.

Enjoy!

Recipes that are not capitalized (here and on pages 288–302) are variations of recipes that can be found in the Staple Recipes chapter.

Day 1

Breakfast
  Morning Bliss Shake
  Breakfast Bar

Main Meal
  Tomato Florentine Soup
  Rainbow Risotto
  Nutty Spinach Greens
  Almond Tart

Light Meal
  Vegetable Hummus Wrap
  Ginger Cookie

Day 2

Breakfast
  Vegetable Tofu Scramble
  Cilantro Mint Sauce
  Apple Raisin Muffin

Main Meal
  Tofu Fajitas
  Mandarin Tomato Salsa
  Spanish Pilaf
  sautéed carrots and cauliflower*
  Apple Custard Pie

Light Meal
  Italian White Bean Stew
  Oatmeal Power Cookie

*Staple Recipe

Day 3

Breakfast
Rolled Oats Hot Cereal
Blueberry Banana Syrup
Zucchini Pecan Bread

Main Meal
Spinach Soup
Vegetable Paella
Eggplant Tapenade
Dilled Asparagus
sautéed strawberries*

Light Meal
Vegetable White Bean Chili
Simple Great Whole Grain
    Bread*
Peanut Butter Cookie

Day 4

Breakfast
Coffee Bliss Shake
Nutty French Toast
sautéed apples*

Main Meal
Summertime Tomato Basil Soup
Spinach Polenta
Ratatouille Stew
sautéed swiss chard*
Walnut Chocolate Chip Cookie

Light Meal
Egg-less Tofu Salad or Sandwich
Lemon Poppy Seed Cake

Day 5

Breakfast
Chai Bliss Shake
Chopra Granola
fresh blueberries and sliced
    bananas*

Main Meal
Vegetable Hot and Sour Soup
Buddha's Delight Vegetable
    Stir-Fry
steamed rice*
Kim Chi Chutney
Unbelievable Double Chocolate
    Cake

Light Meal
Roasted Tofu and Yams
Garden Salad with Cilantro
    Pecan Sauce
sautéed apricots*

*Staple Recipe

Day 6

Breakfast
Broccoli Tofu Scramble
Mandarin Tomato Salsa
Simple Great Whole Grain
    Bread with Almond Butter

Main Meal
Potato Leek Soup
French Vegetable Stew
toasted millet*
steamed carrots and green
    beans*
Linzertorte Cookie

Light Meal
split pea dahl*
Indian Rice
Apple Leek Chutney
Cardamom Butter Cookie

Day 7

Breakfast
  Almond Bliss Shake
  Apple and Rice Hot Cereal

Main Meal
  Italian Vegetable Soup
  Curry Filo Tarts
  Walnut Yogurt Sauce
  roasted sweet potatoes*
  Berry Tofu Sorbet

Light Meal
  Marinated Tofu Thai Wrap with
    Nutty Dipping Sauce
  Cranberry Bliss Balls

Day 8

Breakfast
  Mango Yogurt
  Tempeh and Potato Hash
  Orange Pear Chutney

Main Meal
  Butternut Squash Soup
  Eggplant and Yam Curry
  Curried Potatoes
  Cucumber Raita
  sautéed apples and
    blackberries*

Light Meal
  Asian Clear Broth
  Thai Tofu Vegetable Stew
  Coconut Cookie

Day 9

Breakfast
  Chopra Granola
  Very Berry Yogurt

Main Meal
  Italian Vegetable Soup
  fresh spinach pasta*
  Tofu "Meat Balls" with Roasted
    Tomato Sauce
  sautéed arugula and roasted
    eggplant*
  Lemon Birthday Cake

Light Meal
  Potato Leek Soup
  poached peaches and
    blueberries*

Day 10

Breakfast
  Mango Bliss Shake
  Vegetable Tofu Scramble
  Russian Borscht Chutney
  Cinnamon Roll

Main Meal
  Vegetable Barley Soup
  Tofu Burger with Leek Sauce
  steamed broccoli*
  Berry Tofu Sorbet

Light Meal
  Roasted Tofu and Yams
  steamed asparagus*
  Blueberry Lemon Cake
    (Variation of Blueberry
    Orange Cake)

*Staple Recipe

Day 11

Breakfast
 Tofu and Potato Italiano
 Homemade Chili Sauce
 Zucchini Pecan Bread

Main Meal
 red lentil dahl*
 Eggplant Cauliflower Curry
 steamed green beans*
 Orange Pear Chutney
 sautéed pears with cardamom*

Light Meal
 Black Bean and Vegetable Stew
 Oat Groat Pilaf with Spinach
 Apricot Pecan Cookie

Day 12

Breakfast
 Chai Bliss Shake
 Breakfast Burrito
 whole apple*

Main Meal
 Tortilla Soup with Avocado and
   Cilantro
 Braised Tofu with Mango
   Tomato Salsa
 sautéed corn, peppers, and
   broccoli*
 sautéed greens*
 Banana-Cocoa-Tofu Frozen
   Mousse

Light Meal
 Black Bean and Rice Wrap
 simple carrot soup*
 Traditional Awesome Brownie

Day 13

Breakfast
 Traditional French Toast
 sautéed apples and
   blackberries*

Main Meal
 Vegetable Barley Soup
 Moroccan Vegetables
 Dilled Lemon Zucchini
 Hummus
 Banana-Cocoa-Tofu Frozen
   Mousse

Light Meal
 Roasted Winter Vegetable Stew
 Organic Mixed Field Greens
   Salad with olive oil
 Kabocha Pumpkin Pie

Day 14

Breakfast
 Masala Potatoes
 Apple Leek Chutney
 Mango Yogurt

Main Meal
 Tomato Florentine Soup
 Mediterranean Pasta
 Savory Swiss Chard
 steamed asparagus*
 Ginger Cookie

Light Meal
 Tofu, Eggplant, and Yukon
   Gold Stew
 Greek Goddess Salad
 Blueberry Orange Cake

*Staple Recipe

Day 15

Breakfast
  Broccoli Tofu Scramble
  Russian Borscht Chutney
  Blueberry Muffin

Main Meal
  Rosemary White Bean Soup
  Vegetable Paella
  sautéed green beans and
    almonds*
  Raspberry Lemon Cake
    (variation of Blueberry
    Orange Cake)

Light Meal
  Curried Chickpea Stew
  steamed rice*
  Ginger Cookie

Day 16

Breakfast
  Whole Wheat Crepes
  Blueberry Banana Syrup
  Country Potatoes

Main Meal
  Sweet Potato Ginger Soup
  broccoli almond stir-fry*
    and Basic Asian-Style Sauce
  Szechwan Baked Egg Rolls
  Spicy Lime and Red Pepper
    Dipping Sauce
  Chinese Five-Spice Garden Pilaf
  sautéed peaches with nutmeg*

Light Meal
  Mexican Tofu Stew
  Garden Salad with no olive oil
  Cilantro Pecan Sauce
  Peanut Butter Cookie

Day 17

Breakfast
  Coffee Bliss Shake
  Hot Quinoa Breakfast Cereal
  Pumpkin Muffin

Main Meal
  Nutty Broccoli Soup
  Simple Whole Grain Pizza with
    Basil and Friends Pesto and
    zucchini
  baked spaghetti squash*
  sautéed swiss chard*
  Almond Tart

Light Meal
  Thai Tofu Vegetable Stew
  steamed rice*
  Oatmeal Power Cookie

Day 18

Breakfast
  Chopra Granola
  Apple Syrup
  Strawberry Banana Yogurt

Main Meal
  Vegetable Hot and Sour Soup
  Thai-Style Noodles with Tofu
  Nutty Spinach Greens
  Kim Chi Chutney
  Double Almond Cookie

Light Meal
  Tofu, Eggplant, and Yukon
    Gold Stew
  Green Quinoa Pilaf
  sautéed pears with cardamom*

*Staple Recipe

Day 19

Breakfast
  Simple Great Whole Grain
    Bread with Almond Butter
  sautéed peaches and currants*
  Very Berry Yogurt

Main Meal
  Zucchini Tofu Bisque
  Curry Filo Tarts
  Cauliflower and Braised Tomato
  Sweet Mixed Fruit Chutney
  Mother Earth's Apple Pie

Light Meal
  French lentil dahl*
  steamed rice*
  steamed carrots, broccoli, and
    zucchini*
  Cranberry Bliss Ball

Day 20

Breakfast
  Toasted Millet Hot Cereal
  Pear Syrup

Main Meal
  Spinach and Lentil Soup
  Winter Vegetables with Couscous
  zucchini, tomatoes, feta, and
    fresh dill*
  Walnut Chocolate Chip Cookie

Light Meal
  Curried Potatoes
  Cucumber Raita
  Organic Mixed Field Greens
    Salad with olive oil
  Berry Tofu Sorbet

Day 21

Breakfast
  Tempeh and Potato Hash
  Tomato Salsa
  Zucchini Pecan Bread

Main Meal
  Spinach Soup
  Tuscany Bulgur Pilaf with
    stuffed acorn squash
  Leek Sauce
  braised carrots and fennel*
  Almond Tart

Light Meal
  Eggplant and Yam Curry
  Greek Goddess Salad
  Oatmeal Power Cookie

Day 22

Breakfast
  Chai Bliss Shake
  Seasonal Fruit Salad
  Strawberry Banana Yogurt

Main Meal
  Very Simple Pumpkin Soup
  Rainbow Risotto
  sautéed spinach*
  steamed asparagus with
    lemon*
  Unbelievable Double Chocolate
    Cake

Light Meal
  Asian Clear Broth
  Lettuce Wrap with two sauces
  Peanut Butter Cookie

*Staple Recipe

Day 23

Breakfast
Whole Wheat Crepes
Sweet Mixed Fruit Chutney
Strawberry Syrup

Main Meal
Italian Vegetable Soup
Spinach Polenta
Roasted Tomato Sauce
Garden Salad with olive oil
Linzertorte Cookie

Light Meal
Cajun Bean and Tempeh Stew
steamed rice*
steamed broccoli*
Apple Cinnamon Cake (variation
of Blueberry Orange Cake)

Day 24

Breakfast
Seasonal Fruit Salad
Apple Maple Yogurt

Main Meal
Tortilla Soup with Avocado and
Cilantro
Mexican Tofu Stew
Spicy Mexican Rice
steamed yellow and zucchini
squash*
Apricot Pecan Cookie

Light Meal
Vegetable Hummus Wrap
Apple Cobbler

Day 25

Breakfast
Couscous Hot Cereal
sautéed apples and
blackberries*

Main Meal
Cuban Black Bean and Sweet
Potato Soup
French Vegetable Stew
Oat Groat Pilaf with Spinach
Dilled Asparagus
Chocolate Tofu Mousse with
Walnut Coconut Praline

Light Meal
Spinach and Lentil Soup
Cashew Tempeh
Coconut Cookie

Day 26

Breakfast
Coffee Bliss Shake
Cardamom Whole Wheat
Pancakes
fresh blueberries and sliced
bananas*

Main Meal
Nutty Broccoli Soup
Tuscany Bulgur Pilaf
roasted sweet potatoes*
steamed yellow and zucchini
squash*
Apple Custard Pie

Light Meal
Vegetable White Bean Chili
sautéed spinach*
Traditional Chocolate Chip
Cookie

*Staple Recipe

Day 27

Breakfast
  Country Potatoes
  Krazy Ketchup
  Traditional French Toast
  Strawberry Syrup

Main Meal
  Vegetable Barley Soup
  Simple Whole Grain Pizza with
    roasted tomato and spinach
  steamed carrots and green
    beans*
  Traditional Awesome Brownie

Light Meal
  Butternut Squash Soup
  Eggless Tofu Salad on Simple
    Great Whole Grain Bread
  Oatmeal Power Cookie

Day 28

Breakfast
  Morning Bliss Shake
  Pumpkin Muffin

Main Meal
  yellow split pea dahl*
  Tofu Burger with Leek Sauce
  steamed rice*
  steamed broccoli, carrots and
    zucchini*
  sautéed strawberries with
    cinnamon*

Light Meal
  Thai Tofu Vegetable Stew
  Kabocha Pumpkin Pie

Day 29

Breakfast
  Nutty French Toast
  Nectarine and Blueberry
    Syrup

Main Meal
  Sweet Potato Ginger Soup
  Buddha's Delight Vegetable
    Stir-fry with Tofu Cubes
  Chinese Five-Spice Garden Pilaf
  Lemon Birthday Cake

Light Meal
  Roasted Eggplant and Spinach
    Pasta with Beans
  Organic Mixed Field Greens
    Salad with olive oil
  sautéed mango and blueberries*

Day 30

Breakfast
  Polenta Hot Cereal
  Apple Syrup
  Cinnamon Roll

Main Meal
  Summertime Tomato Basil Soup
  Mediterranean Pasta
  roasted butternut squash rings*
  braised fennel, green beans,
    almonds*
  poached peaches with
    blackberry sauce*

Light Meal
  Very Simple Pumpkin Soup
  Marinated Tofu Thai Wrap with
    Nutty Dipping Sauce
  Double Delight Cookie

*Staple Recipe

Staple Recipes

Pray for peace and grace and spiritual food, for wisdom and guidance, for all these are good, but don't forget the potatoes.

JOHN TYLER PETTEE

In a perfect world, you would have freshly baked bread and steaming, wholesome soup waiting for you as you walked through the door each night. Unfortunately, this scenario is not available to most of us. With a little planning, however, you will be able to create delicious, healthy meals easily and quickly. Our goal is to make your life easier. We encourage you to learn the basic Staple Recipes for soups, sauces, and sautés described in this section. Having mastered these staples, you will have a foundation for creating wholesome, healthy meals.

These recipes are ripe for personal adaptation. Become familiar with each of the Staple Recipes so you can increase your personal repertoire and create simple basic meals using the ingredients that you have on hand.

Remember: Delicious meals begin with wholesome basic ingredients. Approach cooking as a unique opportunity to express your creativity. Like any artistic endeavor, cooking will yield wonderful results if the ingredients are the best quality and the artist (you, the cook) has the intention to create something wonderful.

Staple Recipes

Ghee: The Golden Oil

Ginger Tea

Ginger Elixir

Vegetable Stock

Basic Dahl

Simple Basic Soup

Sautéed Fruits and Syrups

    Simple Fruit Sauté

    Simple Frozen Fruit Syrup

Whole Grain Baked Goodies

    Simple Great Whole Grain Bread

    Very Best Dairy-Free Muffins

Soy: The Perfect Food

    Simple Marinade for Tofu or Tempeh

Simple White Sauce: Basic Roux

Greens

    Simmered Greens

Simply Vegetables

    Basic Mixed-Vegetable Sauté

    Basic Roasted Vegetables

Cooked Grains

Ghee: The Golden Oil

Ghee is clarified butter. Ordinary butter contains about 80 percent butterfat, 15 percent water, 3 percent salt, and 1 to 2 percent milk solids or curds. During the process of making ghee, water is boiled off and the curds are cooked into a sediment that is easily removed. The result is a fragrant, flavorful oil that does not become rancid, even without refrigeration. In the tradition of Ayurveda, ghee is prized for its unique medicinal and balancing qualities. Even those with sensitivity to dairy products can usually enjoy ghee, as it is free of milk proteins and sugars. Ghee plays an important role in Indian and Ayurvedic cuisine, lending a subtle taste and fragrance to the food. It is heat tolerant, making it useful for quick sautéing and browning.

A teaspoon of ghee contains 5 grams of fat, of which 3 are saturated, and a little more than 8 milligrams of cholesterol. Because it is so flavorful, you can usually use less ghee than an equivalent amount of another oil. If you are concerned about high cholesterol and prefer to avoid any unnecessary saturated fat and cholesterol, feel free to substitute olive oil for ghee in any recipe.

You will need the following to make 1½ cups of ghee:
> 3- or 4-quart heavy-bottomed stainless steel pot
> 4-inch wire mesh strainer lined with terry cloth or a flour-sack dish towel
> heat-resistant bowl or pot to strain hot ghee into
> clear glass container with tight-fitting lid
> 1 pound of organic unsalted butter

Place the butter in the pot. Bring the butter to a boil, and then reduce the heat to produce a slow, steady, rolling boil. Keep an eye on the butter to avoid burning it. Allow the foam that forms to settle to the bottom of the pot. As the foam is reduced, it produces a crackling sound, which is caused by moisture evaporating from the butter. Let the butter simmer for up to 30 minutes. Keep the heat on your stove as low as possible. The ghee is complete when you see browned butterfat caramelized on the bottom of the pan, while the top portion of the ghee is mostly clear. Allow the mixture to cool slightly, then strain it through a cloth-lined strainer or a flour-sack dish towel into a heat-resistant container. Allow the ghee to cool completely before storing it in a clear glass jar. You can keep the ghee for up to one month without the need for refrigeration.

You can also make ghee in an electric slow cooker without the risk of burning it. Place the butter in the cooker on the lowest possible setting. It usually requires about 6 hours for the solids and moisture to completely cook out, leaving the pure golden ghee.

Ghee is delicious drizzled on toast, oatmeal, or rice; it adds flavor and character to any sautés for soups, sauces, and stews. A teaspoon of ghee each day in your cooking supplies 7.5 percent of your recommended daily fat, 15 percent of your saturated fat, and 3 percent of your daily cholesterol intake. If your diet is otherwise low in saturated fat and cholesterol, ghee will make a minor contribution.

If you wish to avoid completely the saturated fat and cholesterol of ghee, we recommend olive oil as a useful and tasty alternative. Olive oil is rich in oleic acid, a monounsaturated fatty acid. Diets rich in olive oil may help reduce cholesterol levels, lower high blood pressure, and reduce the risk for colon cancer. Always use "extra virgin" olive oil, which meets the highest standards for purity. Most of the recipes in this book call for ghee or olive oil, which can be used interchangeably except for baking sweet recipes, for which canola oil is preferable to olive oil.

Unless specific amounts are given in a recipe, when using ghee or olive oil to coat a pan, please use as little as possible, only adding more to avoid burning your food.

Ginger Tea

Ginger is known as the universal medicine and can be found in regional cuisines worldwide. Ginger tea has a strong cleansing effect on the body, helping to mobilize toxins and restore balance. Ginger tea benefits the digestive system and can help reduce cravings for sweet and salty items. Ginger helps soothe and cleanse the respiratory tract, making it a valuable tea during cold and flu season. We recommend that you drink two to three cups of hot ginger tea a day. Make it a habit. For variety, try sweetening your tea with raw organic honey or adding chopped mint or lemon slices.

One Quart of Ginger Tea

Coarsely chop an unpeeled 2-inch piece of whole ginger. Place the pieces into a 2- or 3-quart pot with one quart of purified water. Bring the water just to a boil and reduce the heat to a simmer. Let the tea simmer for 15 minutes. Strain the tea and pour it into a thermos bottle or store in a glass jar. Reheat the tea as needed. Use the ginger pieces from the tea in your vegetable stockpot (see page 42).

One Cup of Ginger Tea

Grate 1 heaping teaspoon of an unpeeled ginger root into a cup of hot water. Let the tea steep for 2 minutes. Strain or let the ginger settle to the bottom of the cup.

Ginger Elixir

A great way to fire up the digestive system is with a ginger elixir. Consider the ginger elixir your jump start to a sluggish digestive system. Take one ounce of fresh ginger elixir before lunch and dinner to kindle your digestive fire.

> 1 3- to 4-inch piece of unpeeled fresh gingerroot
> 4 to 6 lemons
> 1 cup purified water
> ¾ cup raw organic honey
> ¼ teaspoon black pepper

Cut the unpeeled fresh ginger into ½-inch pieces. Using a powerful juicer, push the ginger through the juicer and juice enough to make 1 cup. In a citrus juicer, juice the lemons to make 1 cup of juice. Combine the juices in a large bowl. With a wire whisk, mix the water, honey, and black pepper into the ginger and lemon juice. Whisk until well blended. Store in a pitcher or glass jar in the refrigerator.

Vegetable Stock

One of the most nutritious and practical kitchen projects is making a vegetable stock. Your homemade vegetable stock will be fresh and salt-free and will add valuable nutrients to your diet. Buy a large flat plastic container that fits in your refrigerator and begin collecting the outer layers of vegetables that you would normally toss into the trash. These "scraps" will make a delicious stock for your soups, sauces, and sautés.

Every time you prepare vegetables for a dish, save the peeling, cores, ends, tops, outer leaves, stems, and anything else that is not actually eaten. Save the ends and peels from the following vegetables: broccoli, carrots, cauliflower, leeks (use onion skin sparingly). Save apple cores, lemon and orange peels, and any green ends such as lettuce or unappealing cooking greens. Just about any type of fruit, herb, or vegetable scraps can go into a stockpot. Avoid large amounts of green or red cabbage, beets, beet greens, and banana peels, however, as they will all cause the stock to be cloudy or discolored. Save your usable scraps in a plastic container for up to five days in the refrigerator.

When you have a good supply, place all of the scraps into a large stockpot. Cover with water to 2 inches above the scraps. Bring to a boil, then reduce the heat and simmer for 1 hour or more. Cool the liquid, then strain it and pour into recycled glass or plastic juice containers. Label the tops of the containters with a bold "STOCK" sign. Store them in the refrigerator. If you are an avid gardener, the vegetable scraps will be very welcome in your compost pile.

Use the stock in place of extra oil for a low-fat cooking process. Keep the stock handy for use in making dahl, soups, and sauces. Stock can also be taken as a relaxing and healing cup of nutritious broth—add a small amount of Bragg Liquid

Aminos to each cup as it heats up. After a few days, water your plants with the stock and make a new batch.

Equipment needed to make stock:
- 1 8- to 10-quart plastic container that fits in the refrigerator
- 1 large soup pot
- Strainer
- 2 recycled glass or plastic juice containers

Basic Dahl

We consider Dahl to be a staple in a well-balanced diet. Dahl is a very nutritious soup made of legumes and a simple masala curry paste. Dahl is easy to digest and low in fat. Eaten with rice, it provides a complete protein. Dahl includes all six tastes and is made with many prized healing spices. Legume choices include: green lentils, brown lentils, French lentils, red lentils, yellow or green split peas, mung beans or split mung beans.

4 SERVINGS

1 cup dry lentils (see list above) rinsed and sorted
Vegetable stock or water
½ teaspoon ground cumin
1 pinch asafetida (hing)
1 pinch turmeric
1 2- to 3-inch piece kombu seaweed (found in Asian markets and health food stores)
1 recipe Curry Paste (recipe follows)

In a 4-quart soup pot, place the lentils and enough vegetable stock or water to cover lentils, plus 3 inches. Bring the lentils to a boil until the foam rises. At regular intervals, remove foam from the top and discard. To help reduce gas and aid in digestion, and to add flavor, add the cumin, asafetida, turmeric, and kombu to the lentils as they cook.

Continue to cook the lentils until they are tender, approximately 1 hour.

Add the Curry Paste to the cooked lentils and simmer together for 5 to 10 minutes. Stir until well heated.

Serve with steamed basmati rice and steamed vegetables for a simple, delicious, and healthy meal.

Curry Paste

1 teaspoon ghee or olive oil
½ teaspoon brown or yellow mustard seeds
½ teaspoon fenugreek seeds
5 cardamom seeds removed from whole, green pods and crushed with a mortar and pestle, or ½ teaspoon ground cardamom
1 pinch red chili flakes
1 stick cinnamon, or ½ teaspoon ground cinnamon
½ cup chopped leeks or onions
1 inch fresh ginger, finely chopped, or ½ teaspoon ground ginger
¼ cup golden raisins, chopped coarsely
½ cup vegetable stock or water
1 teaspoon ground cumin
½ teaspoon turmeric
1 pinch asafetida (hing)
½ teaspoon ground coriander
1 tablespoon tomato paste
1 teaspoon Bragg Liquid Aminos or tamari
¼ cup chopped cilantro
½ cup low-fat coconut milk or vanilla soymilk
1 tablespoon lemon juice

In a medium sauté pan, heat ghee or olive oil and add the mustard seeds. Let the mustard seeds pop briefly. (Caution: the seeds may pop out of the pan.) Add the next seven ingredients (fenugreek through raisins) in order. Add vegetable stock as the mixture begins to dry. Sauté for 5 minutes, and then add cumin, tumeric, asafetida, and coriander. Add more stock if necessary, then add the tomato paste and aminos. Simmer in the sauté pan for 2 to 3 minutes. Add the cilantro, coconut, and lemon juice.

NUTRITIONAL FACTS | *Per 1-cup serving*
Using ghee
Calories 262, Total fat 2.6 g, Saturated fat 1.4 g, Carbohydrates 43.9 g, Protein 16 g

Simple Basic Soup

This basic soup is perfect fare for a light dinner or as part of a hearty lunch. Select two or three different vegetables to create a soup. Choose from any of the following: acorn squash, asparagus, broccoli, butternut squash, carrots, cauliflower, celery, cooking greens, corn, potato, pumpkin, spinach, sweet potato, tomatoes, yams, or zucchini.

SERVES 4

- 1 teaspoon ghee or olive oil
- ¼ cup chopped leeks, onions, or celery
- 1 pinch black pepper
- 1 teaspoon dill
- 1 teaspoon thyme
- ½ teaspoon nutmeg
- 1 tablespoon Bragg Liquid Aminos or tamari
- 3 cups vegetables, washed and cut into bite-size pieces
- 4 to 5 cups vegetable stock
- 1 recipe Tofu Cream, optional (recipe follows)

In a 4-quart soup pot, heat the oil. Add the leeks. Add the pepper, dill, thyme, nutmeg, and aminos. Simmer until the vegetables begin to brown, 1 or 2 minutes. Add the remaining vegetables and sauté for another 3 or 4 minutes, stirring to coat the vegetables well with the spices and leeks. Pour in the stock and bring to a boil. Reduce the heat and allow the soup to simmer at a gentle rolling boil for 10 minutes or until the vegetables are cooked. Don't overcook. The soup can be left chunky or puréed to a smooth consistency with a hand blender, blender, or food processor. If desired, add the tofu cream (for additional protein) and continue to blend together. If the mixture is too thick, add more vegetable stock. Gently reheat and serve.

Tofu Cream

½ cup vegetable stock
½ cup low-fat silken tofu, cubed
1 teaspoon lemon juice or rice vinegar

Combine in a blender and process slowly until well mixed.

NUTRITIONAL
FACTS

Per 1-cup serving
Using olive oil, without tofu cream
Calories 72, Total fat 1.5 g, Saturated fat .3 g,
Carbohydrates 11.6 g, Protein 2.9 g

Tofu cream only
Calories 79, Total fat 2.6 g, Saturated fat 0 g,
Carbohydrates 5.1 g, Protein 8.8 g

Sautéed Fruits and Syrups

Look in your fruit bowl. Toward the end of the week, you may discover overly ripe pieces of fruit that no one may want to eat: bananas with brown spots, softening apples, peaches with mushy spots. You might think these fruits belong in the trash, but actually, these are just the type of fruits that make the most flavorful fruit syrups, breakfast fruit chutneys, and dessert fruit sautés.

Common fruits to sauté include apples, apricots, bananas, berries, peaches, pears, and strawberries. Wash the fruit, and cut into slices or bite-size pieces. You may want to peel the fruit first, especially if the skin looks less than desirable. If it is not too bad, leave the skin on, as it provides important dietary fiber. Sautéed fruits are easy to digest and make a great complement to any meal. Including fruit chutney or sautéed fruit in a meal is one way to ensure that you are incorporating the six tastes. Fruits are generally sweet or sour and, when sautéed with spices and savory foods like leeks, can balance any meal.

Keep a few bags of frozen berries in the freezer. Buy the best quality product you can find. Use the frozen fruits in desserts, muffins, and as a wonderful complement to hot morning cereal. Some great combinations include blueberries and bananas, raspberries and apples, mixed berries, cherries and apricots, and strawberries and mangos. Also try different sweet spices to create new tastes. Experiment with allspice, cloves, cardamom, ginger, cinnamon, and nutmeg to enhance the flavor in fruit sautés.

Simple Fruit Sauté

1 teaspoon ghee
2 cups fruit, sliced or cubed (see choices below)
2 tablespoons apple juice or other fruit juice
½ teaspoon cinnamon
½ teaspoon nutmeg
2 tablespoons golden raisins, cranberries, or currants, optional
2 tablespoons maple syrup

Heat the ghee in a small sauté pan over medium heat. Add the fruit and simmer for 2 minutes. Add the juice, cinnamon, nutmeg, and the dried fruit if desired, and continue to simmer for 4 to 5 minutes or until the fruit is almost soft. Add a little bit more juice if the mixture appears to dry out. Pour the maple syrup in just before serving. Use this simple sauté as a dessert fruit or breakfast fruit.

Recommended fruit choices are apples, pears, apricots, nectarines, peaches, strawberries, blackberries, blueberries, figs, persimmons, and plums.

NUTRITIONAL FACTS

Per ½-cup serving
Using apples
Calories 99, Total fat 1.4 g, Saturated fat .8 g,
Carbohydrates 21.1 g, Protein .3 g

Simple Frozen Fruit Syrup

SERVES 4

1   teaspoon ghee
1   10-ounce bag frozen organic fruit, about 1½ cups
    (see choices below)
½   teaspoon cinnamon
½   teaspoon nutmeg or cloves
1   teaspoon arrowroot powder, if needed
1   tablespoon apple juice or other fruit juice, if needed
2   tablespoons maple syrup

In a sauté pan, heat the ghee and add the frozen fruit. As the fruit defrosts, liquid will begin to fill the pan; allow the liquid to reduce, by simmering at a low heat for approximately 3 or 4 minutes. As the fruit simmers, add the cinnamon and nutmeg. If the fruit is too juicy, add 1 teaspoon arrowroot powder dissolved in 1 tablespoon fruit juice to the syrup as it simmers. If the mixture begins to dry out, add more juice. Simmer until the syrup is the consistency of maple syrup. Add the maple syrup to the hot fruit just before serving. Serve on pancakes, hot cereal, dessert cakes, and ice cream.

Recommended frozen fruit choices are blueberries, cherries, blackberries, raspberries, mango, and strawberries.

NUTRITIONAL
FACTS

Per ½-cup serving
Using frozen strawberries
Calories 90, Total fat 1.4 g, Saturated fat 0.8 g,
Carbohydrates 18.9 g, Protein .6 g

Whole Grain Baked Goodies

Open thine eyes, and thou shalt be
satisfied with bread.

PROVERBS 20:13

Bread is the staff of life, the foundation of our soul, the memory of ancient wisdom, and the treasure of the ages. In every culture, tradition, religion, and cuisine, bread has always captured the human heart and soul with aroma, taste, texture, romance, and intrigue—always challenging our resistance to indulge in more. Why do we love homemade bread so? Someone—our mother, wife, lover, or friend—has put much love and attention into the bread: carefully and gently combining the yeast and the sugar with not too hot nor too cool water; mixing the stone-ground wheat, fresh herbs, salt, oil, all combined in a large earthen bowl, then kneading with the energy that comes only from within. With every stroke of attention creating soft and flexible dough to sculpt into a vision of perfection—a loaf of bread, a batch of sweet cinnamon rolls, an abundant pizza, pita bread for a dip, a pastry filled with savory delight.

Baking is a gift. You don't need to be gifted to bake; baking is a gift to be shared. As part of a healthy balanced diet, freshly baked breads, muffins, cookies, cakes, fresh pastas, and freshly cooked whole grains bring sweetness into our lives, adding comfort and pleasure. Using the highest-quality organic ingredients—whole grains, fresh organic butter and milk, raw and natural sugars and spices—your baked goods will be not only delicious but also very nutritious and fulfilling.

Simple Great Whole Grain Bread

MAKES 3
LOAVES,
8 SLICES
PER LOAF

2 tablespoons active yeast
2 tablespoons turbinado sugar
4 cups very warm water
4 cups whole wheat pastry flour
4 cups whole wheat bread flour
1 tablespoon salt
Seasonings
1 tablespoon olive oil, optional

In a medium bowl, dissolve the yeast and sugar in the warm water and proof—the yeast will expand and foam. In a separate, large bowl, whisk together the flours, salt, and your choice of seasonings (see the next page for suggestions). When the yeast mixture has foamed, add it to the flour mixture. With clean hands, combine the yeast and flour together and knead the dough for 5 minutes on a clean surface dusted with flour. Place the dough in an oiled bowl and cover it. Place the bowl in a warm area and let the dough rise until doubled in size, about 1 hour.

When the dough has risen, punch it down with your hand to release the air and flatten it out. Knead the dough for another 3 or 4 minutes, then form it into loaves—or rolls, flat bread, or pizza—and place on oiled baking sheets or pans.

Preheat the oven to 350 degrees. Let the dough rest for another 10 to 15 minutes before baking. Bake for about 30 minutes or until browned and crusty. Spray water or oil on the bread toward the end of the baking time for a more crusty texture.

Any of the following optional items may be added to the flour before adding the yeast:

1 cup sautéed apples and 1 tablespoon cinnamon or sage

1 tablespoon cinnamon and 1 cup raisins

½ cup cranberries, ½ cup almonds, and 1 teaspoon nutmeg

½ cup chopped dates, ¼ cup chopped walnuts, 1 tablespoon basil, and 1 teaspoon allspice

2 tablespoons flaxseed, sesame seeds, roasted fennel seeds, or caraway seeds

¼ cup chopped fresh basil, thyme, cilantro, rosemary, or marjoram—alone or in combination

½ cup sautéed leeks or onions

¼ cup sliced kalamata olives and 1 tablespoon dried rosemary

2 tablespoons dried basil

NUTRITIONAL FACTS

Per slice
Using olive oil and no optional items
Calories 156, Total fat 1.4 g, Saturated fat .3 g, Carbohydrates 30.4 g, Protein 5.8 g

Very Best Dairy-Free Muffins

MAKES 12
MUFFINS

1¾ cups whole wheat pastry flour or spelt flour
½ cup turbinado sugar
1 teaspoon cinnamon
1 teaspoon grated lemon rind
2 teaspoons baking powder
½ teaspoon baking soda
½ teaspoon salt
1 cup low-fat vanilla soymilk or rice milk
2 tablespoons canola oil
¼ cup maple syrup
¾ cup mango purée (or mashed banana or applesauce)
½ cup fresh, defrosted, or dried fruit

Preheat the oven to 350 degrees. Spray a muffin pan with oil and set aside. In a large bowl, whisk together the flour, sugar, cinnamon, lemon rind, baking powder, baking soda, and salt. In a separate bowl, combine the soymilk, oil, maple syrup, fruit purée, and fruit. Add the dry ingredients to the wet ingredients and combine gently with a rubber spatula. Scoop into the muffin pan and bake for 15 to 20 minutes or until golden brown. An inserted toothpick should come out clean.

NUTRITIONAL
FACTS

Per muffin
Calories 178, Total fat 2.7 g, Saturated fat .4 g, Carbohydrates 36.1 g, Protein 2.5 g

Soy: The Perfect Food

Nonvegetarians and vegetarians alike will benefit from including soy-based products in their daily meal planning. Over the past thirty years, the taste, texture, and quality of soy-based products has greatly improved. Some of the soy products available in markets today include: soy cheese, soymilk, soy burgers, tofu ice cream, tofu breakfast sausage, ground "meat," soy cold cuts and tofu hot dogs.

Soybeans are an important source of phytoestrogens. Phytoestrogens are naturally occurring plant-based substances that contain chemicals related to the hormones produced by mammals. One type of phytoestrogen, isoflavones, has been credited with many health-promoting benefits. Including soy products in your diet may help reduce the risk of osteoporosis and some of the uncomfortable symptoms of menopause. Studies have shown that the daily use of soy products may also help lower cholesterol levels and protect against certain types of cancer. Soybeans are rich in protein, iron, B vitamins, and zinc. Soy products also provide a good source of omega-3 and omega-6 fatty acids. We recommend the regular use of soy products in a well-balanced diet.

Soy Products

Tempeh is a type of fermented soybean cake that is originally from Indonesia. Tempeh is made from the whole soybean and is high in protein. Like tofu, tempeh can be marinated to enhance the flavor. Use tempeh as a ground meat replacement in chili, Italian sauces, savory casseroles, and Mexican dishes.

Tofu is composed of fermented soybeans made into a concentrated cheeselike form. It is originally from Japan. Tofu is astringent, sweet, cooling, heavy, and mild tasting. Tofu is very versatile and will take on the flavors of any food with which it is cooked. It is high in calcium, iron, and phosphorus. Tofu is easy to digest and is well suited to combine with flavorful warming spices. There are two types of tofu: fresh tofu, packaged in water, and silken tofu, which is best used in sauces. We generally recommend using firm or extra-firm low-fat tofu.

Soymilk is the liquid that comes from soybeans that are cooked and pressed. Soymilk is naturally high in calcium and contains no cholesterol. Soymilk comes in full-fat, low-fat, and nonfat varieties. You can find it flavored with vanilla, cocoa, carob, or just plain. Soymilk can be used to replace milk in many recipes. We recommend the use of low-fat soymilk products.

Textured vegetable protein (TVP) is made from defatted soy flakes. It is a dried, granular product, often sold in bulk at natural food stores. TVP needs to be reconstituted in liquid to become soft and flavorful. Marinades work well with TVP. Use in recipes as a ground meat substitute.

Fresh soybeans (edamame), high in protein and phytoestrogens, look much like Chinese snow peas. They are best eaten steamed. Steam the pods for 20 minutes. They can be found in most food stores and Asian markets, either fresh or frozen.

Cooking Tofu and Tempeh

Marinating tofu or tempeh overnight allows the flavors to incorporate into these otherwise bland foods. To speed up the process, place tofu or tempeh and the marinade in a baking pan and bake at 350 degrees for 20 to 30 minutes. Keep some marinated tofu on hand, stored in the refrigerator. Use slabs of marinated tofu in sandwiches, cube it for stir-fry, and crumble it for breakfast sautés.

Simple Marinade
for Tofu or Tempeh

SERVES 4

1 16-ounce package fresh, low-fat, firm or extra-firm tofu
   or tempeh
¾ cup Bragg Liquid Aminos or tamari
¾ cup rice vinegar
2 tablespoons balsamic vinegar
2 tablespoons maple syrup
1 teaspoon ginger powder
1 teaspoon cumin
½ teaspoon red chili flakes
1 teaspoon sesame oil

Slice the tofu or tempeh into ¼-inch slabs or cut into cubes. Combine the rest of the ingredients in a shallow baking pan. Add the tofu or tempeh. Soak overnight. To speed up the process, bake the tofu or tempeh in a 350-degree oven for 20 to 30 minutes, then cool. Remove the tofu or tempeh from the marinade and use it in a variety of different dishes. Store in a resealable plastic bag or container with a tight-fitting lid.

NUTRITIONAL
FACTS

Per ½-cup serving
Calories 215, Total fat 6.5 g, Saturated fat .2 g,
Carbohydrates 16.5 g, Protein 22.5 g

Simple White Sauce: Basic Roux

Use this sauce as a base for soups, stews, and casseroles. There are many variations that can be utilized to change the character of this basic sauce. Add cheese, herbs, marinated tofu cubes, and steamed vegetables. You can blend it with vegetable soup, add it to thicken stew, use it as the base of your favorite Alfredo sauce, or make a cheesy sauce for macaroni and cheese. There are endless creative uses for this simple sauce.

 1 tablespoon ghee or olive oil
½ cup chopped leeks or onions
 1 pinch black pepper or red chili flakes
 1 tablespoon Bragg Liquid Aminos or tamari
 2 tablespoons whole wheat pastry flour or unbleached white flour
 1 cup low-fat or plain vanilla soymilk

Heat the oil in a saucepan, then add the leeks. Sauté for 1 minute, then add the pepper and aminos. Continue to sauté until the leeks are slightly browned. Using a wire whip, stir in the flour. Allow the flour to brown slightly. Slowly begin to pour the soymilk into the mixture, stirring with the wire whisk as you pour. Use the amount of soymilk that creates the thickness you desire—less for a thick sauce, more for a thinner sauce.

NUTRITIONAL FACTS | *For ¼ of recipe*
Using ghee
Calories 79, Total fat 4.5 g, Saturated fat 2.8 g, Carbohydrates 7.3 g, Protein 2.5 g

Greens

There are numerous benefits to incorporating greens into your diet, and there are many varieties of greens available in the market these days. Greens are high in calcium, vitamin A, vitamin C, vitamin K, vitamin E, and numerous phytonutrients. In a healthy, well-balanced diet, greens play an important role in reducing the risk of heart disease, cancer, and other ailments. We recommend that a serving of greens be part of your daily diet.

Let's look at some of the common greens available. Purchase organic greens whenever possible. Green choices can also include spinach, mustard, and beet greens.

Arugula has a sharp, bitter, and peppery taste. It is originally from the Mediterranean region, where it is considered an aphrodisiac. This tasty green is excellent for stimulating digestion. Arugula is easy to grow and mixes well with other greens.

Bok choy is a sweet, crisp, cooling, and mild-tasting green. It comes from China and is beneficial in cooling the body and reducing mucus in the system.

Chard has a slightly bitter, yet mild taste. Swiss chard, as it is commonly called, is a member of the beet family. The leaves can be red, green, white, or rainbow in color. It is good for improving bowel function. Chard is easy to grow in the garden.

Collards are part of the kale and cabbage family. They are mild and very popular in southern cuisine. *Kale* has a crisp and sweet taste when young, and gets bitter as it matures. It is helpful in building immune strength, easing congestion, and aiding digestion. Kale is an excellent source of calcium, iron, and vitamins A and C.

Simmered Greens

Very fast and easy to cook, greens provide a source of the "bitter" taste in your meals. Use about 2 cups of fresh greens per person. Using a large sauté pan, heat 1 teaspoon ghee or olive oil and 1 tablespoon vegetable stock. Add a pinch of pepper and 6 to 8 cups assorted cooking greens. Sauté the greens until they are slightly wilted but still maintain a vibrant green color. Sprinkle with balsamic vinegar.

NUTRITIONAL
FACTS

Per ½-cup serving
Using olive oil
Calories 32, Total fat 1.3 g, Saturated fat .2 g,
Carbohydrates 3.7 g, Protein 1.4 g

Simply Vegetables

Eat your vegetables! Vegetables play a predominant role in a healthy, well-balanced diet. If you really try to include 5 to 9 servings of fruits and vegetables each day into your diet, you will need to eat a variety of them. How can you cook vegetables so you and your family (even the kids) will really like them and want to eat them? Be creative; mix colors and flavors that appeal to you. Our favorite combinations include: carrots and broccoli, cauliflower and greens, eggplant and sweet potatoes, and zucchini and tomatoes. There are many different ways to cook vegetables; for example, roasting, sautéing, steaming, braising, and blanching. You can also include vegetables in many soups, stews, sauces, and casseroles.

In the Ayurvedic approach to eating, we recommend that most vegetables and fruits be lightly cooked or steamed to aid in digestibility. This does not mean that you should avoid fresh salads made with beautiful organic cucumbers, tomatoes, shredded carrots, sprouts, and organic field greens. For ease in digestion, we recommend that cold foods, such as a salad, always be eaten before a soup or hot main dish. People with delicate digestive systems should mostly eat slightly cooked or steamed vegetables for ease of digestion and comfort. A wonderful way to add greens to your meal is to place a handful of salad greens—such as field greens, spinach, watercress, or arugula—on the plate, then add hot, steaming grains or vegetables on top to lightly steam the greens. It also makes the plate look beautiful.

Preparing Vegetables

Plan on 1 to 1½ cups of different vegetables per person at each meal. For cooking greens, use 2 cups per person, as greens reduce in volume during the cooking process. Start with your favorite vegetables. Peeling vegetables is not necessary if you are using organic vegetables. The skins of most vegetables have abundant vital nutrients and fiber so it is best to keep them on whenever possible. Wash all fruits and vegetables, organic or nonorganic, before you use them. (Remember to keep all the washed ends and scraps for your stockpot.) Most varieties of squash are peeled, unless you are using the squash as a boat.

Use lots of fresh and dried herbs with your vegetables. Not only will the vegetables taste better, you will benefit from the medicinal qualities found in them. As mentioned in the Condiments and Baking Supplies in the Basics of Nourishment (page 23), we also recommend the use of a product called Bragg Liquid Aminos, found in most health food stores. It is a nonfermented soy-based product that provides a savory and salty taste similar to soy sauce. Use it to flavor vegetables.

Vegetables should always be cooked al dente, or almost tender. Cook them a little longer for those with delicate digestive systems. Begin your sauté or steaming process with the vegetables that will take the longer time to cook. For example: cauliflower, asparagus, carrots, potatoes, squash, and other hard vegetables will take 5 to 6 minutes to cook to a tender stage, whereas zucchini, broccoli, and green beans will take only 3 to 4 minutes. Time your vegetables accordingly.

Basic Mixed-Vegetable Sauté

SERVES 4

1 teaspoon ghee or olive oil
¼ cup coarsely chopped leeks or onions
½ teaspoon black pepper
1 tablespoon Bragg Liquid Aminos or tamari
1 cup small cauliflower florets
2 medium carrots, sliced thinly
¼ to ½ cup vegetable stock
1 cup broccoli florets
1 medium zucchini, quartered vertically, then sliced
2 cups fresh baby spinach, washed
1 teaspoon dill
1 teaspoon cumin

Heat the oil in a large sauté pan. Add the leeks, pepper, and aminos. Sauté for 2 minutes or until the leeks begin to clear. Add the cauliflower and carrots. Pour in ¼ cup vegetable stock to help speed up the cooking process. When the liquid has begun to disappear, in about 4 to 5 minutes, add the broccoli and zucchini. Continue to sauté for another 2 minutes, then add the spinach, dill, and cumin. Add a small amount of additional stock if necessary. For even cooking, keep the vegetables moving by tossing or stirring. Remove from heat. A teaspoon of aminos or balsamic vinegar sprinkled on top of the sautéed vegetables will add to the character of the vegetables. Serve with a chutney or spicy sauce.

NUTRITIONAL FACTS

Per 1-cup serving
Using ghee
Calories 54, Total fat 1.6 g, Saturated fat .8 g, Carbohydrates 7.4 g, Protein 2.7 g

Basic Roasted Vegetables

SERVES 4

2 teaspoons ghee or olive oil
1 tablespoon Bragg Liquid Aminos or tamari
1 tablespoon balsamic vinegar
1 tablespoon dried basil
½ teaspoon black pepper
1 teaspoon dried dill
1 cup peeled, cubed eggplant
1 large yam, peeled and cut into ½-inch cubes
1 cup asparagus, cut into 1-inch pieces (approximately 10 spears)
2 medium carrots, cut into ¼-inch slices

Preheat the oven to 350 degrees. Spray a sheet pan with olive oil. In a large bowl, combine the oil, aminos, vinegar, basil, pepper, and dill and whisk together with a fork. Add the prepared vegetables to the mixture. With plastic sandwich bags on your hands, combine the vegetables and the oil mixture until the vegetables are well coated. Spread the vegetables on the oiled sheet pan and place in the oven for 20 to 30 minutes. As an alternative, you can thinly slice the vegetables, toss on the oil mixture, and barbecue the vegetables on an oiled outdoor grill.

SPICING VARIATION

Replace the basil with 1 teaspoon curry powder and 1 teaspoon garam masala.

NUTRITIONAL FACTS

Per ¾-cup serving
Using ghee
Calories 95, Total fat 2.8 g, Saturated fat 1.6 g,
Carbohydrates 14.8 g, Protein 2.6 g

Cooked Grains

Freshly cooked whole grains provide an excellent source of carbohydrates, nutrients, and fiber. Grains also provide a sweet taste for balancing the diet. All grains can be cooked on the stovetop and most grains can be cooked in a rice cooker. Most grains require two to four parts water to one part dry grain, but read the recommended ratio on the package or in the chart below. If you prefer a rice cooker, try to find one with a stainless steel insert rather than aluminum. Rinse and drain the grains in a wire mesh strainer before cooking and be on the lookout for small rocks or twigs.

Cooking on the Stovetop

Bring the water and grains to a boil, according to the cooking directions. Reduce the heat to the lowest possible temperature. Most grains cook best when left alone. Don't be tempted to raise the lid and look inside. If your temperature is as low as possible and the appropriate amount of water is used, the grains will cook to a perfect consistency if you resist looking inside. Try lightly sautéing the grains in a dry pan before adding the water. The heat will release the flavor and lightly toast the grains, imparting a rich, nutty flavor. Experiment with your favorite grains.

Cooking Grains Table

MAKES 4 $^{1}/_{2}$-CUP SERVINGS

Use vegetable stock or purified water in the cooking of grains. Add a pinch of salt, herbs, or spices to enhance the flavors.

Grain (1 cup)	Liquid (cups)	Cooking Time (minutes)
Basmati rice	2	15–20
Pearl barley	4	45
Millet	2½	30
Quinoa	2	15–20

Grain (1 cup)	Liquid (cups)	Cooking Time (minutes)
Buckwheat (kasha)	2	20–30
Polenta	3½	15
Rolled oats	3	15
Oat groats, steel cut	3	40
Brown rice	2	45
Couscous and Bulgur		
Couscous	1½	7*
Bulgur wheat	1½	15*

*Couscous and bulgur wheat are not cooked, but absorb heated liquid. To prepare, bring the liquid to a boil, add the grain, and remove from the heat. Stir and cover. Set aside and let the grain rest for the appropriate time. Fluff with a fork and use in your favorite recipe.

NUTRITIONAL FACTS
Per 1 cup of uncooked grain

Grains	Calories (g)	Total Fat (g)	Sat. Fat (g)	Carbs (g)	Protein (g)
Rice	171	0.3	.1	38.7	3.2
Pearl barley	181	0.6	.1	38.9	5.0
Millet	187	2.1	.4	36.4	5.5
Quinoa	158	2.9	0	28.0	5.0
Groats/kasha	152	1.1	.2	30.7	4.8
Polenta	124	0.6	.1	26.8	2.9
Rolled oats	154	2.7	.5	25.8	6.6
Brown rice	170	1.4	.3	35.7	3.7
Couscous	158	0.3	.1	33.5	5.5
Bulgur	147	0.6	.1	32.0	3.5

Breakfast and Baked Goodies

Breakfast is a forecast of the whole day:
Spoil that and all is spoiled

LEIGH HUNT

We provide breakfast recipes for every occasion. For a breakfast on the run try Breakfast Bars and Almond Bliss Shake. For a morning when you are hungry and crave a big healthy meal, there is Broccoli Tofu Scramble, Strawberry Banana Yogurt, and Zucchini Pecan Bread. For a Sunday morning brunch extravaganza try Whole Wheat Crepes with Blueberry Syrup, Country Potatoes with Mandarin Tomato Salsa, and Coffee Bliss Shakes. Listen to your body's signal of hunger in the morning and eat accordingly.

One of our favorite breakfasts at the Chopra Center includes a small bowl of Hot Grain Cereal served with sautéed mixed berries, topped with a sprinkle of Chopra Granola, soymilk, and maple syrup. This breakfast includes all the six tastes, is balanced nutritionally, and is very satisfying.

Breakfast Recipes

Almond Bliss Shake

Apple and Rice Hot Cereal

Apple Syrup (Variations: Apricot, Pear, Nectarine)

Apple Maple Yogurt

Apple Raisin Muffins

Blueberry Muffins

Blueberry Banana Syrup (Variations: Strawberry, Raspberry, Blackberry)

Breakfast Bar

Breakfast Burritos

Broccoli Tofu Scramble

Cardamom Whole Wheat Pancakes

Chai Bliss Shake

Chopra Granola

Cinnamon Rolls

Country Potatoes

Coffee Bliss Shake

Homemade Almond Butter

Masala Potatoes

Hot Breakfast Cereal (Rolled Oats, Rice, Coucous, Polenta, Quinoa, Millet)

Mango Bliss Shake

Mango Yogurt

Morning Bliss Shake
Nutty French Toast
Pumpkin Muffins
Seasonal Fruit Salad
Strawberry Banana Yogurt
Tempeh and Potato Hash
Tofu and Potato Italiano
Traditional French Toast
Whole Wheat Crepes, Sweet or Savory
Vegetable Tofu Scramble
Very Berry Yogurt
Zucchini Pecan Bread

Almond Bliss Shake

Serves 1

1 tablespoon almond butter
2 teaspoons organic raw honey or maple syrup
1 ounce soy protein powder, plain or vanilla
1 pinch nutmeg
1 pinch cardamom
1 cup low-fat vanilla soymilk or rice milk
1 medium banana, peeled and sliced

Place all the ingredients in a blender and blend until smooth.

Nutritional Facts

Per 12-ounce serving
Calories 487, Total fat 12.4 g, Saturated fat 3.3 g,
Carbohydrates 61.1 g, Protein 32.9 g

Apple and Rice Hot Cereal

SERVES 4

2½ cups low-fat vanilla soymilk or rice milk
1 cup basmati rice, rinsed
1 stick cinnamon
3 whole cardamom pods
¼ to ½ cup apple juice
3 large apples, Granny Smith or pippin, unpeeled and cubed
¼ cup currants
1 tablespoon lemon juice
1 teaspoon cinnamon
½ teaspoon nutmeg
1 teaspoon vanilla extract
1 tablespoon maple syrup
1 tablespoon toasted coconut
¼ cup roasted walnuts

In a 2-quart saucepan, bring the soymilk and rice to a boil; add the cinnamon stick and the cardamom. Reduce the heat, cover, and simmer for 15 to 20 minutes at the lowest possible heat. Fluff with a fork and set aside. In a medium sauté pan, bring the apple juice to a boil; add the apples, currants, lemon juice, cinnamon, and nutmeg. Simmer for 5 minutes, adding more juice if necessary. Remove from the heat and stir in the vanilla and maple syrup. Place the rice in a serving bowl or individual bowls. Spoon the apple mixture over the rice and drizzle some of the juice on top. Garnish with the toasted coconut and walnuts.

NUTRITIONAL
FACTS

Per ¾-cup serving
Calories 382, Total fat 6.8 g, Saturated fat 2 g,
Carbohydrates 71.9 g, Protein 8.2 g

Apple Syrup

SERVES 4

1 teaspoon ghee
2 large apples, unpeeled and chopped
2 tablespoons currants, raisins, or dried cranberries
1 teaspoon cinnamon
¼ teaspoon nutmeg
½ cup apple juice
1 tablespoon lemon juice or orange juice
2 tablespoons maple syrup

Heat the ghee in a small saucepan. Add the apples, currants, cinnamon, nutmeg, and apple juice. Sauté for 2 minutes. Add the lemon juice or orange juice, and continue to simmer for 3 to 4 more minutes. The apples should be lightly cooked. Just before serving, add the maple syrup and stir to coat the apples well with the syrup. Serve warm or chilled. All of the ingredients and spices can be adjusted according to your taste.

VARIATION
Use 6 apricots, 3 pears, or 3 nectarines instead of the apples.

NUTRITIONAL FACTS

Per ½-cup serving
Using apples
Calories 124, Total fat 1.6 g, Saturated fat .9 g,
Carbohydrates 27.1 g, Protein .3 g

Apple Maple Yogurt

SERVES 4

1 teaspoon ghee
1 large apple, peeled or unpeeled, chopped into ½-inch pieces
1 teaspoon cinnamon
½ teaspoon nutmeg
1 tablespoon apple juice
2 tablespoons maple syrup
2 cups vanilla yogurt, low-fat

Heat the ghee in a small sauté pan. Add the apple, cinnamon, and nutmeg. Sauté for 3 to 4 minutes. Add the apple juice when the mixture gets dry. Remove the apples from the heat and place in a mixing bowl. Allow the apples to cool slightly. Pour the maple syrup and yogurt over the apples and stir until well combined. Serve for breakfast with fruits, granola, and hot cereals, and also as a cooling side dish to an entrée.

NUTRITIONAL FACTS

Per ¾-cup serving
Calories 184, Total fat 3.1 g, Saturated fat 1.9 g, Carbohydrates 33 g, Protein 6.1 g

Apple Raisin Muffins

MAKES 12
MUFFINS

2 cups whole wheat pastry flour or spelt flour
¼ cup turbinado sugar
2 teaspoons baking powder
½ teaspoon baking soda
½ teaspoon nutmeg
1 teaspoon cinnamon
1 cup raisins or currants
½ cup chopped walnuts
1 cup apple juice
¼ cup applesauce
1 tablespoon canola oil
¼ cup maple syrup
1 teaspoon vanilla extract
1 large egg, beaten, or 2 egg whites
3 medium apples, unpeeled, grated or finely chopped

Preheat the oven to 350 degrees. Spray a muffin pan with oil and set aside. In a bowl, combine the flour, sugar, baking powder, baking soda, nutmeg, cinnamon, raisins, and walnuts and stir together thoroughly using a wire whisk. In a separate bowl, combine the apple juice, applesauce, oil, maple syrup, and vanilla. Stir well, then add the egg and apples. Add the dry ingredients to the wet ingredients and combine gently. Scoop into the muffin pan and bake for 15 to 20 minutes or until golden brown. An inserted toothpick should come out clean.

NUTRITIONAL
FACTS

Per muffin
Calories 234, Total fat 5 g, Saturated fat .5 g,
Carbohydrates 42 g, Protein 4.9 g

Blueberry Muffins

MAKES 12
MUFFINS

1¾ cups whole wheat pastry flour or spelt flour
¼ cup turbinado sugar
2 teaspoons baking powder
½ teaspoon baking soda
½ teaspoon salt
1 teaspoon cinnamon
1 tablespoon grated lemon rind
1 cup low-fat vanilla soymilk or rice milk
1 tablespoon canola oil
½ cup mango purée or applesauce
¼ cup maple syrup
10 ounces blueberries, fresh or defrosted

Preheat the oven to 350 degrees. Spray a muffin pan with oil and set aside. In a bowl, combine the flour, sugar, baking powder, baking soda, salt, cinnamon, and lemon rind. Stir together with a wire whisk. In a separate bowl, combine the soymilk, oil, fruit purée, maple syrup, and blueberries. Stir gently to just combine. Add the dry ingredients into the wet ingredients and combine gently. Scoop into the muffin pan and bake for 15 to 20 minutes or until golden brown. An inserted toothpick should come out clean.

NUTRITIONAL
FACTS

Per muffin
Calories 138, Total fat 1.7 g, Saturated fat .4 g,
Carbohydrates 27.6 g, Protein 2.9 g

Blueberry Banana Syrup

SERVES 4

1 teaspoon ghee
1 cup fresh or frozen blueberries
1 cup sliced bananas
½ teaspoon nutmeg
¼ teaspoon ground cloves
1 tablespoon apple juice, orange juice, or lemon juice
1 teaspoon arrowroot powder
2 tablespoons maple syrup

Heat the ghee in a small saucepan. Add the blueberries, bananas, nutmeg, cloves, and juice. Simmer for 3 to 4 minutes if you are using fresh berries or 5 to 8 minutes if you are using frozen, or until the liquid begins to dissipate. To thicken the sauce, dissolve the arrowroot powder in 1 tablespoon of water, add to the berries, and stir until a smooth consistency is achieved. Add the maple syrup just before serving. Pour over breakfast cereal or use as a dessert topping.

VARIATION
Use strawberries, raspberries, peaches, nectarines, or blackberries instead of blueberries.

NUTRITIONAL FACTS | *Per ⅓-cup serving*
Calories 123, Total fat 1.9 g, Saturated fat 1.1 g, Carbohydrates 25.9 g, Protein .8 g

Breakfast Bar

12 SERVINGS

2 cups organic rolled oats
1 cup whole wheat pastry flour or oat flour
1 tablespoon flax seeds
1 tablespoon sesame seeds
1 teaspoon baking powder
½ teaspoon salt
1 cup currants or dried cranberries
1 cup sunflower seeds, pecans, or cashew pieces
1 cup coconut flakes
1 teaspoon cinnamon
1 teaspoon nutmeg
1 teaspoon ginger
¼ cup turbinado sugar
1½ cups low-fat vanilla soymilk or rice milk
¼ cup maple syrup
¼ cup canola oil or ghee
¾ cup mango purée or applesauce

Topping

1 tablespoon turbinado sugar
1 tablespoon cinnamon

Preheat the oven to 350 degrees. Spray a 9-by-13-inch baking pan with oil. Place all the dry ingredients (rolled oats through sugar) in a bowl. Using a wire whisk, combine the mixture well. Place all the wet ingredients (soymilk through fruit purée) in a large bowl and combine with a wire whisk. Add the dry ingredients to the wet ingredients and combine gently, using a rubber spatula. Transfer the mixture to the prepared pan and distribute evenly, gently patting the batter into place with the spatula. Combine the sugar and the cinnamon and sprinkle over the batter. Bake for approximately 30 minutes or until golden brown and an inserted toothpick comes out clean. Cool, then cut into 12 bars. Wrap individually. Breakfast bars are great as a breakfast on the run or as a handy, healthy snack.

NUTRITIONAL FACTS

Per 2-by-2-inch bar
Calories 339, Total fat 11.4 g, Saturated fat 3 g, Carbohydrates 50.9 g, Protein 8.2 g

Breakfast Burritos

SERVES 4

Be creative. This is a great way to make quick healthy meals and snacks. Great for children's lunch boxes, too.

4   large whole wheat tortillas (8 inches or larger)
8   tablespoons grated jack or cheddar cheese, optional
2   cups burrito filling, see suggestions on next page
4   tablespoons tomato salsa

Preheat the oven to 350 degrees. On an oiled sheet pan, lay out the tortillas and sprinkle with cheese. In the center of each tortilla, place ½ cup filling of your choice. Add the salsa and spread all the ingredients out to the edges of the tortilla. Place the pan in the oven for 5 minutes or until the cheese has melted. Remove from the oven and gently roll each tortilla into a rectangle by folding in two of the sides and then rolling over into a box shape.

To prepare one burrito, place the tortilla in a heated sauté pan, add the ingredients, and heat until the cheese has melted.

Burrito Filling Suggestions

Tempeh and Potato Hash (see page 100)

Tofu and Potato Italiano (see page 101)

Vegetable Tofu Scramble (see page 104)

vegetable sautés

refried pinto beans, rice, and guacamole

Country Potatoes (see page 86) with chopped soy "bacon" or soy sausage

black beans, rice, and tomato salsa

sautéed apples

rice and bananas with Almond Butter (see page 89), drizzled with honey

NUTRITIONAL
FACTS

Per 8-inch burrito
Using tortillas, salsa, and cheese
Calories 213, Total fat 8.6 g, Saturated fat 4.3 g,
Carbohydrates 25.8 g, Protein 8 g

Broccoli Tofu Scramble

SERVES 4

16 ounces fresh low-fat tofu, firm or extra firm
1 teaspoon ghee or olive oil
1 cup chopped leeks or onions
1 pinch black pepper
1 tablespoon Bragg Liquid Aminos or tamari
1 large red or green bell pepper, chopped
1 cup 1-inch broccoli florets
1 medium zucchini, sliced and cut into ¼-inch pieces
1 teaspoon curry powder
1 teaspoon ground cumin
½ teaspoon garam masala
1 teaspoon dried dill
Vegetable stock

Drain the tofu and crumble into a bowl and set aside. Heat a large sauté pan and add the oil, leeks, pepper, and aminos. Add the bell pepper, sauté for 2 minutes, then add the broccoli florets and zucchini. Continue to sauté for 2 or 3 minutes, or until the broccoli begins to soften. Add the tofu and spices. Add a small amount of vegetable stock, if the mixture gets too dry. Combine well and continue to sauté until heated through. Serve with country potatoes (page 86) and simple great whole grain bread (page 52).

NUTRITIONAL
FACTS

Per 1¼-cup serving
Using olive oil
Calories 181, Total fat 6.9 g, Saturated fat .2 g,
Carbohydrates 13.9 g, Protein 15.9 g

Cardamom Whole Wheat Pancakes

Serves 4

1½ cups whole wheat pastry flour
1½ teaspoons baking powder
½ teaspoon cardamom, ground
½ teaspoon nutmeg
½ teaspoon salt
1 egg
2 tablespoons ghee or canola oil
¼ cup maple syrup
1¼ cups low-fat soymilk or rice milk

In a bowl, combine the flour, baking powder, cardamom, nutmeg, and salt. Stir together with a whisk or fork. In a separate larger bowl, place the egg, oil, maple syrup, and soymilk. Lightly whip with a whisk or fork. Add the dry ingredients to the wet ingredients and stir until smooth. Don't overmix. Heat a griddle or sauté pan to medium hot. The griddle will be hot enough when a sprinkle of water sizzles in the pan. Brush the pan with the oil. Using a ¼-cup measure, pour the batter into the hot pan. After bubbles form on top of the cakes, turn them over and continue to cook for another 2 minutes or until the cakes are golden brown. Keep the pancakes warm in a 250-degree oven. Serve with fruit, fruit syrup, or maple syrup.

Nutritional Facts

Per serving of 3 3-inch pancakes
Calories 333, Total fat 10.4 g, Saturated fat 5.8 g, Carbohydrates 50.7 g, Protein 9.1 g

Chai Bliss Shake

SERVES 1

1 cup chai (traditional masala chai, yogi tea, or Chopra Center tea), made by steeping 2 bags in 8 ounces of boiling water for 10 minutes, or 2 tablespoons chai concentrate
1 medium banana, peeled and sliced
1 pinch nutmeg
1 pinch cinnamon
2 teaspoons organic raw honey or maple syrup
1 scoop soy protein powder, plain or vanilla
2 tablespoons low-fat vanilla soymilk

Combine all ingredients in a blender and blend until smooth.

NUTRITIONAL FACTS

Per 12-ounce serving
Calories 289, Total fat 1.2 g, Saturated fat .7 g, Carbohydrates 43.6 g, Protein 26 g

Chopra Granola

SERVES 10

2 cups organic rolled oats
¼ cup sunflower seeds
¼ cup pine nuts
¼ cup flaxseed
¼ cup sesame seeds
½ cup almonds or pecans, slices or pieces
2 tablespoons poppy seed
½ cup coconut flakes
1 tablespoon cinnamon
1 teaspoon nutmeg
1 teaspoon allspice
2 tablespoons ghee or canola oil
2 tablespoons apple juice
2 teaspoons vanilla extract
½ cup maple syrup
¼ cup dried cranberries
½ cup currants or chopped dates

Preheat the oven to 350 degrees. Oil a sheet pan and set aside. Combine all the dry ingredients, excluding the cranberries and the currants, in a bowl. Combine all the wet ingredients in a large bowl, add the dry ingredients, and, with plastic sandwich bags on your hands, toss together until well combined. Spread out on the oiled sheet pan. Bake for 30 minutes or until golden brown. Stir often with a spatula for even cooking. Add the currants and cranberries after the granola is baked. Cool completely, then store in a resealable plastic bag. Enjoy with soymilk. Chopra granola makes a good snack at any time of the day.

NUTRITIONAL FACTS

Per ½-cup serving
Calories 353, Total fat 15.6 g, Saturated fat 4.4 g,
Carbohydrates 43.8 g, Protein 9.8 g

Cinnamon Rolls

MAKES 24 ROLLS

**Basic
Dough**

1 tablespoon plus ½ cup turbinado sugar
1 tablespoon active yeast
1 cup very warm water
2 cups whole wheat pastry flour or unbleached organic white flour
2 cups whole wheat bread flour
1 teaspoon salt
1 tablespoon cinnamon
1 tablespoon ghee, melted butter, or canola oil
1 cup milk, soymilk, or rice milk
1 egg, optional

**Cinnamon
Filling**

2 tablespoons ghee or melted butter
2 tablespoons apple juice
2 tablespoons maple syrup
¼ cup turbinado sugar
2 tablespoons cinnamon
¼ cup chopped walnuts or raisins or both

Combine the 1 tablespoon sugar, yeast, and water in a small bowl and set aside until the yeast expands and foams.

Place the flours, salt, remaining ½ cup sugar, and cinnamon in a large bowl and whisk well. Add the ghee, milk, and egg (if using). Add the yeast when it has expanded. Combine and knead for 5 minutes. Place the dough in an oiled bowl. Cover and place in a warm spot to rise, about 45 to 60 minutes. When the dough has risen, punch it down to release the air, knead for 4 minutes, then roll out in a rectangular shape until the dough is ¼ inch thick.

Preheat the oven to 350 degrees. Oil a baking pan and set aside. Combine the ghee, apple juice, and maple syrup in a small bowl. In another small bowl, combine the sugar and cinnamon. Using a pastry brush, brush the rolled-out dough with the ghee, apple, and maple mixture. Sprinkle the sugar and cinnamon mixture over the ghee mixture, then sprinkle the nuts and/or raisins over the surface. Starting at a short end, gently begin to roll up the dough into a log. Cut the log into 1½-inch-thick slices and set them on the baking pan, about 1 inch apart. Let rise for 10 to 15 minutes, then bake for 20 to 25 minutes or until golden brown. Remove from the oven, turn the rolls over, and glaze the tops with maple syrup while they are hot.

NUTRITIONAL FACTS | *Per roll*
Calories 149, Total fat 3.9 g, Saturated fat 1.5 g, Carbohydrates 24.8 g, Protein 3.6 g

Country Potatoes

4	medium potatoes, russets or Yukon, unpeeled or peeled, cubed
3	teaspoons ghee or olive oil
1½	cups chopped leeks or onions
1	cup chopped red or green bell pepper
1	teaspoon salt
1	teaspoon black pepper
1	teaspoon cumin
1	teaspoon dill

Stovetop Method: Bring 4 quarts of water to a boil, add the potatoes and blanch until al dente, 4 or 5 minutes. Drain and set aside. Heat a large sauté pan on medium heat and add 1 teaspoon oil. Add the leeks, bell pepper, and spices. Sauté until the vegetables are tender, 3 minutes. Remove from the sauté pan, place in a bowl, and set aside. Reheat the sauté pan with 1 teaspoon oil and add the drained potatoes. Sauté until golden brown. Keep turning the potatoes and continue to drizzle the remaining teaspoon oil into the pan to prevent sticking. Add the leek and pepper mixture and reheat just before serving.

    Oven Method: Oil a sheet pan and preheat the oven to 350 degrees. Combine the raw, cubed potatoes and the vegetables in a large bowl. In a small bowl, combine the oil and the spices and whisk together with a fork. Pour the oil mixture over the vegetables and, with your hands in plastic sandwich bags, toss together until well combined and the vegetables are coated with the oil mixture. Spread on the oiled sheet pan and bake for 20 to 30 minutes or until the potatoes are tender, yet crispy and golden brown.

NUTRITIONAL
FACTS

Per 1¹/₄-cup serving
Stovetop
Using ghee
Calories 218, Total fat 7.9 g, Saturated fat 4.6 g,
Carbohydrates 32.5 g, Protein 4 g

Oven
Using olive oil
Calories 180, Total fat 3.8 g, Saturated fat .5 g,
Carbohydrates 32.5 g, Protein 4 g

Coffee Bliss Shake

SERVES 1

½ cup strong brewed coffee, or 1 shot espresso
1 pinch ground cardamom
1 medium banana, peeled and sliced
2 teaspoons organic raw honey or maple syrup
2 tablespoons low-fat vanilla soymilk

Place all ingredients in a blender and blend until smooth.

NUTRITIONAL
FACTS

Per 1-cup serving
Calories 194, Total fat 1 g, Saturated fat .6 g,
Carbohydrates 44.2 g, Protein 2.1 g

Homemade Almond Butter

MAKES $^1/_2$ CUP   1   cup raw almonds, sliced
                    2   teaspoons ghee

Dry-roast the almonds on a sheet pan in a 350-degree oven for 20 minutes or until golden brown and aromatic. Place the roasted almonds in a blender and begin to process into a coarse grind. Slowly drizzle the ghee onto the almonds as they purée. Scrape down the sides of the blender and then continue to purée until a smooth consistency is achieved. Cool and store in a jar with a tight-fitting lid. Spread 1 or 2 teaspoons on slices of toasted bread.

NUTRITIONAL FACTS | *Per 1-tablespoon serving*
Calories 75, Total fat 3.7 g, Saturated fat .7 g, Carbohydrates 1.2 g, Protein 1.2 g

Masala Potatoes

SERVES 4

3 large russet potatoes, peeled and cubed, soaked in salted water
1 teaspoon ghee or olive oil
1 teaspoon cumin seeds or 2 teaspoons ground cumin
1 teaspoon brown mustard seeds (caution, the seeds will pop when cooking)
1 teaspoon fenugreek seeds
1 cup chopped leeks or onions
2 inches of finely chopped fresh ginger or 1 teaspoon ground ginger
½ teaspoon turmeric
1 tablespoon Bragg Liquid Aminos or tamari
2 teaspoons coriander
1 teaspoon garam masala
½ cup fruit chutney or apricot jam
¼ cup plus ¼ cup vegetable stock
2 teaspoons lemon juice
¾ cup "lite" coconut milk or low-fat vanilla soymilk
1 10-ounce package frozen peas
¼ cup chopped fresh cilantro

Bring 4 quarts of water to a boil. Drain the cubed potatoes, add to the boiling water, and cook until al dente, 4 or 5 minutes. Drain the potatoes and set aside. Heat the oil in a large saucepan over medium heat and begin to add the next 12 ingredients (cumin through lemon juice) in the order listed. Keep the remaining ¼ cup vegetable stock close at hand to add as the mixture begins to dry out. Stir in the potatoes and simmer for 2 minutes, then add the coconut milk and the peas. Simmer for another 2 minutes, then add the cilantro. Stir well and continue to cook for another 3 or 4 minutes or until the potatoes are heated through. Serve as a breakfast dish, an entrée side dish, or in a breakfast burrito or calzone. Serve with cucumber raita (see page 233).

NUTRITIONAL FACTS	*Per 1-cup serving* Calories 372, Total fat 6.2 g, Saturated fat 2.5 g, Carbohydrates 67.7 g, Protein 11.2 g

Hot Breakfast Cereal

SERVES 4

Rolled oats or other grain of your choice, uncooked
4   cups water
½   teaspoon salt, optional
½   teaspoon nutmeg
1   teaspoon cinnamon
1   cup low-fat vanilla soymilk or rice milk
2   tablespoons maple syrup

Using the measurement listed in the Nutritional Facts chart below, combine your choice of grain with the salt and water in a 2-quart saucepan. (Toasting the grains until golden brown first in a dry sauté pan lends a nutty flavor to the cereal.) Bring to a boil, reduce heat, and simmer. Add the spices and begin to add the soymilk or rice milk as the mixture begins to thicken. Be prepared to add more milk if needed to create a thick and creamy cereal. Let the cereal cook for 5 to 7 minutes for oats, couscous, and polenta and 10 to 15 minutes for rice, quinoa, and millet. Just before serving, add maple syrup. Serve with sautéed fruit or fruit syrup.

NUTRITIONAL FACTS
4 servings per measurement of uncooked grain

Grain	Cups	Calories	Total Fat (g)	Sat. Fat (g)	Carbs (g)	Protein (g)
Rolled oats	2	208	3.3	.1	37.3	7.5
Rice	1.5	296	1.2	.7	65.7	5.9
Quinoa	1.5	293	4.4	.1	54.1	9.4
Couscous	1.5	289	1.1	.7	60.4	9.3
Polenta	1.5	221	2.3	.8	45.4	4.7
Millet	1.5	330	3.9	1.1	64.8	9.3

Mango Bliss Shake

SERVES 1

1 cup low-fat plain yogurt

1 fresh mango, cubed, or ½ cup mango purée, or ½ cup frozen mango cubes

¼ cup apple juice

2 teaspoons organic raw honey or maple syrup

¼ teaspoon cardamom, ground

Place all the ingredients in a blender and blend until smooth.

NUTRITIONAL FACTS

Per 2-cup serving
Calories 281, Total fat 4.1 g, Saturated fat 2.6 g, Carbohydrates 47.5 g, Protein 13.4 g

Mango Yogurt

SERVES 4

1 fresh mango
¼ cup mango purée or applesauce
2 tablespoons maple syrup or organic raw honey
1 pinch cloves
½ teaspoon cinnamon
¼ teaspoon cardamom
1½ cups low-fat vanilla yogurt

Cut the mango lengthwise on each side of the pit. Cut each half into cubes inside the skin, then remove the cubes with a paring knife. In a mixing bowl, place the cubed mango and the fruit purée. Add the maple syrup and the spices. Add the yogurt and blend together well by hand or with a hand mixer. You can also do this in a food processor for a smooth finish. Serve for breakfast with fruit, granola, and hot cereal— or as a creamy sauce or a cooling side dish with an entrée.

NUTRITIONAL FACTS

Per ¾-cup serving
Calories 178, Total fat 1.5 g, Saturated fat .8 g,
Carbohydrates 36.4 g, Protein 5 g

Morning Bliss Shake

SERVES 1

5 whole almonds, skin on, soaked overnight in ½ cup water
2 teaspoons organic raw honey or maple syrup
1 ounce soy protein powder, plain or vanilla
1 pinch cinnamon
1 cup low-fat vanilla soymilk
1 teaspoon Biochavan herbal supplement, optional
1 medium banana, peeled and sliced
1 tablespoon aloe vera juice

Drain the almonds and discard the water. Place almonds in a blender, add the other ingredients, and blend until smooth. Take as a morning protein supplement and digestive aid.

NUTRITIONAL
FACTS

Per 1¼-cup serving
Calories 424, Total fat 6.8 g, Saturated fat 2.8 g,
Carbohydrates 61.3 g, Protein 29.8 g

Nutty French Toast

SERVES 4

½ cup almonds or cashews, whole or pieces
2 tablespoons sunflower seeds
2 tablespoons sesame seeds
2 tablespoons flaxseed
1 teaspoon cinnamon
1 teaspoon nutmeg
2½ cups low-fat vanilla soymilk or rice milk
1 teaspoon vanilla extract
8 slices whole wheat bread

Combine the first 6 ingredients (almonds through nutmeg) in a food processor and pulse into a coarse meal. Slowly add the soymilk and vanilla. Purée into a smooth, thick consistency. Pour the mixture into a shallow baking pan or bowl. Soak bread slices in the mixture for about 1 minute on each side, allowing the liquid to soak in. Heat a skillet or griddle over medium heat. It is ready when a sprinkle of water sizzles. Spray or drizzle the skillet with oil. Carefully lay the bread slices down onto the hot skillet. Keep the heat moderate, not too hot. Cook approximately 2 to 4 minutes on each side until the toast is golden brown. Serve with maple syrup and sautéed fruit.

NUTRITIONAL
FACTS

Per 2-slice serving
Calories 360, Total fat 15.3 g, Saturated fat 4 g,
Carbohydrates 43 g, Protein 12.5 g

Pumpkin Muffins

MAKES 12
MUFFINS

2 cups whole wheat pastry flour or spelt flour
½ cup turbinado sugar
1 teaspoon cinnamon
1 teaspoon nutmeg
2 teaspoons baking powder
½ teaspoon baking soda
½ teaspoon salt
½ cup sliced almonds
½ cup raisins or dried cranberries
1 cup low-fat vanilla soymilk or rice milk
1 tablespoon canola oil
¼ cup maple syrup
¾ cup pumpkin purée

Preheat the oven to 350 degrees. Spray a muffin pan with oil and set aside. In a bowl, stir together with a wire whisk the flour, sugar, cinnamon, nutmeg, baking powder, baking soda, salt, almonds, and raisins. In a separate, larger bowl, combine the soymilk, oil, maple syrup, and pumpkin purée. Add the dry ingredients to the wet ingredients and combine gently. Scoop into the muffin pan and bake for 20 to 25 minutes or until golden brown. An inserted toothpick should come out clean.

NUTRITIONAL
FACTS

Per muffin
Calories 200, Total fat 3.7 g, Saturated fat .6 g, Carbohydrates 37.9 g, Protein 3.7 g

Seasonal Fruit Salad

SERVES 4

1 mango
1 peach, unpeeled
1 pear, unpeeled
1 apple, Granny Smith or pippin, unpeeled
½ cup blueberries, fresh or defrosted
½ cup orange juice
1 tablespoon maple syrup
1 teaspoon nutmeg

Cube all the fruit into bite-size pieces and put into a mixing bowl. Combine the orange juice, maple syrup, and nutmeg and pour over the fruit. Put into a single serving bowl or individual bowls.

NUTRITIONAL FACTS

Per 1¼-cup serving
Calories 142, Total fat .8 g, Saturated fat .2 g,
Carbohydrates 32.4 g, Protein 1.1 g

Strawberry Banana Yogurt

SERVES 4

1 banana, peeled and sliced
1 cup fresh strawberries, sliced
1 teaspoon cinnamon
½ teaspoon ginger powder
1 tablespoon apple or orange juice
2 cups low-fat vanilla yogurt
2 tablespoons maple syrup or organic raw honey

Heat a small sauté pan on medium heat. Add the bananas and the strawberries. Simmer for 1 or 2 minutes; add the cinnamon, ginger, and juice, then sauté for 3 or 4 minutes. Remove from the heat, place in a mixing bowl, and allow the fruit to cool slightly. Add the yogurt and the maple syrup and mix until well combined. Adjust sweetness according to your tastes by adding more maple syrup. Serve for breakfast with fruit, granola, and hot cereal.

NUTRITIONAL FACTS

Per 1-cup serving
Calories 186, Total fat 1.8 g, Saturated fat 1.1 g, Carbohydrates 35.7 g, Protein 6.6 g

Tempeh and Potato Hash

SERVES 4

12 ounces tempeh, cubed and marinated overnight (see page 57)
2 cups cubed red, Yukon, or russet potatoes, skin on
1 teaspoon ghee or olive oil
1 cup leeks or onions, chopped
1 tablespoon Bragg Liquid Aminos or tamari
1 cup chopped red or green bell pepper
½ teaspoon black pepper
1 teaspoon marjoram
1 teaspoon thyme
2 teaspoons sage
½ teaspoon nutmeg
½ cup vegetable stock
1 10-ounce package frozen peas

Heat the oven to 350 degrees and bake the marinated tempeh for 20 to 30 minutes. Remove from the oven and set aside. Bring 4 quarts of water to a boil and blanch the potatoes until al dente, 4 minutes. Drain and set aside. Heat the oil in a large sauté pan over medium heat, add the leeks, aminos, bell pepper, and spices. Add the drained potatoes and sauté for 3 or 4 minutes. Add ¼ cup vegetable stock and the peas. Remove the tempeh from the marinade and add to the sauté pan with the remainder of the stock. Allow the mixture to heat through. Serve with scrambled tofu, or use in a breakfast burrito (page 78).

NUTRITIONAL FACTS

Per 1½-cup serving
Calories 305, Total fat 6.8 g, Saturated fat 1.1 g, Carbohydrates 38.4 g, Protein 22.6 g

Tofu and Potato Italiano

SERVES 4

16 ounces cubed marinated firm tofu
2 cups cubed red, Yukon, or russet potatoes, skin on
1 teaspoon ghee or olive oil
1½ cups leeks or onions, chopped
½ teaspoon black pepper
1 pinch red chili flakes
2 tablespoons Italian herbs
2 tablespoons Bragg Liquid Aminos or tamari
1 cup chopped green bell pepper
2 cups diced tomatoes

Heat the oven to 350 degrees and bake the marinated tofu for 20 to 30 minutes. Remove from the oven, drain, and set aside. Bring 4 quarts of water to a boil and blanch the potatoes until al dente, 4 minutes. Drain and set aside. Heat the oil in a large sauté pan over medium heat. Add leeks, spices, aminos, and bell pepper. Sauté for 3 or 4 minutes. Add the drained potatoes and tomatoes. Simmer for another 3 minutes, then add the baked tofu cubes. Simmer for another 2 or 3 minutes until the tofu is heated through. Serve for breakfast as an entrée or in a breakfast burrito (page 78).

NUTRITIONAL FACTS

Per 2-cup serving
Calories 272, Total fat 7 g, Saturated fat .3 g,
Carbohydrates 33.8 g, Protein 18.3 g

Traditional French Toast

SERVES 4

2 eggs or 4 egg whites
½ cup low-fat milk, soymilk, or rice milk
2 teaspoons cinnamon
½ teaspoon ginger powder
1 teaspoon vanilla extract
1 teaspoon ghee
8 slices whole grain bread

In a medium-size flat bowl, combine eggs, milk, spices, and vanilla. Whisk the mixture together for 1 minute with a fork. Heat a griddle or large sauté pan over medium-high heat. Place the ghee on the griddle. The griddle is hot when a sprinkle of water sizzles. Cut the bread slices in half. Working with one piece at a time, dip the bread in the batter, turn it to the other side, and then place on the heated griddle. Continue until the griddle is full or the bread is used up. Toast the bread for 2 or 3 minutes on each side or until it is golden brown. Place in a 250-degree oven to keep warm. Serve with fresh or sautéed fruit and maple syrup.

NUTRITIONAL FACTS

Per 2-slice serving
Calories 277, Total fat 8 g, Saturated fat 3 g, Carbohydrates 39.2 g, Protein 11.9 g

Whole Wheat Crepes, Sweet or Savory

SERVES 4

2 eggs
1½ cups low-fat milk, soymilk, or rice milk
½ teaspoon salt
1 cup whole wheat pastry flour
2 tablespoons ghee or canola oil
1 teaspoon nutmeg

Place all the ingredients into a blender and blend until very smooth. Pour the batter into a mixing bowl and refrigerate for 30 minutes. Heat a griddle or sauté pan over medium-high heat. Place additional oil on the griddle. The griddle will be hot when a sprinkle of water sizzles. Ladle ¼ cup batter onto the griddle. Using the ladle, swirl the batter around into a very thin pancake. Turn when the surface begins to bubble. Being careful not to overcook the pancakes, cook until golden brown. Stuff the crepes with savory or sweet filling. Roll the filling up inside the crepe and then cover with the sauce.

For a sweet crepe: use sautéed fruit and paneer or ricotta cheese and blueberry syrup. For a savory crepe: use sautéed vegetables and serve with a creamy savory sauce flavored with fresh herbs. Enjoy as a main dish or a breakfast dish.

NUTRITIONAL FACTS

Per 2 crepes without filling
Using low-fat milk and canola oil
Calories 248, Total fat 11.1 g, Saturated fat 2.2 g, Carbohydrates 26.8 g, Protein 10.2 g

Vegetable Tofu Scramble

SERVES 4

16 ounces fresh low-fat tofu, firm or extra firm, drained and
  crumbled
1 teaspoon ghee
½ cup chopped leeks or onions
1 tablespoon Bragg Liquid Aminos or tamari
1 pinch black pepper
1 teaspoon cumin
1 teaspoon curry powder
½ teaspoon coriander
½ teaspoon dill
¼ teaspoon nutmeg
½ cup diced tomatoes
½ cup diced zucchini
1 cup fresh spinach
Vegetable stock
¼ cup chopped cilantro

Place the crumbled tofu into a bowl and set aside. Heat a large sauté
pan over medium heat and add the ghee, leeks, aminos, and spices.
Sauté for 2 minutes. Add the tomatoes, zucchini, and spinach and continue to sauté until the vegetables begin to soften, 4 or 5 minutes. Add
some vegetable stock if the mixture becomes dry. Add the crumbled
tofu and stir until well combined. Continue to sauté until the tofu is
heated through. Garnish with the chopped cilantro. Serve in a breakfast
burrito (see page 78) or as an entrée with salsa and country potatoes
(see page 86).

NUTRITIONAL
FACTS

Per 1-cup serving
Calories 160, Total fat 6.7 g, Saturated fat .8 g,
Carbohydrates 9.5 g, Protein 15.2 g

Very Berry Yogurt

SERVES 4

1 teaspoon ghee

1 10-ounce package frozen berries, or 1 pint fresh, any variety

½ teaspoon cloves

½ teaspoon allspice

2 tablespoons maple syrup or organic raw honey

2 cups low-fat vanilla yogurt

In a small sauté pan, heat the ghee and add the berries. Simmer for 1 or 2 minutes, allowing the frozen berries to defrost. Add the spices, and continue to simmer until the berries begin to soften, 3 to 5 minutes. Remove from the heat and place in a mixing bowl to cool slightly. If the berries produce too much liquid, spoon them into the bowl with a slotted spoon. Add the maple syrup and the yogurt and mix until well combined. Adjust sweetness according to your taste by adding more maple syrup. Serve for breakfast with fruit, granola, and hot cereal.

NUTRITIONAL FACTS

Per ¾-cup serving
Calories 173, Total fat 3 g, Saturated fat 1.8 g, Carbohydrates 30.4 g, Protein 6.3 g

Zucchini Pecan Bread

8 SLICES

1½ cups whole wheat pastry flour
¾ cup turbinado sugar
1 teaspoon baking powder
½ teaspoon baking soda
½ teaspoon salt
1 teaspoon cinnamon
1 teaspoon nutmeg
Grated rind of 1 orange
½ cup chopped pecans
2 large eggs, or 4 egg whites
2 tablespoons canola oil
¼ cup mango purée or applesauce
1½ cups grated zucchini

Preheat the oven to 350 degrees. Spray a 4-by-9-inch loaf pan with oil and set aside. In a medium bowl, place the flour, sugar, baking powder, baking soda, salt, cinnamon, nutmeg, orange rind, and pecans. In another large bowl, combine the eggs, oil, fruit purée, and zucchini and mix together with a wire whisk. Using a spatula, very gently fold the dry mixture into the wet mixture. Place the thick batter in the loaf pan. Bake for 50 minutes or until an inserted toothpick comes out clean. Cool and slice.

NUTRITIONAL FACTS

Per slice
Using whole eggs
Calories 269, Total fat 10.1 g, Saturated fat 1.1 g,
Carbohydrates 39 g, Protein 5.5 g

Entrées

To lengthen thy life, lessen thy meals.

BENJAMIN FRANKLIN

We have divided the Chopra Center 30-Day Nutritional Plan to include light meals and main meals. The light meals are meals that are best eaten in the evening, before 6 or 7 P.M. for optimal digestion. Your metabolic activity slows in the evening so you do not need as much fuel to maintain your energy level. Eating lighter at night is particularly beneficial if you are trying to drop a few pounds. You will also tend to sleep better if you have eaten a lighter evening meal.

The main meals are best enjoyed during the midday period. Your digestion is at its peak, and since you are more active during the day, your fuel requirements are higher. Most people in the West are in the habit of having their main meal in the evening when there is more time for meal preparation and the family is together. Try gradually eating more at lunchtime and less at dinner and notice how you feel. You and your family can still spend quality time together in the evening—you just don't need to eat as much.

Helpful Pointers

- Almost all of the recipes can be prepared for 1 or 2 people by dividing the ingredients in half or in quarters. Experiment with your favorites.
- If you are cooking for one, a trip to the salad bar may yield just the right vegetable combination of broccoli, cauliflower, bell peppers, carrots, and celery for a soup, stir-fry, or stew. Look for the freshest produce you can find.
- Use low-fat fresh tofu that is firm or extra firm for the best cooking results.
- Keep some marinated tofu on hand to speed up the process of making a quick stir-fry or sandwich. It also makes a protein-rich snack.
- Keep a cup of vegetable stock nearby whenever you are cooking. If you are tempted to add additional oil or fat to a dish to add moisture, try adding some vegetable stock instead. This will help to reduce extra fat in the diet. We have used only 1 teaspoon of oil in most of our dishes serving four. You can increase or decrease as desired.
- For added variety, you can add chicken or fish to some of the entrées.
- In the entrée recipes, we have used a standard 16-ounce package of tofu or tempeh. Package sizes will vary according to brand. Use the amount of either tofu or tempeh that is available. It does not need to be an exact amount.
- When planning a menu for a meal, a day, or a week, think about what you may be doing. Will you need some extra food to take for lunch the next day? Will you need to have a very quick, eat-on-the-run dinner before a meeting?

Thinking ahead will give you time to prepare foods that will be better for you and more nourishing, and you will be able to resist the temptation to run through a fast-food place or pick up food that may not be very nourishing.

Try to arrange your planning with this intention: Make lunch, whenever possible, the largest meal of the day and dinner the lighter meal of the day.

General Outline for a Day's Entrées

Main Meal

Soup
Grain
Dish with protein
Steamed or sautéed vegetable
Vegetables or stew
Chutney or sauce
Dessert

Light Meal

Soup or stew
Grain or bread
Dessert

Entrée Recipes

Curry Filo Tarts

Braised Tofu with Mango Tomato Salsa*

Buddha's Delight Vegetable Stir-Fry*

Cashew Tempeh or Tofu

Mediterranean Pasta*

Eggplant Cauliflower Curry

Moroccan Vegetables*

Rainbow Risotto

Roasted Eggplant and Spinach Pasta with Beans*

Roasted Tofu and Yams

Simple Whole Grain Pizza

Szechwan Baked Egg Roll

Thai-Style Noodles with Tofu or Tempeh*

Tofu Burgers or Tofu "Meat Balls"

Tofu, Tempeh, or Chicken Fajitas*

Vegetarian Paella

Winter Vegetables with Couscous

Spinach Polenta

*Entrées with optional chicken or fish additions.

Curry Filo Tarts

SERVES 4

1 teaspoon plus 1 teaspoon ghee or olive oil
1 cup chopped leeks or onions
1 tablespoon Bragg Liquid Aminos or tamari
1 pinch black pepper
1 3-inch head cauliflower, coarsely chopped into ½-inch pieces
1 pound carrots, peeled and chopped into ½-inch pieces
¼ cup vegetable stock
2 cups coarsely chopped broccoli
2 teaspoons curry powder
1 teaspoon dried dill
2 teaspoons garam masala
4 sheets whole wheat filo pastry

Preheat the oven to 350 degrees. Spray or brush a cupcake pan or 4 8-ounce custard cups or oven-safe bowls with oil. Heat a large sauté pan over medium heat; add 1 teaspoon oil, and then add the leeks, aminos, and pepper. Sauté until the leeks are translucent. Keeping the heat on high, add the cauliflower and carrots. Sauté for 4 or 5 minutes until the vegetables are cooked but not soft. Add ¼ cup vegetable stock as needed. Add the broccoli and the spices and continue to sauté for another 4 minutes. Be careful not to overcook the vegetables. Turn off the heat, cover, and set aside. Lay out the sheets of filo pastry on the counter. Spray lightly or brush with the remaining teaspoon oil. Fold each sheet in half, then in half again. Line the prepared cups with the folded filo sheets. Using a slotted spoon, fill the pastry cups with the vegetable mixture, straining off excess liquid. Bring up the ends of the filo pastry and twist together at the top. Spray lightly with oil and bake for 15 minutes or until golden brown.

NUTRITIONAL FACTS

Per tart
Calories 227, Total fat 5.2 g, Saturated fat 2.3 g, Carbohydrates 37.8 g, Protein 7.7 g

Braised Tofu with Mango Tomato Salsa

You may use salmon or chicken as an alternative to tofu.

SERVES 4

Marinade

1	cup apple juice
¼	cup lemon juice or rice vinegar
¼	cup Bragg Liquid Aminos, tamari, or soy sauce
¼	cup maple syrup or organic raw honey
1	pinch red chili flakes
1	teaspoon ground cumin
½	teaspoon ground cardamom
1	teaspoon grated fresh ginger or ½ teaspoon ground
1	teaspoon ghee or olive oil
16	ounces fresh firm, or extra firm low-fat tofu, or 4 4-ounce fresh salmon fillets, or 4 4-ounce boneless chicken breasts
1	recipe Mango Tomato Salsa (recipe follows)

Using a wire whisk, combine the marinade ingredients in a shallow baking dish or bowl. Slice the block of tofu into ½-inch-thick slices. Lay the tofu in the marinade and refrigerate overnight, or bake for 20 minutes in a 350-degree oven. If baked, cool the tofu before handling.

Heat the oil in a sauté pan over high heat. Reserving the marinade, remove the tofu. Place the tofu in the pan and sauté it briefly on each side until it is golden brown. Drizzle 1 tablespoon of the marinade over the tofu as it browns. Remove the tofu and arrange on a serving platter. Drizzle some of the marinade over it.

If you are using fish or chicken, marinate overnight first to optimize the flavor, then bake in a 350-degree oven for 20 to 30 minutes or grill until tender just before serving. Baste the chicken or fish with the marinade during grilling or baking. Serve with mango tomato salsa.

Mango Tomato Salsa

1 whole jalapeno or Anaheim chili, roasted and peeled, or 2 tablespoons mild canned chilies
1 ripe mango, cubed
2 medium tomatoes, cubed
1 teaspoon ghee or olive oil
½ cup chopped leeks or onions
2 cloves garlic or 1 teaspoon minced fresh ginger
1 tablespoon Bragg Liquid Aminos, tamari, or soy sauce
1 tablespoon lemon juice
¼ cup chopped cilantro
1 teaspoon ground cumin
½ teaspoon ground coriander

Using a pair of stainless steel tongs, hold the raw chili over the direct flame of a gas burner or place on a grill. Carefully turn the chili continuously, allowing the flame to char the skin of the chili until it blisters. Char as much of the surface area as possible. Seal the charred chili in a plastic bag, allowing the chili to steam inside, which will loosen the charred skin. When cool enough to handle, peel off the skin under running water.

Chop the chili and place in a small mixing bowl. Add the cubed mango and tomato and set aside. Heat the oil in a small sauté pan over medium heat. Add the leeks with the garlic and sauté until soft and transparent. Stir in the liquid aminos. Add the sauté to the mango mixture. Add the remaining ingredients and toss well. Serve on braised tofu or use as a side dish or condiment with other entrée dishes.

NUTRITIONAL FACTS	*Per 4-ounce serving*
	Using tofu
	Calories 309, Total fat 8.2 g, Saturated fat .4 g, Carbohydrates 40.7 g, Protein 18.4 g
	Using salmon fillet
	Calories 343, Total fat 10.2 g, Saturated fat 1.5 g, Carbohydrates 35.4 g, Protein 27.6 g
	Using chicken breast
	Calories 306, Total fat 4.4 g, Saturated fat .8 g, Carbohydrates 35.4 g, Protein 31.3 g

Buddha's Delight Vegetable Stir-Fry

Plan on approximately 1½ cups total of mixed raw vegetables per person before cooking. Choose any of the following vegetables—up to 6 or 7 cups total—for a stir-fry for 4 people. Cook the vegetables in the order given.

Basic Chinese Sauce

(MAKES 2 CUPS)

- 1 teaspoon plus 2 teaspoons sesame oil
- 2 cloves garlic, pressed, or ½ teaspoon garlic powder
- 1 teaspoon grated ginger or 1 teaspoon ground
- ¼ teaspoon red chili flakes
- ¼ cup Bragg Liquid Aminos or tamari
- 3 tablespoons rice vinegar
- 1 tablespoon lemon juice
- 1 tablespoon maple syrup
- 1 teaspoon mustard, dry
- 1½ cups vegetable stock
- 2 tablespoons arrowroot, dissolved in 2 tablespoons water

Vegetable Selections

- 1 cup thinly sliced carrots, cut diagonally
- 1 cup bite-size cauliflower florets
- 1 cup bite-size broccoli pieces, including peeled and sliced stalk
- 1 cup diagonally cut celery
- 1 cup 2-inch pieces asparagus
- 1 cup whole green beans
- 2 cups thinly sliced bok choy, cut diagonally
- 2 cups shredded white or napa cabbage
- 1 cup thinly sliced red or green bell peppers
- 2 cups mung bean sprouts
- 2 cups shredded spinach
- 1 cup whole snow peas
- 1 tablespoon ghee, olive oil, or sesame oil, or 2 tablespoons apple juice or vegetable stock

Sesame seeds and sliced green onions

In a small saucepan, heat 1 teaspoon sesame oil over medium heat. Add the garlic, ginger, and red chili flakes and sauté briefly. Add the aminos, vinegar, lemon juice, maple syrup, and mustard. Whisk together, adding the vegetable stock slowly, and bring the mixture to a rolling boil. Just as the sauce begins to boil, add the remaining 2 teaspoons sesame oil and the dissolved arrowroot, stirring constantly with a whisk until sauce is thickened. Remove from the heat and set aside.

Select your choice of vegetables and cut them into the correct sizes. Place all of the vegetables into separate piles or bowls until you are ready to sauté. In a large wok or sauté pan, heat the oil or apple juice (use apple juice or vegetable stock to reduce the fat content). Keep the heat on high; begin the stir-fry by adding the vegetables that will take the longest to cook. Keep adding the vegetables, one kind at a time in the order listed, until all the vegetables are cooking in the wok or pan. Allow the vegetables to cook until they are al dente—still a little crunchy—no more than 5 to 7 minutes. Pour the sauce over vegetables after they are cooked. Heat through and serve over rice or udon noodles. Garnish with sesame seeds and sliced green onions.

Buddha's Delight with Chicken

Stir-fry ¼ to ½ cup diced chicken per person in 1 teaspoon sesame oil. Sauté for 4 minutes. Add the Chinese sauce and sauté for another 2 minutes. Remove from the wok or sauté pan and set aside. Stir-fry the vegetables, adding the chicken and sauce at the end to reheat briefly.

NUTRITIONAL FACTS

Per 2-cup serving
Using olive oil, vegetables, and sauce
Calories 172 (vegetables and sauce), Total fat 7.5 g,
Saturated fat 1 g, Carbohydrates 20 g, Protein 6.3 g

Per 2½-cup serving
Using chicken
Calories 360, Total fat 18 g, Saturated fat 4 g,
Carbohydrates 20 g, Protein 29.9 g

Cashew Tempeh or Tofu

SERVES 4

1 teaspoon plus 1 teaspoon ghee, olive oil, or sesame oil
8 ounces fresh, low-fat tofu or tempeh, cut into 1-inch triangles, 1 inch thick
2 tablespoons apple juice
2 tablespoons Bragg Liquid Aminos or tamari
1 cup chopped leeks or onions
2 cloves garlic, minced, or ½ teaspoon garlic powder
1 pinch red chili flakes
1 tablespoon chopped fresh ginger
1 teaspoon ground cumin
1 cup diagonally sliced carrots
1 cup diced green bell peppers
1 cup diced red bell peppers
3 cups broccoli florets
½ cup vegetable stock
¼ cup toasted cashews

Heat 1 teaspoon oil in a sauté pan. Add the tofu and sprinkle both sides with apple juice and aminos. Continue until all the tofu is brown. Add more oil (or some vegetable stock) if necessary. Remove the tofu from the heat and set aside.

Heat the remaining 1 teaspoon oil in a large sauté pan or wok. Add the leeks, garlic, red chili flakes, ginger, and cumin. Sauté until leeks are translucent. Add the carrots and peppers and continue to sauté for 2 to 3 minutes. Add the tofu, broccoli, and vegetable stock. Allow the mixture to simmer, adding more vegetable stock if necessary. Heat through and garnish with the cashews. Serve with rice and a lettuce wrap (see page 199).

NUTRITIONAL FACTS

Per 1½-cup serving
Calories 269, Total fat 11.3 g, Saturated fat 3 g,
Carbohydrates 25.3 g, Protein 16.8 g

Mediterranean Pasta

This sauce is also great served over broiled or grilled fish or chicken, over rice or as a side dish stew. Garnish with toasted pine nuts.

SERVES 4

1 teaspoon ghee or olive oil
1 cup chopped leeks or onions
1 tablespoon Bragg Liquid Aminos or tamari
½ teaspoon black pepper
1 teaspoon thyme
1 teaspoon dried basil or 2 tablespoons chopped fresh basil
1 teaspoon oregano
1 cup asparagus, cut into 1-inch pieces
½ cup artichoke quarters, fresh or canned, rinsed
1 cup green beans, cut into 1-inch pieces
¼ cup vegetable stock
2 cups watercress or red Swiss chard, torn into small pieces
2 cups diced tomatoes
2 tablespoons chopped Kalamata olives
½ pound fresh pasta or 6 ounces dried pasta, cooked and drained
Extra virgin olive oil
Balsamic vinegar

In a large sauté pan, heat the oil and add the leeks, aminos, pepper, thyme, basil, and oregano. Simmer for 2 minutes, then add the asparagus, artichokes, green beans, and vegetable stock; stir and cover the pan and continue to simmer for 3 or 4 more minutes. Add the watercress, tomatoes, and additional stock, if necessary. Simmer until the greens are just wilted. Add the olives and serve over your favorite cooked pasta. Drizzle a little extra virgin olive oil and balsamic vinegar over the pasta before adding the sauce to add extra zest.

NUTRITIONAL FACTS

Per 2-cup serving
Using sauce and pasta
Calories 269, Total fat 4 g, Saturated fat .9 g,
Carbohydrates 47.8 g, Protein 10.3 g

Eggplant Cauliflower Curry

SERVES 4

1 teaspoon plus 1 teaspoon ghee or olive oil
1 tablespoon Bragg Liquid Aminos or tamari
2 tablespoons apple juice
1 tablespoon curry powder
1 tablespoon dill weed
3 cups eggplant, cut into 1-inch cubes
3 cups cauliflower florets, rinsed
1 cup chopped leeks or onions
2 teaspoons ginger, fresh, finely chopped
1 tablespoon Bragg Liquid Aminos or tamari
¼ cup vegetable stock
2 teaspoons ground cumin
¼ cup homemade fruit chutney or apricot jam
2 teaspoons coriander
2 teaspoons garam masala
2 teaspoons lemon juice
½ cup coconut milk
1 cup low-fat vanilla soymilk
¼ cup chopped fresh cilantro
Toasted coconut flakes and roasted cashews

Preheat the oven to 350 degrees. In a large bowl, whisk together 1 teaspoon oil, aminos, apple juice, curry powder, and dill. Add the eggplant and gently toss until well covered. Lay the eggplant cubes out on a sheet pan and roast for 20 minutes. Remove from the oven and cool. Meanwhile, bring 4 quarts of water to a boil, add the cauliflower, and blanch for 5 to 6 minutes. Drain and set aside to cool.

Heat the remaining teaspoon oil in a 4-quart soup pot. Add the leeks, ginger, aminos, vegetable stock, cumin, chutney or jam, coriander, and garam masala. Reduce the heat and simmer for 5 minutes, then add the lemon juice, coconut milk, soymilk, and cilantro. Add the eggplant and cauliflower and continue to simmer over medium to low heat for another 4 or 5 minutes. If the mixture gets dry, add some additional vegetable stock. Garnish with toasted coconut flakes and roasted cashews if desired and serve over rice.

| NUTRITIONAL FACTS | *Per 1½-cup serving*
Calories 237, Total fat 4.1 g, Saturated fat 2.2 g, Carbohydrates 44 g, Protein 6.2 g |

Moroccan Vegetables

SERVES 4

Moroccan Chili Sauce

1 teaspoon ghee or olive oil
1 cup chopped leeks or onions
3 cloves garlic, minced, or 1 teaspoon garlic powder
2 teaspoons oregano
1 pinch black pepper
2 teaspoons curry powder
1 teaspoon allspice
2 tablespoons Bragg Liquid Aminos or tamari
1 large green bell pepper, finely chopped
2 ribs celery, finely chopped
2 cups (about 1½ pounds) finely chopped tomato
½ cup vegetable stock or tomato juice

Moroccan Vegetables

2 large carrots, peeled and cut into ¼-inch rounds
1 cup cauliflower florets
¼ cup vegetable stock
2 large zucchini, cut in half lengthwise, then into ¼-inch slices
4 cups fresh spinach, washed and torn into pieces
1 cup broccoli florets
2 tablespoons toasted pine nuts
¼ cup chopped fresh dill
¼ cup crumbled feta cheese

Heat the oil in a large saucepan. Add the leeks, garlic, oregano, black pepper, curry powder, allspice, and aminos and sauté over medium heat for 2 or 3 minutes. Add the bell pepper, celery, and tomatoes and continue to sauté for 2 or 3 minutes. Reduce the heat to low, add the stock and simmer, covered, for up to ½ hour.

Bring 3 quarts of water to a boil in a large pot. Add the carrots and cauliflower and blanch for 2 minutes, or lightly steam in a steamer. Drain the vegetables and set aside. In the same large pot, heat the vegetable stock, add the zucchini, and simmer for 2 or 3 minutes. Add the carrots and cauliflower, the spinach, and the chili sauce. Heat just to the boiling point, add the broccoli, and stir. Reduce the heat to low. Cover and simmer for 3 or 4 minutes. Be careful not to overcook the broccoli. Garnish with toasted pine nuts, freshly chopped dill, and feta cheese. Serve over pasta, couscous, grains, or as a side-dish stew.

VARIATION

Bake 4 4-ounce boneless chicken breasts or 4 4-ounce freshwater bass fillets in the sauce and serve the vegetables on the side.

NUTRITIONAL FACTS

Per 1½-cup serving
Calories 187 (without cheese), Total fat 6.6 g,
Saturated fat .9 g, Carbohydrates 24.4 g, Protein 7.4 g

Using 1 4-ounce chicken breast
Calories 305, Total fat 8 g, Saturated fat 1.3 g,
Carbohydrates 24.4 g, Protein 33.6 g

Using 1 4-ounce water bass fillet
Calories 311, Total fat 10.8 g, Saturated fat 1.8 g,
Carbohydrates 24.4 g, Protein 28.8 g

Rainbow Risotto

This is a perfect dish for a dinner party.

SERVES 8

1 teaspoon plus 1 teaspoon ghee or olive oil
1½ cups leeks, shallots, or onions, chopped
1 tablespoon Bragg Liquid Aminos or tamari
1 teaspoon balsamic vinegar
1 teaspoon black pepper
1 teaspoon dried basil
1 teaspoon thyme
1 teaspoon sage
2 cups arborio rice, rinsed and drained
6 cups hot vegetable stock
1 cup thinly sliced carrots
1 cup thinly sliced celery
1 cup zucchini, cut in half lengthwise, then into ¼-inch slices
1 cup cooked white beans or 1 14-ounce can, drained and rinsed
2 cups arugula, or a mixture of spinach and arugula, coarsely torn
1 tablespoon chopped fresh rosemary
1 tablespoon chopped fresh mint
2 tablespoons fresh basil, thinly sliced
Chopped fresh parsley

Heat 1 teaspoon oil in a 4-quart soup pot over medium heat. Sauté the leeks with the aminos, vinegar, pepper, dried basil, thyme, and sage until the leeks are translucent. Add the rice and sauté, stirring constantly until golden brown or caramelized. Lower the heat. As the rice dries out, begin to add stock, 1 cup at a time, stirring constantly. Allow the rice to absorb the stock each time before adding more. Keep stirring. Risotto should have a soft (not mushy) texture with a creamy consistency. Be careful not to overcook or let the rice dry out. The cooking process will take about 20 to 30 minutes total. Taste the rice for texture.

Heat the remaining teaspoon oil in a sauté pan over medium-high heat and add the carrots, celery, zucchini, and beans. Add some stock if necessary to keep the vegetables moist. Sauté until the carrots are al dente or almost soft. Add the greens and continue to sauté until just wilted. Pour all the ingredients from the sauté pan into the rice, add the fresh herbs and gently combine. Place the rice in a festive serving dish and garnish with freshly chopped parsley. Traditionally, a good quality grated Parmesan or asiago cheese and cream might be added to this dish to achieve a creamy consistency.

Nutritional Facts	*Per 1½-cup serving* Calories 328, Total fat 2.8 g, Saturated fat .4 g, Carbohydrates 55.8 g, Protein 19.7 g

Roasted Eggplant and Spinach Pasta with Beans

You can replace the white beans with small pieces of grilled or baked chicken or fish.

SERVES 4

1   medium eggplant, sliced into ¼-inch rounds
2   tablespoons balsamic vinegar
1   teaspoon olive oil plus 1 teaspoon ghee or olive oil
1   tablespoon plus 2 teaspoons dried basil
1   teaspoon plus ½ teaspoon black pepper
1   cup minced leeks, shallots, or onions
2   cloves fresh garlic, pressed or minced
1   tablespoon Bragg Liquid Aminos or tamari
2   teaspoons dried dillweed or 1 tablespoon minced fresh dill
6   cups fresh spinach, rinsed and coarsely torn or chopped
1   cup cooked white beans or 1 14-ounce can, drained and rinsed
¼   cup vegetable stock
½   pound fresh pasta
½   cup Pesto-Tomato Pasta Sauce (see page 243) or ¼ cup pre-made or store-purchased pesto
¼   cup crumbled feta cheese or good-quality Parmesan cheese, grated
2   tablespoons minced fresh parsley

Preheat the oven to 350 degrees. Place the eggplant in a large bowl with the balsamic vinegar, 1 teaspoon olive oil, 1 tablespoon basil, and 1 teaspoon pepper. Toss until well coated. Lay the eggplant onto an oiled sheet pan and brush any remaining oil mixture on both sides of the eggplant. Bake for 20 minutes.

When eggplant is cool enough to work with, slice it into thin strips and set aside.

Heat the remaining teaspoon oil in a large sauté pan over medium heat. Add, in order, the leeks, garlic, aminos, ½ teaspoon pepper, dill, and 2 teaspoons basil. Add the spinach and sauté until just wilted, then add the reserved sliced eggplant and beans, chicken, or fish. Add the vegetable stock only if necessary to add moisture. Simmer until heated through.

Cook the pasta in boiling water just before serving. Drain pasta and place in a shallow pasta bowl or individual pasta bowls; toss with a little olive oil to prevent sticking. Pour the pesto-tomato pasta sauce into the eggplant mixture, heat briefly, then pour the sauce over the hot pasta. Toss together and serve. Garnish with the cheese and minced parsley.

| NUTRITIONAL FACTS | *Per 2-cup serving*
Calories 395 (includes cheese), Total fat 7.6 g, Saturated fat 2.1 g, Carbohydrates 64.9 g, Protein 16.9 g |

Roasted Tofu and Yams

S ERVES 4

Tofu Marinade

½ cup lemon or orange juice
1 cup apple juice
1 tablespoon Bragg Liquid Aminos or tamari
1 teaspoon olive oil
1 teaspoon garam masala
16 ounces fresh, low-fat tofu, firm or extra firm, cut into 1-inch cubes

Yams

2 large yams or sweet potato
1 teaspoon ghee or olive oil
½ teaspoon black pepper
½ teaspoon oregano
1 teaspoon dill
1 teaspoon curry powder
1 teaspoon garam masala
2 teaspoons Bragg Liquid Aminos or tamari
1 teaspoon lemon juice
½ cup apple juice or vegetable stock
Chopped cilantro

Combine all the marinade ingredients in a shallow bowl and add the tofu cubes. If possible, marinate the tofu overnight. Or, to speed up the process, put the tofu and the marinade in a shallow baking pan and bake in a 350-degree oven for 20 to 30 minutes. Remove from the oven and let cool.

Preheat the oven to 350 degrees. Peel the yams and cut into 1-inch cubes. In a large bowl, whisk together the oil, pepper, oregano, dill, curry powder, garam masala, aminos, lemon juice, and apple juice. Add the cubed yams and toss until well coated with the marinade.

Spread the marinated yams on an oiled sheet pan and bake until they are soft and golden brown, but not mushy, approximately 30 minutes. If the tofu has not been baked yet and has marinated overnight, add it to the yams at the same time on the same sheet pan and bake until golden brown, approximately 30 minutes. If you have already baked the marinated tofu, remove the tofu cubes from the tofu marinade with a slotted spoon and add to the yams for the final 15 minutes of baking. Serve over your favorite grain with some steamed vegetables and sautéed greens. Garnish with freshly chopped cilantro.

NUTRITIONAL FACTS	*Per 1½-cup serving* Calories 305, Total fat 8.2 g, Saturated fat .5 g, Carbohydrates 41.7 g, Protein 16.1 g

Simple Whole Grain Pizza

MAKES 2
10-INCH
PIZZAS

2 tablespoons active yeast
2 tablespoons turbinado sugar
2 cups very warm (not boiling) water
2 cups organic unbleached white flour
2 cups organic whole wheat pastry flour
1 tablespoon olive oil or ghee
1 teaspoon sea salt
1 tablespoon dried basil

Place the yeast and the sugar in a small bowl, add the warm water and dissolve until the yeast expands or "proofs." In a large bowl, combine the flours, oil, salt, and basil. Make a hole in the center of the flour and pour the proofed yeast into it. Mix together with your hands and knead the dough in the bowl until smooth in texture, about 5 minutes. If the mixture is very dry, add ½ cup more water. Place dough into a clean, oiled bowl and cover with a damp dish towel. Let rise until doubled in size, about 1 hour.

When the dough has risen, punch it down with your hand, flattening it out. Preheat the oven to 350 degrees. Divide the dough in half and roll each half into round pizzas. Place on oiled pizza pans. Top with your favorite toppings. Bake for about 20 minutes or until browned and crusty.

SAUCES *(amounts given are per pizza)*

> 2 tablespoons Basil and Friends Pesto (see page 230)
> ½ cup Roasted Tomato Sauce (see page 244)

VEGETABLE CHOICES *(amounts given are per pizza)*

2 cups roasted vegetables cut in bite-size pieces: carrots, zucchini, eggplant, red bell peppers

4 sliced tomatoes with 2 tablespoons thinly sliced fresh basil

3 diced zucchinis sautéed with ¼ cup diced roasted red peppers

½ pound mushrooms sautéed with 1 cup chopped leeks

3 cups sautéed spinach

CHEESES AND EXTRAS

feta, paneer, or jack cheese (¼ to ½ cup cheese per pizza)

black olives

soy pepperoni

artichoke hearts

NUTRITIONAL FACTS | *Per slice (⅛ plain pizza)*
Calories 134, Total fat 1.1 g, Saturated fat .5 g, Carbohydrates 20.9 g, Protein 3.1 g

Szechwan Baked Egg Roll

Serve these with Nutty Dipping Sauce (page 241) or Spicy Lime and Red Pepper Dipping Sauce (page 247).

MAKES 8
ROLLS
(4 SERVINGS)

1 teaspoon ghee or olive oil
1 teaspoon sesame oil
2 medium carrots, diced small
2 teaspoons minced fresh ginger
1 teaspoon coriander
1 teaspoon Chinese five-spice powder
¼ cup minced leeks or green onions
1½ cups shredded cabbage
½ cup finely diced red bell pepper
½ cup chopped mung bean sprouts
¾ cup extra firm, low-fat, silken tofu, marinated and diced small
8 egg roll wrappers
1 egg, whisked into a small bowl
1 tablespoon sesame seeds

Preheat the oven to 425 degrees. In a wok or sauté pan, heat the oils over high heat. Add the carrots, ginger, coriander, five-spice powder, and leeks and sauté for 3 minutes. Add the cabbage, bell pepper, and sprouts. Sauté for another 2 minutes. Add the tofu. Simmer for 2 minutes, then remove from the heat and drain any excess liquid from the pan. Lay the egg wrappers out on the counter. Using a slotted spoon, place ¼ cup of the mixture in the center of each wrapper. Fold the wrapper over the filling, by first tucking in the sides, then rolling over. Place the egg rolls on an oiled baking sheet pan sprinkled with cornstarch. Brush each egg roll with the egg wash and sprinkle with sesame seeds. Bake for 15 to 20 minutes or until golden brown.

Serve with rice and a stir-fry or with Thai-style noodles (page 132).

NUTRITIONAL FACTS	*Per 2 egg rolls*
	For egg rolls only without sauce
	Calories 186, Total fat 5.5 g, Saturated fat 1.1 g,
	Carbohydrates 25.1 g, Protein 9.1 g

Thai-Style Noodles with Tofu or Tempeh

Use this stir-fry sauce in other Asian-style stir-fry dishes.

SERVES 4

1 recipe baked marinated tofu or tempeh (see page 57) or 2 cups cooked diced chicken

Thai Stir-fry Sauce

½ cup vegetable stock
¼ cup rice vinegar
2 tablespoons apple juice
2 teaspoons lemon juice
1 teaspoon miso paste
1 teaspoon paprika
1 teaspoon Chinese five-spice powder
1 tablespoon maple syrup
1 tablespoon Bragg Liquid Aminos or tamari
2 tablespoons thinly sliced fresh basil leaves

Noodles

8 ounces Pad Thai, soba, or rice noodles
1 teaspoon ghee, sesame oil, or olive oil
½ cup sliced leeks, onion, or green onions
1 pinch red chile flakes
1 teaspoon coriander
2 tablespoons finely chopped fresh ginger
2 cloves garlic, pressed or minced, optional
2 tablespoons vegetable stock
2 tablespoons toasted sliced almonds
¼ cup chopped green onions
2 cups mung bean sprouts, rinsed
½ cup chopped cilantro

Remove the tofu or tempeh from the marinade and cut into 1-inch strips. Set aside.

In a blender, combine all the sauce ingredients except the basil and purée until smooth. Add the basil after blending. Set aside.

Cook or soak the noodles according to the package directions. Rinse, place in a large bowl, and sprinkle with sesame oil to keep the noodles from sticking.

Heat the oil in a wok or large sauté pan. Add the leeks, chili flakes, coriander, ginger, and garlic and sauté for 2 minutes, adding the stock after 1 minute. Add 2 cups of the tofu, tempeh strips, or chicken. Cover, reduce the heat, and simmer for 3 or 4 minutes. Add the almonds, green onions, sprouts, and cilantro. Simmer until heated through, 3 or 4 minutes. Add the stir-fry sauce, simmer 2 to 3 minutes, then pour the mixture over the noodles and toss until well combined. Serve with steamed vegetables.

NUTRITIONAL FACTS	*Per 2-cup serving* Calories 414, Total fat 9 g, Saturated fat .5 g, Carbohydrates 64.3 g, Protein 18.9 g
	Using chicken Calories 469, Total fat 7.8 g, Saturated fat 1.6 g, Carbohydrates 59 g, Protein 40.8 g

Tofu Burgers or
Tofu "Meat Balls"

3–4 dry bread slices
1 teaspoon ghee or olive oil
1 cup chopped leeks or onions
½ teaspoon black pepper
16 ounces fresh, low-fat tofu, firm or extra firm, drained and crumbled
¼ cup mixed almonds, pine nuts, and sunflower seeds
1 cup grated zucchini
1 cup grated carrots
1 teaspoon basil, dried
1 teaspoon oregano, dried
1 teaspoon thyme, dried
1 teaspoon minced garlic or 1 teaspoon garlic powder
1 tablespoon Bragg Liquid Aminos or tamari

Preheat the oven to 350 degrees. Place the dry bread in a food processor, and pulse into bread crumbs. Remove from the food processor and set aside. Heat the oil in a small sauté pan; add the leeks and pepper. Sauté for 2 or 3 minutes over high heat. Remove from the heat and cool. Place the tofu, mixed nuts and seeds, grated vegetables, and sautéed leeks in the food processor. Pulse a few times, then add the basil, oregano, thyme, garlic, and aminos. Continue to pulse to a smooth consistency. The mixture should be thick, yet firm. Scoop out the mixture with a ½-cup measure and form into balls. Flatten the balls into burgers and pat the bread crumbs on each side of the burgers. Heat some oil in a pan and sauté briefly to brown both sides of the burgers. Place on an oiled sheet pan and bake for 15 minutes or until firm.

Use this recipe to make "meat balls" for pasta or as an alternative to ground meat in tacos and casseroles. Change the spices according to the use. Serve the tofu burgers with leek sauce (see page 239) or in whole wheat buns with traditional trimmings.

NUTRITIONAL FACTS	*Per serving (2 burgers or 4 meat balls)* Calories 261, Total fat 10.4 g, Saturated fat .7 g, Carbohydrates 24.1 g, Protein 17.5 g

Tofu, Tempeh, or Chicken Fajitas

SERVES 4

Marinade

2 tablespoons chopped cilantro
½ cup lime, lemon, or orange juice
1 cup apple juice
2 teaspoons oregano
1 tablespoon cumin
¼ cup Bragg Liquid Aminos or tamari
1 pinch black pepper
1 pinch red chili flakes
3 cloves garlic, crushed, or 2 teaspoons garlic powder
16 ounces fresh, low-fat tofu or tempeh, firm or extra firm

Filling

1 teaspoon ghee or olive oil
2 tablespoons Bragg Liquid Aminos or tamari
4 large leeks, thinly sliced into long strips
1 medium red bell pepper, cut into thin strips
1 pinch red chili flakes
1 small yellow squash, cut into thin strips
1 medium zucchini, cut into thin strips
1 cup broccoli florets
1 cup vegetable stock
2 cups diced tomatoes
2 teaspoons cumin
1 teaspoon chili powder
1 teaspoon oregano
½ cup chopped cilantro

With a wire whisk or fork, combine all the marinade ingredients except the tofu in a shallow baking dish. Cut the tofu into ¼-inch slabs. Place in the marinade and marinate overnight in the refrigerator and bake the next day for 20 to 30 minutes in a 350-degree oven. Or bake immediately without marinating overnight. Remove from the oven and set aside.

Preheat the oven to 350 degrees. Cut the tofu into ½-inch strips and set aside, reserving the marinade. Heat the oil in a large sauté pan over medium-high heat. Add the tofu strips and brown briefly on each side. Remove the pan from the heat and place the tofu strips back in the marinade. Place into the oven to keep warm. In the heated sauté pan, add the aminos, leeks, and pepper. Sauté for 3 minutes. Add the rest of the ingredients, except for the cilantro, one at a time. Continue to simmer until the vegetables are cooked. Be careful not to overcook the broccoli. Remove the tofu from the oven and strain from the marinade. Add the tofu to the sauté and heat completely. Sprinkle the cilantro on top and serve with corn or flour tortillas, Spanish rice, or spicy Mexican rice (see page 221), and mandarin tomato salsa (see page 240).

Variation: Chicken Fajitas

Chicken can be used in this recipe as follows: Marinate 4 4-ounce chicken breasts overnight. Don't place the marinating chicken into the oven. Just before starting the stir-fry, cut the chicken into thin strips and brown the chicken just as you would brown the tofu. Set aside and add the chicken at the end in place of the tofu.

NUTRITIONAL FACTS

Per serving (3 fajitas, each with ½-cup filling)
Using tofu or tempeh and no tortillas
Calories 282, Total fat 8 g, Saturated fat .2 g, Carbohydrates 34.1 g, Protein 18.4 g

Using chicken and no tortillas
Calories 279, Total fat 4.2 g, Saturated fat 4 g, Carbohydrates 28.8 g, Protein 31.3 g

Vegetarian Paella

A festive party dish.

2 cups basmati rice

4 cups water or vegetable stock

1 teaspoon plus 1 teaspoon ground cardamom

1 pinch saffron threads

1 cinnamon stick

1 tablespoon cumin

1 teaspoon coriander

1 teaspoon turmeric

1 teaspoon dill

1 teaspoon allspice

½ teaspoon ground cloves

1 teaspoon ghee or olive oil

1 cup chopped leeks, shallots, or onions

1 teaspoon black pepper

1 tablespoon Bragg Liquid Aminos or tamari

1 cup roasted red peppers, fresh or canned

1 cup diced green peppers

2 medium zucchini, halved lengthwise, then cut into
¼-inch slices

1 cup quartered marinated artichoke hearts

1½ cups garbanzo beans (chickpeas), cooked or canned,
drained

¼ cup plus ¼ cup vegetable stock

2 cups broccoli florets

1 pound fresh spinach, torn into small pieces

½ pound fresh asparagus, cut into 1-inch pieces

1 cup chopped fresh parsley

½ cup chopped green onions

½ cup kalamata olives, whole or chopped

1 cup chopped fresh tomatoes

1 cup toasted pine nuts

Combine the rice, 4 cups water, 1 teaspoon cardamom, saffron threads, and the cinnamon stick in a 4-quart pot with a tight-fitting lid. Cook the rice until tender, about 20 to 30 minutes. Preheat the oven to 200 degrees. After the rice is cooked, remove the cinnamon stick and fluff the rice with a fork. Place the rice in a stainless steel bowl or large baking dish.

Combine the cumin, coriander, remaining cardamom, turmeric, dill, allspice, and cloves into a small bowl. Sprinkle the spice mixture over the hot rice and toss gently to combine. Cover with foil and place in the oven.

Heat the oil in a large sauté pan over medium-high heat. Add the leeks, black pepper, and aminos. Sauté until the leeks are translucent. Add the red and green peppers, zucchini, and artichoke hearts. Simmer on low heat for 3 to 4 minutes. Add the garbanzo beans and ¼ cup vegetable stock. Bring to a boil, then add the broccoli and the spinach. Remove from the heat immediately and cover. Set aside.

In a separate shallow sauté pan, heat the remaining ¼ cup stock and add the asparagus. Simmer for 4 to 5 minutes or until the asparagus turns light green. Strain the remaining liquid out of the pan.

Remove the rice from the oven. Drain any remaining liquid from the vegetable mixture. Combine the mixture with the rice and toss gently to incorporate all the ingredients. Place the rice and vegetable mixture in a festive serving dish and garnish with the asparagus, parsley, green onions, olives, tomatoes, and pine nuts. Keep warm in a 200-degree oven until ready to serve.

NUTRITIONAL FACTS

Per 1½-cup serving
Calories 348, Total fat 10.4 g, Saturated fat 1.6 g, Carbohydrates 51.7 g, Protein 11.8 g

Winter Vegetables
with Couscous

SERVES 4

2 medium carrots, cut into ½-inch slices
1 medium sweet potato, cut into ¼-inch cubes
1 small acorn squash, peeled and cut into ½-inch pieces
1 cup brussels sprouts or green beans, cut in half
1 teaspoon ghee or olive oil
1 teaspoon brown mustard seeds (seeds may pop from the pan during cooking)
1 teaspoon cumin seeds
1 cup chopped leeks or onions
2 tablespoons Bragg Liquid Aminos or tamari
1 teaspoon ground coriander
½ teaspoon ground turmeric
½ teaspoon ground cardamom
1 teaspoon ground ginger
½ cup vegetable stock
1 cup garbanzo beans, cooked, or 1 14-ounce can, drained and rinsed
1 cup low-fat coconut milk or vanilla soymilk
1 cup couscous, soaked (see page 66)
2 tablespoons currants
2 tablespoons toasted pine nuts
2 tablespoons toasted coconut flakes
2 tablespoons chopped fresh cilantro

Fill a 4-quart soup pot with 3 inches of water and bring to a boil. Add the carrots, sweet potato, acorn squash, and brussels sprouts. Blanch for 4 to 5 minutes. Drain vegetables and set aside. In the same pot, heat the oil, add the mustard and cumin seeds, and pop briefly. Add the leeks, aminos, coriander, turmeric, cardamom, and ginger. Add some stock if the mixture begins to dry. Simmer for 3 or 4 minutes. Add the blanched vegetables and more vegetable stock if necessary. Stir and cover for 5 to 7 minutes until the vegetables are tender but not over-cooked. Stir frequently to incorporate all the spices into the vegetable mixture. Add the garbanzo beans and coconut milk, stir, and continue to simmer until heated through. Serve over couscous. Garnish with currants, toasted pine nuts, toasted coconut flakes, and chopped fresh cilantro.

NUTRITIONAL FACTS | *Per 1½-cup serving*
Calories 352, Total fat 14.6 g, Saturated fat 3.8 g, Carbohydrates 43.9 g, Protein 11 g

Spinach Polenta

SERVES 4

2 cups plus 1 to 1½ cups water or vegetable stock
½ teaspoon salt
1 tablespoon dried basil
1 cup polenta (coarse corn meal)
1 10-ounce package frozen spinach, defrosted and drained,
   or 4 cups sautéed fresh spinach

Preheat the oven to 350 degrees. Prepare a baking dish, 8-by-8-inch or 9-by-13-inch, by spraying or brushing with olive oil. Bring 2 cups water to a boil in a medium-size pot. Add the salt and the basil. Slowly begin to pour in the polenta, stirring with a wire whisk as you pour. Reduce the heat to a low simmer, and continue to stir, while adding the 1 to 1½ cups remaining water. Keep stirring until the mixture begins to thicken. Use more water for a smooth creamy texture; use less for a more solid finished dish. Stir in the spinach. Pour the polenta mixture into the prepared baking dish. The polenta will begin to solidify. Bake the polenta for 20 minutes or until heated through. Serve with roasted tomato sauce (see page 244) or ratatouille stew (page 186).

NUTRITIONAL
FACTS

Per 2-slice serving
Calories 172, Total fat 1.9 g, Saturated fat .2 g,
Carbohydrates 28 g, Protein 10.8 g

Soups

Of soup and love, the first is best.

SPANISH PROVERB

The base of a good soup is the stock. Make a tasty vegetable stock and keep it in your refrigerator. See Staple Recipes for the instructions for vegetable stock. The second most important item is the soup pot or kettle. You should have a good stainless steel pot—18 to 20 gauge steel—from 6 to 9 quarts in size, and a good long spoon to go with it. A large pot will allow room for movement and will be perfect to use for your vegetable stock. A smaller, 4-quart soup pot will also come in handy for small batches of soup and will also be good for cooking rice and other grains. Be sure to have tight-fitting lids for your pots.

Helpful Pointers

- Be creative. Make simple soups by trying different vegetables and mixing and matching herbs and spices. A general rule about spices: *you can always add more.* Start simple, and then go from there.

- Use Bragg Liquid Aminos or tamari to help create a rich savory flavor. Use a good stock, some aminos, leeks or onions, spices, and a dash of pepper to make just about any vegetable taste great in a soup.

- Soup makes the perfect light supper after a long day. Learn to make several simple soups in 20 minutes time. See Staple Recipes for examples and ideas about simple soups.

- One of the most useful tools for blending soups is a hand blender, which makes blending soups and cleaning up easy.

- Using a slow cooker is also an easy and carefree way to make soup. If you are adding dried beans, for the best results soak all dried hard beans overnight in water to make them easier to digest. Drain the beans and place them into the slow cooker. Add vegetable stock or water to cover the beans up to 2 to 3 inches above the level of the beans. The uncooked beans will absorb a lot of liquid as they cook. To enhance the flavor, briefly sauté some vegetables—such as leeks, celery, and carrots—with the spices before adding them to the cooker. Combine all the ingredients in the cooker and place the setting on low. Cook for 4 to 6 hours, or until the beans and vegetables are tender. Keep in mind that a soup with vegetables only, without meat or beans, will take only 2 to 4 hours to cook in a slow cooker. With that in mind, don't leave a vegetable soup to cook for 8 hours while you are at work for the day.

- Time saver: Pre-cook dried beans in the slow cooker the day before or during the day. Keep canned or jarred beans on hand to speed up the cooking process.

Soup Recipes

Asian Clear Broth*

Cuban Black Bean and Sweet Potato Soup*

Italian Vegetable Soup

Butternut Squash Soup

Nutty Broccoli Soup

Rosemary White Bean Soup

Spinach and Lentil Soup

Potato Leek Soup

Spinach Soup

Summertime Tomato Basil Soup

Sweet Potato Ginger Soup

Tomato Florentine Soup

Tortilla Soup with Avocado and Cilantro*

Vegetable Barley Soup*

Vegetable Hot and Sour Soup*

Very Simple Pumpkin Soup

Zucchini Tofu Bisque

*Soups with optional chicken or fish additions.

Asian Clear Broth

Tofu and Marinade

1 teaspoon ghee or olive oil
1 tablespoon Bragg Liquid Aminos or tamari
1 pinch red chili flakes
½ teaspoon cumin
½ teaspoon coriander
2 tablespoons lemon, apple, or orange juice
1½ cups fresh, low-fat tofu, firm or extra firm, cut into small cubes

Soup

1 teaspoon ghee or sesame oil
½ cup chopped leeks or onions
1 tablespoon finely chopped fresh ginger
½ teaspoon black pepper
1 teaspoon coriander
1 tablespoon Bragg Liquid Aminos or tamari
½ cup diagonally sliced celery
½ cup thinly sliced carrot sticks
½ cup thinly sliced red cabbage
1 cup thinly sliced bok choy
1 teaspoon Chinese five-spice powder
4 cups vegetable stock
½ cup sunflower sprouts
½ cup bean sprouts
¼ cup sliced green onions
Cooked shrimp or chicken to taste

Preheat the oven to 350 degrees. In a bowl, combine the oil, aminos, chili flakes, cumin, coriander, and juice. Add the tofu cubes and toss to combine. Place the tofu cubes on an oiled sheet pan and bake for 30 minutes or until golden brown. Remove from the oven and set aside.

Heat the oil in a wok or large soup pot. Add the leeks, ginger, pepper, coriander, and aminos, and sauté for 2 or 3 minutes. Add the vegetables and continue to sauté for 3 or 4 more minutes. Add the Chinese five-spice powder and sauté for another 2 minutes. Add the vegetable stock and bring just to a boil. Reduce the heat, add the tofu cubes, and simmer for 5 minutes. Ladle into individual bowls and garnish with the sprouts and green onions. Add cooked shrimp or chicken pieces to the soup as an additional garnish, if desired.

NUTRITIONAL FACTS | *Per 1½-cup serving*
Calories 158, Total fat 6.5 g, Saturated fat .4 g,
Carbohydrates 11.6 g, Protein 13.3 g

Cuban Black Bean and Sweet Potato Soup

SERVES 4

1 cup black beans, sorted, rinsed, and soaked overnight in water
2 bay leaves
1 teaspoon ghee or olive oil
1 cup chopped leeks or onions
1 cup chopped celery
1 teaspoon black pepper
2 tablespoons Bragg Liquid Aminos or tamari
1 pinch red chili flakes
1 teaspoon cinnamon
1 teaspoon oregano
2 teaspoons cumin
1 large sweet potato, peeled and cut into ½-inch cubes
1 cup cubed carrots
1 cup chopped or diced tomatoes
4 cups vegetable stock
2 cups coarsely torn greens, spinach, red chard, or kale
½ cup chopped fresh cilantro
1 to 2 cups cubed cooked chicken, optional

Drain the soaked beans and place in a large soup pot. Add water to 3 inches above the beans, add the bay leaves, and bring to a boil. Reduce the heat and let the beans simmer until soft, about 1 to 1½ hours. Drain the beans, reserving 1 cup of the liquid bean stock, and set aside. Discard the bay leaves. In the same soup pot, heat the oil. Add the leeks, celery, pepper, and aminos. Simmer for 3 minutes, then add the next six ingredients (chili flakes through carrots). Sauté for 5 minutes, stirring until well coated. Allow the mixture to brown slightly. Add the beans and the tomatoes. Simmer for 2 or 3 minutes, then add the vegetable stock and reserved cup of liquid bean stock to cover the contents in the soup pot. Simmer the soup until the sweet potatoes are soft. Add the greens and wilt in the hot soup.

Leave the soup chunky or purée to a smooth texture. Garnish with the cilantro just before serving.

Grilled or smoked chicken makes a flavorful addition to this soup. If desired, use 1 to 2 cups of cubed chicken for four people, adding it in with the beans and tomatoes.

NUTRITIONAL FACTS

Per 1½-cup serving
Calories 294, Total fat 2.6 g, Saturated fat .1 g, Carbohydrates 53.7 g, Protein 14 g

Using 1¾ cups chicken
Calories 471, Total fat 6.6 g, Saturated fat 2.1 g, Carbohydrates 53.7 g, Protein 49.4 g

Italian Vegetable Soup

SERVES 4

1 cup white beans, sorted, rinsed, and soaked overnight in water
4 bay leaves
1 teaspoon ghee or olive oil
½ cup chopped leeks, shallots, or onions
1 tablespoon Bragg Liquid Aminos or tamari
½ teaspoon black pepper
1 teaspoon basil, dried
1 teaspoon marjoram, dried
1 teaspoon dill, dried
1 teaspoon oregano, dried
1 cup diced carrots
1 cup sliced celery
1 cup cauliflower florets
5 cups vegetable stock
1 cup zucchini, halved lengthwise, then sliced
1 cup coarsely torn greens: mixed spinach, kale, Swiss chard
2 tablespoons tomato paste
1 tablespoon thinly sliced fresh basil
1 tablespoon chopped fresh parsley

Drain the beans and place in a large soup pot. Fill the pot with water to a level that is 2 inches above the beans and add 2 of the bay leaves. Bring to a boil and cook until the beans are soft, about 1 to 1½ hours. Replenish the water as needed to maintain a rolling boil. Drain the beans and set aside. Discard the liquid.

In the same large soup pot, heat the oil and add the leeks, aminos, herbs and spices, and carrots. Sauté for 3 or 4 minutes, then add the celery and cauliflower. Add ½ cup vegetable stock if the mixture begins to dry out. Continue to sauté for 4 or 5 minutes, then add the white beans and zucchini. Stir frequently and combine well with the herbs and spices. Add the greens and simmer for 3 minutes, then add the remaining vegetable stock to just cover the mixture. Add the 2 remaining bay leaves and bring to a boil, then reduce the heat and simmer for 10 minutes. Add the tomato paste and simmer another 10 minutes. Remove the bay leaves before serving. Ladle the soup into bowls and garnish with fresh basil and parsley.

NUTRITIONAL FACTS | *Per 1¼-cup serving*
Calories 268, Total fat 2.1 g, Saturated fat .4 g, Carbohydrates 46.3 g, Protein 15.9 g

Butternut Squash Soup

SERVES 4

1 teaspoon ghee or olive oil
½ cup chopped leeks or onions
½ teaspoon black pepper
1 teaspoon Bragg Liquid Aminos or tamari
4 cups butternut squash, peeled and cut into ½-inch cubes (about 2 pounds)
1 teaspoon curry powder
1 pinch garam masala
5 cups vegetable stock
½ cup vanilla soymilk or rice milk
Nutmeg

Heat a large soup pot and add the oil, leeks, pepper, and aminos. Sauté over high heat for 3 or 4 minutes. Add the squash, curry powder, and garam masala. Stirring frequently, allow the squash to brown in the spices. Add the vegetable stock to just cover the squash. Bring to a boil and then reduce the heat to medium. Simmer until the squash becomes soft. With a hand blender, food processor, or blender, purée the soup until smooth and add the soymilk to create a creamy consistency. Garnish with a sprinkle of nutmeg.

NUTRITIONAL FACTS

Per 1¼-cup serving
Calories 123, Total fat 2.9 g, Saturated fat 1.1 g, Carbohydrates 20 g, Protein 4.3 g

Nutty Broccoli Soup

SERVES 4

1 large head broccoli
1 teaspoon ghee or olive oil
1 cup chopped leeks or onions
2 teaspoons Bragg Liquid Aminos or tamari
1 teaspoon thyme
1 teaspoon marjoram
1 teaspoon nutmeg
1 teaspoon dill
½ teaspoon black pepper
½ cup almonds, finely chopped, or substitute 2 tablespoons almond butter for a richer taste
4 cups vegetable stock
2 teaspoons lemon juice
2 tablespoons chopped fresh parsley

Cut the broccoli head into florets. Peel and chop the stalk. Heat the oil in a soup pot. Add the leeks, aminos, herbs, and spices. Sauté for 2 or 3 minutes, then add the broccoli and the finely chopped almonds. If you are using almond butter, add later. Sauté the almonds and broccoli with the herbs and spices for several minutes, stirring frequently. Add the stock, bring to a boil (if you are using almond butter, add it now), then reduce the heat. Simmer the soup until the broccoli is almost soft. Be careful not to overcook the broccoli. Let the soup cool for about 10 minutes, then purée with a hand blender or food processor. Reheat, then add the lemon juice. Ladle into bowls and garnish with chopped parsley. Use different vegetables in this soup recipe such as carrots, squash, potato, and cauliflower. Each makes a delicious soup combination.

NUTRITIONAL FACTS

Per 1½-cup serving
Using almond pieces, not almond butter
Calories 187, Total fat 8.9 g, Saturated fat 1.5 g, Carbohydrates 18.6 g, Protein 8.1 g

Rosemary White Bean Soup

SERVES 4

Beans

1 cup navy beans or other white beans, sorted, rinsed, and soaked overnight
Water or vegetable stock
4 sprigs fresh rosemary
2 bay leaves
½ teaspoon salt
2 tablespoons tomato paste

Soup

1 teaspoon ghee or olive oil
3 cloves garlic, pressed, or ½ teaspoon garlic powder
1 cup chopped leeks, shallots, or onions
½ teaspoon black pepper
1 tablespoon Bragg Liquid Aminos or tamari
1 cup carrots, cut into ¼-inch rounds
1 cup zucchini, cut into ¼-inch rounds
1 teaspoon dried thyme or 1 tablespoon fresh
1 teaspoon dried dill or 1 tablespoon fresh
½ cup vegetable stock
2 tablespoons freshly chopped parsley or dill

Drain and rinse the beans, then place them in a soup pot. Add water to at least 2 inches above the beans. Add the rosemary, bay leaves, and salt. Bring to a boil, then reduce the heat and simmer until the beans are tender, about 1 to 1½ hours. Be prepared to add more water if necessary. The soup should always have enough liquid in it to allow the beans to move around. As the beans cook, foam will appear on top. Skim off the foam from the soup with a spoon and discard. Do not drain the liquid after the beans are cooked. Stir frequently and keep the soup at a low simmer. Add the tomato paste. Add enough water to cover the mixture plus 1 inch. Bring to a boil.

Heat the oil in a large sauté pan. Add the remaining soup ingredients in order, except for the parsley or the dill garnish.

Sauté all the ingredients together until the leeks are translucent. Add the vegetable mixture to the beans and bring to a boil. Reduce the heat and allow the soup to cook until the carrots are tender and a smooth consistency is achieved. Remove the bay leaves before serving. Garnish with freshly chopped parsley or dill.

| NUTRITIONAL FACTS | *Per 1¼-cup serving*
 Calories 307, Total fat 4 g, Saturated fat 1.6 g, Carbohydrates 53 g, Protein 14.7 g |

Spinach and Lentil Soup

To make this soup wheat-free, do not add the bulgur.

SERVES 4

- 1 teaspoon ghee or olive oil
- 1 cup chopped leeks or onions
- 1 cup celery, cut into ¼-inch slices
- 2 cloves garlic, pressed, or ½ teaspoon garlic powder
- 1 teaspoon fresh minced ginger
- 1 pinch red chili flakes
- ½ teaspoon black pepper
- 1 teaspoon chopped fresh rosemary
- 1 tablespoon Bragg Liquid Aminos or tamari
- 1 cup diced carrots
- ½ cup bulgur wheat, optional
- 1 teaspoon cumin
- ½ teaspoon allspice
- 1 cup brown lentils, sorted, rinsed, and drained
- 5 to 6 cups vegetable stock
- 2 bay leaves
- 2 tablespoons tomato paste
- 4 cups coarsely chopped fresh spinach
- ¼ cup chopped fresh parsley
- 1 cup diced tomatoes

Heat a soup pot, add the oil, then add the leeks, celery, garlic, ginger, red chili flakes, black pepper, and rosemary. Add the aminos and carrots. Sauté for 3 minutes, then add the bulgur (if using), sautéing until golden brown. Add the cumin and allspice, stirring frequently. Add the lentils, 5 cups vegetable stock, and the bay leaves. Bring the soup to a boil, then reduce the heat and continue to simmer until the lentils are tender, 30 to 40 minutes. Add more stock as necessary. Add the tomato paste and the spinach, and simmer another 5 minutes or until the spinach is wilted. Remove the bay leaves before serving. Ladle into soup bowls and garnish with the fresh parsley and diced tomatoes.

NUTRITIONAL FACTS	*Per 1¼-cup serving* Calories 319, Total fat 3 g, Saturated fat 1 g, Carbohydrates 55 g, Protein 17.7 g

Potato Leek Soup

SERVES 4

6 medium red or white potatoes, peeled or unpeeled, cubed
1 teaspoon ghee or olive oil
2 to 3 cups chopped leeks or shallots
½ teaspoon black pepper
1 teaspoon Bragg Liquid Aminos or tamari
1 tablespoon tarragon
2 teaspoons thyme
1 teaspoon salt
5 cups vegetable stock
Nutmeg
2 tablespoons chopped fresh parsley

Place the cubed potatoes in a bowl of cold water and set aside until needed. Heat the oil in a large soup pot. Add the leeks, pepper, and aminos. Over medium-high heat, sauté the leeks until golden brown, then add the tarragon, thyme, and salt. Drain the potatoes and add to the sauté. Stir the potatoes until well coated with the herbs and continue to sauté for 4 minutes or until the potatoes begin to brown. Cover the potatoes with vegetable stock and bring to a boil. Reduce the heat and simmer until the potatoes are tender. Let the soup cool for 10 minutes, then purée the soup using a hand blender, blender, or a food processor. Garnish soup with a sprinkle of nutmeg and freshly chopped parsley.

NUTRITIONAL FACTS

Per 1½-cup serving
Calories 279, Total fat 3.4 g, Saturated fat .3 g,
Carbohydrates 37.3 g, Protein 24.4 g

Spinach Soup

SERVES 4

1 teaspoon ghee or olive oil
1 cup chopped leeks, shallots, or onions
2 cups celery, sliced in ¼-inch pieces
½ teaspoon black pepper
1 tablespoon tarragon
2 teaspoons thyme
½ teaspoon allspice
1 tablespoon Bragg Liquid Aminos or tamari
16 cups fresh spinach, rinsed well, torn coarsely, and drained
4 cups vegetable stock
½ cup low-fat vanilla soymilk or rice milk
Nutmeg

Heat the oil in a large soup pot over medium-high heat. Add the leeks, celery, herbs, and spices. Add the aminos and sauté for 4 or 5 minutes until the leeks are translucent. Add the spinach by the handful, continuing to stir after each addition. Wilt the spinach, keeping it a light green color. Do not overcook it. Add the vegetable stock to just cover the spinach. Bring to a boil, then remove from the heat. Let the soup cool slightly, then purée until a smooth, creamy texture is achieved. Add additional stock as necessary to create the desired consistency. Add the soymilk. Reheat. Sprinkle with nutmeg just before serving.

NUTRITIONAL FACTS

Per 1½-cup serving
Calories 112, Total fat 2.9 g, Saturated fat 1.1 g, Carbohydrates 15.2 g, Protein 6.3 g

Summertime Tomato Basil Soup

SERVES 4

½ cup garbanzos, sorted, rinsed and soaked overnight in water, or 1 14-ounce can, rinsed and drained
2 bay leaves
1 teaspoon ghee or olive oil
1 cup chopped leeks, shallots, or onions
1 tablespoon Italian herb mix
½ teaspoon black pepper
1 teaspoon dill
1 tablespoon Bragg Liquid Aminos or tamari
1 cup cubed red bell pepper
1 cup zucchini, halved lengthwise, then sliced
1 large tomato, chopped
2 cups tomato juice
2 cups vegetable stock
½ cup basil leaves, packed into the cup

Drain and rinse the garbanzos and place in a soup pot. Add enough liquid to cover the beans by 2 inches. Bring to a boil, add the bay leaves, then reduce the heat to a low rolling boil. Cook the beans until they are tender, 40 to 50 minutes. Drain the beans and set aside.

Heat the oil in a soup pot. Add the leeks, herb mix, pepper, dill, and aminos. Sauté for 3 or 4 minutes. Add the bell pepper and the zucchini. Sauté for another 5 minutes. Add the tomato and continue to sauté for another 3 or 4 minutes. Add the cooked or canned garbanzo beans, and simmer for another 5 minutes, stirring frequently. Add the tomato juice and the vegetable stock. Bring to a boil. Reduce the heat. Slice the basil leaves thinly, add to the soup, and simmer for another 4 or 5 minutes. Remove the bay leaves before serving.

NUTRITIONAL FACTS

Per 1¼-cup serving
Calories 257, Total fat 4.2 g, Saturated fat .5 g, Carbohydrates 37.5 g, Protein 17.1 g

Sweet Potato Ginger Soup

SERVES 4

1 teaspoon ghee or olive oil
1 pinch red chili flakes
1 cup chopped leeks or onions
1 tablespoon minced fresh ginger or 1 teaspoon powdered ginger
2 tablespoons Bragg Liquid Aminos or tamari
5 cups sweet potatoes, peeled and cubed
1 teaspoon coriander
1 teaspoon garam masala
6 cups vegetable stock
¼ cup chopped fresh cilantro

Heat the oil in a soup pot over medium-high heat. Add the red chili flakes, leeks, ginger, and aminos. Sauté for 2 or 3 minutes. Add the sweet potatoes and sauté until they are well coated and begin to brown slightly. Add the coriander and garam masala. Sauté another 2 minutes, stirring frequently. Add the vegetable stock to cover the sweet potatoes and bring to a boil. Reduce the heat and simmer until the sweet potatoes are tender. Blend with a hand blender or food processor into a smooth consistency, adding more stock as necessary. Reheat before serving and garnish with the chopped cilantro.

NUTRITIONAL FACTS

Per 1½-cup serving
Calories 247, Total fat 2.9 g, Saturated fat .3 g, Carbohydrates 50.5 g, Protein 5 g

Tomato Florentine Soup

SERVES 4

4 large tomatoes
Black pepper, thyme, and rosemary
Olive oil spray
2 bunches spinach, or 1 10-ounce package frozen
   spinach, defrosted
1 teaspoon ghee or olive oil
1 cup chopped leeks or onions
4 stalks celery, chopped
½ teaspoon black pepper
1 teaspoon tarragon
1 teaspoon thyme
1 teaspoon basil
1 teaspoon marjoram
½ teaspoon nutmeg
1 tablespoon Bragg Liquid Aminos or tamari
4 cups vegetable stock

Preheat the oven to 350 degrees. Cut off the vine end and make a small **X** with a paring knife on the top of the smooth side of each tomato. Place the tomatoes in a shallow baking pan, **X** side up. Sprinkle generously with black pepper, thyme, and rosemary and spray lightly with olive oil. Roast for 20 to 30 minutes. Cool the tomatoes, then gently peel off and discard the skin. Place the tomatoes and their juice in a bowl and break them up or mash into small pieces with a fork. Set aside.

Clean, rinse, and drain the fresh spinach. If you are using defrosted frozen spinach, place it in a strainer and push out the excess liquid. Set aside. Heat a soup pot over medium heat and add the oil, leeks, celery, herbs and spices, and aminos. Sauté for 3 or 4 minutes. Add the tomatoes and the spinach and simmer for another 5 minutes. Add the stock to just cover the tomato mixture. Bring to a boil, then reduce the heat. Simmer for 5 more minutes. Add more stock to create desired consistency.

NUTRITIONAL FACTS	*Per 1½-cup serving* Calories 223, Total fat 4.1 g, Saturated fat .4 g, Carbohydrates 24.8 g, Protein 22 g

Tortilla Soup with Avocado and Cilantro

SERVES 4

1 teaspoon plus 1 teaspoon ghee or olive oil
2 corn tortillas, cut in half, then cut into long, thin strips
1 cup chopped leeks or red onions
1 tablespoon Bragg Liquid Aminos or tamari
1 teaspoon black pepper
1 pinch red chili flakes
1 teaspoon mild chili powder
1 tablespoon cumin
1 teaspoon coriander
1 teaspoon marjoram
1½ cups carrots, cut into bite-size pieces
½ cup chopped green bell pepper
¼ cup roasted red pepper, diced
1 cup fresh or frozen corn
4 cups vegetable stock
¼ cup chopped cilantro, reserve 4 large sprigs for garnish
1 cup avocado, cut into cubes and sprinkled with lemon juice
1 cup sautéed shrimp or cubed grilled fish of your choice, optional

Over medium-high heat, heat 1 teaspoon oil in a large sauté pan. Layer the tortilla strips evenly in the pan and sauté until the tortilla strips are hard. Remove the strips from the pan and place on paper towels. Set aside.

Heat the remaining 1 teaspoon oil in a soup pot and add the leeks, aminos, herbs, and spices. Sauté for 3 or 4 minutes. Add the carrots and sauté for another 3 minutes. Add the bell pepper, roasted pepper, and corn. Reduce the heat and simmer for 4 or 5 minutes. If the mixture gets dry, add ¼ cup vegetable stock. Allow the vegetables to cook until the carrots are almost soft. Add the remaining vegetable stock to cover the vegetables and bring to a boil. Reduce the heat and cook for another 4 or 5 minutes. Add the chopped cilantro. Divide the avocado between four individual bowls. Ladle the soup over the avocado and garnish with the cilantro sprigs and the crispy tortilla strips. Serve right away.

As part of the garnish, divide 1 cup of sautéed shrimp or cubed grilled fish to this tasty soup, if desired.

NUTRITIONAL FACTS	*Per 1-cup serving* *Using vegetables only* Calories 347, Total fat 14.7 g, Saturated fat 1.8 g, Carbohydrates 32.6 g, Protein 21.1 g *Using 1½ cups cooked shrimp* Calories 401, Total fat 15.3 g, Saturated fat 2 g, Carbohydrates 32.6 g, Protein 33 g *Using 1½ cups cooked freshwater bass* Calories 426, Total fat 17.4 g, Saturated fat 2.4 g, Carbohydrates 32.6 g, Protein 34.8 g

Vegetable Barley Soup

A traditional barley soup is usually made with beef. For added flavor without the additional fat, add 1½ cups diced uncooked chicken to this soup if you wish.

SERVES 4

- 1 teaspoon ghee or olive oil
- 1 teaspoon mustard seeds, yellow or brown
- 1 pinch red chili flakes
- ½ teaspoon black pepper
- 1 cup chopped leeks or onions
- 1 cup celery, sliced to ¼-inch pieces
- 1 tablespoon Bragg Liquid Aminos or tamari
- 1½ cups cubed uncooked chicken breasts, optional
- ½ cup pearled barley, rinsed and drained
- 1 teaspoon cumin
- 1 teaspoon coriander
- ½ teaspoon allspice
- 1 cup carrots, cut into bite-size pieces
- 1 cup red or russet potato, cut into small cubes
- 1 teaspoon marjoram
- 4 to 6 cups vegetable stock
- 2 bay leaves
- 3 cups coarsely torn spinach or arugula or both
- ¼ cup chopped fresh parsley

Heat the oil in a soup pot over medium-high heat. Add the mustard seeds and allow them to pop briefly in the hot oil. Add the chili flakes, black pepper, leeks, celery, and aminos. If using chicken, add it now. Sauté until the leeks are translucent, 2 or 3 minutes. Add the barley and stir until well combined. Add the cumin, coriander, and allspice and continue to sauté for another 2 or 3 minutes or until the barley browns slightly. Stir frequently. Add the carrots, potato, and marjoram. Simmer another 3 minutes. Add some vegetable stock if the mixture gets dry.

When well browned, add 4 cups vegetable stock and the bay leaves. Bring to a boil, then reduce the heat and simmer until the carrots and potatoes are cooked and the barley is soft. Add the spinach. Add more vegetable stock if necessary as the barley absorbs the liquid. Remove the bay leaves before serving. Garnish with freshly chopped parsley.

NUTRITIONAL FACTS

Per 1¼-cup serving
Calories 280, Total fat 4 g, Saturated fat .4 g, Carbohydrates 38.8 g, Protein 22.5 g

Using 1½ cups chicken
Calories 367, Total fat 5.1 g, Saturated fat .7 g, Carbohydrates 38.8 g, Protein 42.1 g

Vegetable Hot and Sour Soup

SERVES 4

1 cup Japanese eggplant, julienned (cut into long thin strips)

Lemon juice

1 cup fresh low-fat tofu, extra firm

1 teaspoon plus 2 teaspoons Bragg Liquid Aminos or tamari

1 teaspoon ghee or sesame oil

1 pinch red chili flakes

1 cup thinly sliced carrots

4 cups vegetable stock

2 tablespoons apple cider vinegar

1 tablespoon arrowroot powder dissolved in ¼ cup cold vegetable stock

2 tablespoons chopped green onions

1½ cups sunflower sprouts

1½ cups mung bean sprouts

1 cup grilled fish or chicken or cooked bay shrimp, optional

Place eggplant in a bowl and cover with water and a sprinkle of lemon juice. Cut the tofu into thin strips, place in a bowl, and toss with 1 teaspoon aminos. Set aside. Drain the eggplant.

Heat the oil in a soup pot over medium heat. Add the red chili flakes and the eggplant. Sauté for 2 or 3 minutes, then add the carrots. Sauté for another 3 or 4 minutes or until carrots are almost soft. Add the vegetable stock and bring to a boil. Add the tofu, vinegar, and remaining 2 teaspoons aminos and simmer for 5 minutes. Drizzle the dissolved arrowroot mixture into the soup, stirring constantly. Very quickly, the soup will begin to thicken. Remove the soup from the heat. Ladle the soup into bowls and garnish with the green onions and sprouts.

A traditional garnish used in hot and sour soup is chicken pieces or small bay shrimp. If desired, divide 1 cup of grilled fish, chicken, or cooked bay shrimp along with the green onions and sprouts.

NUTRITIONAL FACTS	*Per 1½-cup serving* Calories 148, Total fat 4.8 g, Saturated fat .2 g, Carbohydrates 16.1 g, Protein 10.1 g
	Using 1 cup grilled freshwater bass Calories 221, Total fat 7.5 g, Saturated fat .8 g, Carbohydrates 16.1 g, Protein 23.8 g
	Using 1 cup cooked shrimp Calories 202, Total fat 5.4 g, Saturated fat .4 g, Carbohydrates 16.1 g, Protein 22 g

Very Simple Pumpkin Soup

SERVES 4

1 large pumpkin (about 3 pounds) or 3 cups canned pumpkin
1½ cup water
1 teaspoon ghee or olive oil
1 cup chopped leeks or onions
½ teaspoon black pepper
1 teaspoon cinnamon
1 teaspoon cumin
1 teaspoon curry powder
½ teaspoon cloves, ground
2 to 3 cups vegetable stock
1 tablespoon Bragg Liquid Aminos or tamari
1 cup low-fat vanilla soymilk
Nutmeg

If using a fresh pumpkin, preheat the oven to 350 degrees. Wash the pumpkin, cut in half, and remove the seeds. Place the pumpkin halves face down in a baking pan. Pour in the water and cover with foil. Bake for 30 minutes or until an inserted knife pulls out easily from the pumpkin. Cool, then remove the pumpkin pulp from the rind with a spoon. Place into a bowl and set aside. You should have about 3 cups of pumpkin pulp.

Heat a soup pot over medium heat and add the oil. Add the leeks and spices. Sauté for 4 or 5 minutes or until the leeks are translucent. Add some stock if the mixture begins to dry. Add the pumpkin pulp and continue to sauté for another 3 or 4 minutes. Add the aminos and brown the pumpkin pulp slightly. Add the vegetable stock to cover the pumpkin and bring to a boil. Reduce the heat and simmer for 10 minutes. Using a hand blender, blender, or food processor, purée the soup to a smooth and creamy consistency, adding the vanilla soymilk as you purée the soup. Return the soup to the pot and reheat if necessary. Garnish with a sprinkle of nutmeg.

NUTRITIONAL FACTS | *Per 1¼-cup serving*
Calories 172, Total fat 3 g, Saturated fat .4 g,
Carbohydrates 23.8 g, Protein 12.2 g

Zucchini Tofu Bisque

SERVES 4

1   teaspoon ghee or olive oil
1   cup chopped leeks or onions
1   pinch red chili flakes
2   tablespoons Bragg Liquid Aminos or tamari
½   teaspoon black pepper
1   teaspoon tarragon
1   teaspoon dill
¼   teaspoon nutmeg
1   teaspoon marjoram
½   teaspoon thyme
4   cups zucchini, halved lengthwise, then sliced
4   cups vegetable stock
6   ounces low-fat silken tofu, firm or extra firm, cut
    into cubes
1   tablespoon fresh lemon juice

Heat a soup pot over medium heat and add the oil. Add the leeks, red chili flakes, aminos, black pepper, tarragon, dill, nutmeg, marjoram, and thyme. Sauté for 4 to 5 minutes, stirring frequently. Add the zucchini and simmer in the herbs and spices until well coated. Add the vegetable stock to cover the zucchini mixture and bring to a boil. Reduce the heat and simmer until the zucchini is cooked, approximately 5 more minutes. Be careful not to overcook. In a blender or food processor, place the tofu and just enough stock to purée it to a thick, smooth consistency. Add the tofu purée to the soup and blend with a hand blender. Taste for seasonings. Reheat if necessary. Add the lemon juice just before serving.

NUTRITIONAL
FACTS

Per 1¼-cup serving
Calories 142, Total fat 3.5 g, Saturated fat 1 g,
Carbohydrates 17.9 g, Protein 9.8 g

Stews

Small cheer and great welcome makes a merry feast.

SHAKESPEARE

One of the greatest pleasures at the end of a day is coming home to a meal ready and waiting for you. Especially during the cold months, a warm stew and a piece of good bread make the perfect light meal. Making a stew in a slow cooker in the morning will ensure that a hearty and healthy meal is available for the whole family later in the day. Stews provide us with an abundance of tastes and textures, all found in a convenient one-pot meal that is hearty, warm, healthy, comforting, and very nurturing.

Stews are easily made from a mixture of beans, vegetables, spices, and fresh herbs. Traditional stews are stewed with large cuts of meats and vegetables for long periods of time. The modern twist on stew cuisine decreases the stewing time to a quick and delicious stew in less than 30 minutes using previously cooked beans. Using either the soup kettle on the stove or an electric slow cooker, you can create wonderful, hearty stews with a variety of beans, legumes, root vegetables, seasonal vegetables, and fresh herbs. Vegetable and bean stews without meats can be cooked in a slow cooker for from 4 to 6 hours. Stews with added meats such as beef or chicken can take longer, from 6 to 8 hours.

Presoaking your beans overnight before placing them in the cooker will aid in digestion, and the beans will not absorb as much liquid during the cooking process.

If you want to add meat to a stew, always brown the meat first before adding the beans and the vegetables.

Helpful Pointers

- Keep marinated tofu or tempeh on hand to add to a stew.
- Canned beans shorten the cooking time of a stew.
- Use good-quality vegetable stock for the best flavor.
- Use minced or crushed fresh garlic instead of garlic powder in most recipes. The use of garlic is always optional. Granulated garlic can also be used. Use 2 or 3 whole cloves of garlic to ½ teaspoon garlic powder or granulated garlic.
- Use fresh or dried herbs. Generally, use twice the amount of fresh herbs as you would dried herbs. For example: 1½ teaspoon dried basil equals 1 tablespoon finely sliced fresh basil.
- Be creative. Use what you have in your refrigerator and pantry to create your own stew recipes.
- Use a slow cooker for effortless cooking.
- If you are using beans in your stew, for the best results soak the beans overnight. Place all of the ingredients in the cooker, making sure there is at least 3 inches of vegetable stock above the level of the beans. Sauté the leeks and the spices together first, and then add the leek mixture to the slow cooker with the other ingredients. Leave out quick-cooking vegetables like spinach until the end. Cook approximately 6 hours on

the low setting or 4 hours on the high setting. Slow cookers vary in temperature range. Make sure the beans are tender to the touch and taste to ensure completion.

Using Beans

Always drain and rinse soaked beans before using them. The benefit of using already cooked beans is to speed up the cooking process. Use them in the slow cooker and reduce the cooking time to 4 hours on low. On the stovetop, add the beans along with the heavier vegetables, such as squash, carrots, and potatoes. You can also use 1 14- or 15-ounce can of organic beans to replace 1 cup of dried beans. If you are using canned beans, the cooking process will take less than 30 minutes.

Stew Recipes

Curried Chickpea Stew
Black Bean and Vegetable Stew*
Cajun Bean and Tempeh Stew*
Eggplant and Yam Curry
French Vegetable Stew
Italian White Bean Stew*
Ratatouille Stew*
Roasted Winter Vegetable Stew
Thai Tofu Vegetable Stew
Tofu, Eggplant, and Yukon Gold Stew
Vegetable White Bean Chili*
Mexican Tofu Stew

*Stews with optional chicken or fish additions.

Curried Chickpea Stew

SERVES 4

1 cup chickpeas, sorted, rinsed, and soaked overnight in water
4 to 6 cups vegetable stock
1 teaspoon ghee or olive oil
2 teaspoons cumin seeds
1 cup chopped leeks or onions
1 pinch red chili flakes
1 teaspoon ginger powder
2 teaspoons curry powder
2 cups cubed sweet potatoes
2 cups cauliflower, cut into large florets
1 cup peas, fresh or frozen
1 cup low-fat coconut milk
2 tablespoons coconut flakes
2 tablespoons chopped cilantro

Drain the soaked chickpeas and place in a soup pot with the vegetable stock. Bring to a boil, then reduce the heat and simmer at a rolling boil until tender, about 1 hour.

Heat a sauté pan with the oil over medium heat. Add the cumin seeds and leeks. Sauté for 3 minutes. Add the red chili flakes, ginger powder, and curry powder. Sauté for another 2 minutes, stirring frequently. Add the sweet potatoes and cauliflower and continue to sauté for another 5 minutes, stirring frequently to coat the vegetables well with the spices. Add the vegetable mixture in the sauté pan to the cooking beans about halfway into the cooking process. Bring to a boil again, then reduce the heat and simmer until the beans and the sweet potatoes are tender to the touch. Add the peas and coconut milk. Simmer for 3 to 4 more minutes until heated through. Serve over basmati rice and garnish with coconut flakes and chopped cilantro.

NUTRITIONAL FACTS

Per 1½-cup serving
Calories 498, Total fat 12.6 g, Saturated fat 5.1 g, Carbohydrates 64.9 g, Protein 31.4 g

Black Bean and Vegetable Stew

SERVES 4

1 cup black beans, sorted, rinsed, and soaked overnight in water
4 cups vegetable stock
1 teaspoon plus 2 teaspoons cumin
2 bay leaves
1 teaspoon ghee or olive oil
1 cup chopped leeks or onions
½ teaspoon black pepper
1 pinch red chili flakes
1 tablespoon Bragg Liquid Aminos or tamari
1 medium yam, peeled and cubed
2 cups carrots, cut into ¼-inch slices
1 cup diced tomatoes
1½ cups cubed smoked chicken, optional
½ cup fresh corn or frozen, defrosted
2 teaspoons cinnamon
2 teaspoons oregano
1 cup chopped fresh cilantro
2 tablespoons tomato paste

Drain the beans. In a soup pot, bring the vegetable stock and beans to a boil. Add 1 teaspoon cumin and the bay leaves, reduce the heat, and simmer at a low rolling boil until the beans are tender, about 1 hour. Meanwhile, heat the oil over medium heat in a large sauté pan; add the leeks, pepper, red chili flakes, and aminos. Sauté for 3 to 4 minutes. Add the yam and carrots. Continue to sauté for 5 minutes, then add the tomatoes and the chicken, if using. Add the remaining 2 teaspoons cumin, the cinnamon, oregano, cilantro, and tomato paste. Add the yam mixture to the beans after the beans have cooked 30 minutes, and continue to simmer. Add more vegetable stock if necessary. The stew will be done when the beans, yams, and carrots are soft to the touch. Remove the bay leaves before serving.

NUTRITIONAL FACTS

Per 1½-cup serving
Calories 418, Total fat 4.5 g, Saturated fat 1.1 g, Carbohydrates 64 g, Protein 31.1 g

Using chicken
Calories 551, Total fat 7.5 g, Saturated fat 2 g, Carbohydrates 64 g, Protein 57.5 g

Cajun Bean and
Tempeh Stew

SERVES 4

1 cup red kidney, small red, or pinto beans, sorted, rinsed, and soaked overnight in water
4 to 6 cups vegetable stock
2 bay leaves
1 teaspoon ghee or olive oil
1 cup chopped leeks, shallots, or onions
1 pinch red chili flakes
2 cloves garlic, minced, or ½ teaspoon garlic powder
1 cup chopped celery
1 tablespoon Bragg Liquid Aminos or tamari
1 cup diced green bell pepper
2 cups diced tomatoes
1½ cups thinly sliced andouille chicken sausage, optional
1 teaspoon turmeric
1 teaspoon thyme
1 teaspoon oregano
1 teaspoon coriander
1 teaspoon cumin
2 teaspoons paprika
1½ cups marinated tempeh, cubed (see page 57)
2 tablespoons maple syrup

Drain the beans. In a soup pot, bring the beans, vegetable stock, and bay leaves to a boil. Reduce the heat and simmer at a rolling boil until the beans are tender, about 1 hour. Heat a sauté pan with the oil over medium heat, then add the leeks, red chili flakes, garlic, and celery. Sauté for 2 minutes. Add the aminos, bell pepper, and tomatoes. If using chicken sausage, add it now. In a small bowl, combine the turmeric, thyme, oregano, coriander, cumin, and paprika. Add the spice mixture to the vegetables, stirring to incorporate. Sauté another 4 to 5 minutes. Add the vegetable mixture to the cooking beans about halfway into the cooking process. Continue to cook, stirring frequently and adding more stock if necessary. Add the tempeh cubes and the maple syrup just before serving and reheat gently. The stew will be finished when the beans are soft to the touch. Remove the bay leaves before serving.

NUTRITIONAL FACTS	*Per 1½-cup serving* *Using tempeh only* Calories 449, Total fat 9.4 g, Saturated fat 1.9 g, Carbohydrates 61.9 g, Protein 29.6 g

Eggplant and Yam Curry

SERVES 4

Vegetables

1	tablespoon olive oil
1	tablespoon curry powder
1	tablespoon garam masala
1	tablespoon Bragg Liquid Aminos or tamari
¼	cup vegetable stock or apple juice
1	large eggplant, cut into 1-inch cubes, skin on
2	large yams, peeled and cut into 1-inch cubes

Curry Masala Sauce

1	teaspoon ghee or olive oil
1	cup chopped leeks or onions
¼	cup finely chopped fresh ginger
2	cups plus 1 tablespoon Bragg Liquid Aminos or tamari
2	cups plus 1 tablespoon vegetable stock
1	pinch asafetida
2	bay leaves
1	tablespoon mild chili powder
1	tablespoon cumin
1	tablespoon coriander
1	tablespoon garam masala
1	teaspoon cardamom
1	teaspoon turmeric
4	cups diced tomatoes
¼	cup finely chopped fresh parsley
¼	cup finely chopped fresh mint
1	cup currants, raisins, or diced dried apricots
1	tablespoon lemon juice

Preheat the oven to 350 degrees. In a large bowl, combine the olive oil, curry powder, garam masala, aminos, and stock. Whisk together, then add the eggplant and yams and toss gently. Place eggplant and yams on an oiled sheet pan and roast for 30 minutes. Remove from the oven and set aside.

Heat the oil in a soup pot over medium heat. Add the leeks, ginger, aminos, and 1 tablespoon vegetable stock. Sauté for 2 to 3 minutes, then add the asafetida and bay leaves. Sauté until the leeks and ginger are tender, 2 to 3 more minutes. Add the chili powder, cumin, coriander, garam masala, cardamom, turmeric, remaining 2 cups stock, and tomatoes. Simmer for 4 or 5 minutes, then add the roasted eggplant and yams. Simmer another 3 to 4 minutes, then add the parsley, mint, currants, and lemon juice.

Continue to simmer the stew until heated thoroughly. Remove the bay leaves and serve with rice and cooling yogurt.

NUTRITIONAL FACTS	*Per 1½-cup serving* *Does not include rice and yogurt* Calories 424, Total fat 7.5 g, Saturated fat 1.1 g, Carbohydrates 73.1 g, Protein 15.9 g

French Vegetable Stew

SERVES 4

1 teaspoon ghee or olive oil
1 cup leeks or onions, chopped
1 tablespoon Bragg Liquid Aminos or tamari
½ teaspoon black pepper
1 teaspoon coriander
1 teaspoon balsamic vinegar
1 teaspoon tarragon
1 teaspoon marjoram
1 teaspoon dried basil
1 cup vegetable stock
1 tablespoon whole wheat pastry flour, oat flour, or rice flour
2 cups carrots, halved lengthwise, then sliced
½ cup peas, fresh or frozen
2 cups cauliflower florets
1 cup French green beans, cut in 1-inch pieces
2 cups broccoli florets
Sliced fresh basil leaves or chopped parsley

Heat the oil in a soup pot over medium heat. Add the leeks, aminos, pepper, coriander, vinegar, tarragon, marjoram, and basil. Sauté for 2 minutes, or until the leeks become translucent. Add 2 tablespoons vegetable stock and the flour. Stirring with a whisk, work the flour into the leek mixture. As the flour begins to brown, add the remaining vegetable stock. Add the carrots and simmer until the carrots are tender. Add the peas, remove from the heat, and cover. Add more stock if necessary to maintain a slightly thickened sauce.

Bring 4 quarts of water to a boil. Add the cauliflower and blanch for 2 minutes. With a slotted spoon, remove the cauliflower and add to the carrots and replace the cover. Place the green beans in the boiling water and blanch for 3 minutes. Remove the beans and add to the carrots and cauliflower. Place the broccoli in the boiling water and blanch for 1 minute. Add to the rest of the vegetables. Keep stirring the stew frequently, coating the vegetables well after each addition. Completely heat through, being careful not to overcook the broccoli. Serve over toasted millet or rice pilaf and garnish with freshly sliced fresh basil or chopped parsley.

NUTRITIONAL FACTS | *Per 1³/₄-cup serving*
Calories 145, Total fat 2.1 g, Saturated fat .2 g, Carbohydrates 24.1 g, Protein 7.7 g

Italian White Bean Stew

The addition of thinly sliced gourmet-quality Italian chicken sausage or diced chicken breast will create a hearty winter stew.

SERVES 4

1 cup navy beans, sorted, rinsed, and soaked overnight
4 cups vegetable stock
2 bay leaves
1 teaspoon ghee or olive oil
1 cup chopped leeks or onions
1 cup chopped red or green bell pepper
1 teaspoon black pepper
1 tablespoon Italian herb mix
1 teaspoon garlic powder
1 tablespoon Bragg Liquid Aminos or tamari
2 cups carrots, cut into ¼-inch slices
1 cup zucchini halved lengthwise, then sliced
2 cups coarsely torn washed spinach
¾ cup Roasted Tomato Sauce (see page 244)
1½ cups thinly sliced cooked chicken sausage or cubed cooked chicken, optional
Freshly grated Parmesan cheese and chopped fresh parsley

Drain the soaked beans. In a soup pot bring the vegetable stock, beans, and bay leaves to a boil. Reduce the heat and let simmer until the beans are tender, about 1 hour.

Heat the oil in a sauté pan over medium heat; add the leeks, bell pepper, black pepper, Italian herbs, garlic, and aminos. Sauté for 2 to 3 minutes, then add the carrots and continue to sauté another 2 minutes. Add the vegetable mixture in the sauté pan to the cooking beans about halfway through the cooking process. Add additional stock if necessary to just cover and then bring back to a boil. Reduce to a simmer. When the beans and the carrots are tender, add the zucchini, spinach, and roasted tomato sauce. If you are using sausage or chicken, add it now. Continue to simmer for another 5 minutes. Remove the bay leaves before serving. Garnish with freshly grated Parmesan cheese and chopped parsley.

NUTRITIONAL FACTS

Per 1-cup serving
Calories 349, Total fat 5.2 g, Saturated fat 1 g, Carbohydrates 59 g, Protein 16.8 g

Using 1½ cups cooked chicken breast
Calories 482, Total fat 8.2 g, Saturated fat 1.9 g, Carbohydrates 59 g, Protein 43.2 g

Ratatouille Stew

Ratatouille makes a wonderful base for an Italian fish stew. Add 1 to 2 cups of marinated and grilled fish such as salmon, halibut, or cod cut into bite-size pieces.

SERVES 4

- 1 large eggplant, cut into 1-inch cubes
- 1 teaspoon ghee or olive oil
- 2 large leeks or onions, chopped
- 2 teaspoons Italian herb mix
- 1 teaspoon marjoram
- 1 teaspoon thyme
- ½ teaspoon black pepper
- 1 teaspoon garlic powder
- 1 tablespoon Bragg Liquid Aminos or tamari
- 2 large zucchini, cut into 1-inch cubes
- 3 large bell peppers, green and red, cut into 1-inch pieces
- 2 cups diced tomatoes
- 1½ cups vegetable stock
- ½ cup thinly sliced fresh basil leaves
- 1 to 2 cups cubed grilled marinated salmon, halibut, or cod, optional

Submerge the eggplant in a bowl of water with a sprinkle of salt in it. Set aside. Heat the oil in a large soup pot over medium heat. Add the leeks, Italian herb mix, marjoram, thyme, black pepper, garlic powder, and aminos. Drain the eggplant and add with the zucchini and bell peppers. Sauté for 4 to 5 minutes. Add the tomatoes and continue to simmer another 3 to 4 minutes. If using fish, add it now. Add the vegetable stock any time the vegetable mixture begins to dry out. The liquid should just cover the vegetables. Simmer the stew for 20 to 30 minutes over low heat. Add the fresh basil just before serving.

NUTRITIONAL FACTS

Per 1-cup serving
Calories 215, Total fat 6.8 g, Saturated fat 3.4 g, Carbohydrates 27.1 g, Protein 11.5 g

Using 1½ cups Atlantic Salmon
Calories 370, Total fat 14 g, Saturated fat 4.5 g, Carbohydrates 27.1 g, Protein 34 g

Roasted Winter Vegetable Stew

Make this hearty stew for guests on a cold winter's day.

SERVES 6

Vegetables

1 cup navy beans, rinsed, and soaked overnight in water
4 to 6 cups plus 1 tablespoon vegetable stock
1 teaspoon plus 1 teaspoon olive oil
1 tablespoon dried sage
1 tablespoon dried thyme
1 tablespoon plus 1 tablespoon Bragg Liquid Aminos or tamari
2 cups russet or sweet potatoes, cubed
2 cups butternut squash, peeled and cubed
2 cups cauliflower florets
1 cup chopped leeks, shallots, or onions
3 sprigs chopped fresh rosemary leaves
½ teaspoon black pepper

Sauce

1 teaspoon ghee or olive oil
½ cup leeks
1 teaspoon black pepper
1 pinch salt
1 teaspoon dried thyme
1 teaspoon dried sage
1 tablespoon finely chopped fresh rosemary
2 tablespoons vegetable stock
2 tablespoons whole wheat pastry flour or unbleached white flour
3 to 4 cups low-fat vanilla soymilk or rice milk
¼ cup thinly sliced fresh basil leaves

Drain the soaked beans and place in a soup pot, with 4 to 6 cups vegetable stock. Bring to a boil, reduce the heat to a rolling simmer, and cook the beans until tender, about 1 hour. When tender, drain and set aside. Discard the liquid.

Preheat the oven to 350 degrees. In a large bowl, whisk together 1 teaspoon oil, sage, thyme, the remaining 1 tablespoon vegetable stock, and 1 tablespoon aminos. Add the cubed potatoes and squash and toss until well coated. Place on an oiled sheet pan and roast for 20 to 30 minutes. Remove from the oven and set aside.

Bring 4 quarts of water to a boil. Add the cauliflower and blanch for 3 minutes. Drain the cauliflower and set aside. Reheat the soup pot over medium heat and add the remaining teaspoon oil. Add the leeks, remaining tablespoon aminos, rosemary, black pepper, and the drained cooked beans. Sauté for 4 to 5 minutes. Add additional vegetable stock if necessary. Add the blanched cauliflower and the roasted vegetables; stir well and continue to sauté over very low heat for 3 to 4 more minutes. Remove from the heat, cover, and set aside.

Heat the oil in a small saucepan. Add the leeks, black pepper, salt, thyme, sage, and rosemary. Sauté for 2 to 3 minutes. Using a whisk, add the vegetable stock and flour while stirring frequently, allowing the flour to brown. Slowly begin to add the soymilk, stirring continuously. Add additional soymilk as the sauce begins to thicken. Add more soymilk if the sauce is too thick. The sauce should have a creamy consistency. Add the sauce to the stew and garnish with the basil just before serving.

| NUTRITIONAL FACTS | *Per 1¼-cup serving*
Calories 368, Total fat 7.1 g, Saturated fat 2.1 g,
Carbohydrates 61.3 g, Protein 14.5 g |

Thai Tofu Vegetable Stew

SERVES 4

Tofu Marinade

1 cup apple juice
½ cup Bragg Liquid Aminos or tamari
¼ cup lemon juice
1 teaspoon cumin
1 teaspoon coriander
1 teaspoon ginger powder
16 ounces fresh low-fat tofu, firm or extra firm

Vegetable Stew

2 cups broccoli florets
1 teaspoon ghee or sesame oil
1 teaspoon cumin seeds
½ cup chopped leeks or onion
1 inch gingerroot, minced or grated
3 cloves garlic, minced, or 1 teaspoon garlic powder
1 jalapeno pepper, stem cut off and seeds removed
2 tablespoons Bragg Liquid Aminos or tamari
1 teaspoon turmeric
½ cup apple juice
2 cups sweet potatoes, peeled and cut into ½-inch cubes
1 teaspoon cumin
1 teaspoon coriander
½ teaspoon ginger powder
14 ounces low-fat coconut milk or vanilla soymilk
1 cup vegetable stock
2 tablespoons chopped cilantro
½ cup fresh bean sprouts

Preheat the oven to 350 degrees. Combine the apple juice, aminos, lemon juice, and spices in a shallow baking dish. Cut the tofu into small cubes and add to marinade. Bake for 20 to 30 minutes. Remove and set aside.

Bring 4 quarts of water to a boil. Add the broccoli and blanch for 1 minute. Be careful not to overcook. Drain the broccoli, rinse in cold water, and set aside.

In the same 4-quart pot, heat the oil and add the cumin seeds. Brown slightly, then add the leeks, gingerroot, garlic, and jalapeno. Sauté for 1 to 2 minutes. Add the aminos, turmeric, and 2 tablespoons apple juice. Add the sweet potatoes, cumin, coriander, and ginger powder. Stir frequently as you begin to brown the sweet potatoes in the leeks and spices. Sauté for 4 to 5 minutes until the sweet potatoes look caramelized. Add the coconut milk and the remaining apple juice. Bring to a boil, then reduce the heat. Add the vegetable stock. Simmer until the sweet potatoes are soft but not mushy, approximately 10 minutes. Add the broccoli and the tofu cubes and combine well. Garnish with the chopped cilantro and fresh bean sprouts. Remove the jalapeno before serving.

NUTRITIONAL FACTS	*Per 1½-cup serving* Calories 444, Total fat 15.6 g, Saturated fat 6.1 g, Carbohydrates 48.6 g, Protein 27.5 g

Tofu, Eggplant, and Yukon Gold Stew

SERVES 4

1 tablespoon olive oil
1 teaspoon plus 1 teaspoon allspice
2 teaspoons coriander
1 teaspoon dill
1 tablespoon plus 1 teaspoon Bragg Liquid Aminos or tamari
2 cups eggplant, cut into 1-inch cubes, skin on
3 medium Yukon gold potatoes, cubed, skin on
2 cups fresh low-fat tofu firm or extra firm, cubed
1 teaspoon ghee or olive oil
1 cup leeks or onions, chopped
½ teaspoon black pepper
1 cup diced carrots
1 cup diced red bell pepper
1 cup diced tomato
1 to 2 cups vegetable stock
½ cup chopped fresh basil or cilantro

Preheat the oven to 350 degrees. In a large bowl, whisk together the olive oil, 1 teaspoon allspice, the coriander, dill, and 1 tablespoon aminos. Add the cubed eggplant, potatoes, and tofu and toss together with your hands until well coated. Place the vegetables and tofu on an oiled sheet pan and roast for 20 to 30 minutes. Remove and set aside.

Heat the oil in a soup pot over medium heat. Add the leeks, black pepper, remaining teaspoon aminos, and remaining teaspoon allspice. Sauté for 2 to 3 minutes. Add the carrots, red pepper, and tomato and continue to sauté for another 5 minutes. Add enough vegetable stock to just cover the tomato. Sauté another 3 to 4 minutes or until the carrots are tender. Add the roasted eggplant, potatoes, and tofu. Add more stock if necessary. Add the fresh basil or cilantro just before serving.

NUTRITIONAL FACTS	*Per 1½-cup serving* Calories 318, Total fat 8.6 g, Saturated fat .7 g, Carbohydrates 40.1 g, Protein 19.8 g

Vegetable White Bean Chili

S E R V E S 4

1 cup Great Northern beans, rinsed and soaked overnight in water
4 to 6 cups vegetable stock
1 teaspoon ghee or olive oil
1 cup leeks or onions, chopped
2 tablespoons Anaheim mild chilies, canned or freshly roasted, seeds removed and diced
2 cloves garlic, minced
1 tablespoon chili powder
1 teaspoon cumin
1 teaspoon coriander
2 medium carrots, cut into 1-inch pieces
1 cup chopped tomatoes
1 cup zucchini, cut in ¼-inch slices
1 cup washed fresh spinach
1 cup corn, fresh or frozen
2 green onions, chopped
¼ cup chopped cilantro
1½ cups cubed smoked chicken or turkey breast, or southwestern-style chicken sausage; or ground turkey or chicken, optional

Drain the soaked beans and place in a soup pot with the vegetable stock. Bring to a boil, then reduce the heat and simmer at a low rolling boil until the beans are tender. Heat the oil in a sauté pan over medium heat. Add the leeks, chilies, garlic, chili powder, cumin, and coriander. If you are using ground chicken or turkey, add it now. Sauté for 3 minutes, then add the carrots and the tomatoes. If you are using smoked chicken or turkey breast or chicken sausage, add it now. Simmer the stew for 5 to 7 minutes or until the carrots are tender. Add the zucchini during the last 2 minutes. Add the vegetable mixture in the sauté pan to the cooking beans when the beans are almost tender. Stir in the spinach and corn. Continue to simmer for another 5 minutes. Garnish with the green onions and chopped cilantro.

NUTRITIONAL FACTS

Per 1½-cup serving
Calories 364, Total fat 4.2 g, Saturated fat .5 g, Carbohydrates 53.2 g, Protein 28 g

Using smoked turkey breast
Calories 445, Total fat 5.1 g, Saturated fat .8 g, Carbohydrates 54.6 g, Protein 44.8 g

Mexican Tofu Stew

SERVES 4

16 ounces fresh low-fat tofu, firm or extra firm, drained
2 teaspoons plus 1 tablespoon Bragg Liquid Aminos or tamari
1 teaspoon plus 1 teaspoon chili powder
1 teaspoon ghee or olive oil
1 cup chopped leeks or onions
1 teaspoon black pepper
1 teaspoon turmeric
1 teaspoon cumin
2 teaspoons oregano
2 carrots, sliced
1 cup diced celery
2 cups diced tomatoes
1 to 2 cups vegetable stock
¼ cup chopped cilantro

Preheat the oven to 350 degrees. Cube the tofu and place in a bowl. Add 2 teaspoons aminos and 1 teaspoon chili powder and toss gently. Place the tofu on an oiled sheet pan and roast for 20 minutes. Remove from the oven and set aside.

Heat the oil in a soup pot over medium heat. Add the leeks, remaining tablespoon aminos, black pepper, remaining teaspoon chili powder, turmeric, cumin, and oregano. Sauté for 3 minutes, then add the carrots, celery, and tomatoes. Continue to sauté for 5 minutes. Add the tofu and enough vegetable stock to just cover the mixture. Simmer for another 5 minutes or until the carrots are tender. Add the chopped cilantro to the mixture and combine. Serve with Spanish pilaf (page 220).

NUTRITIONAL FACTS

Per 1¼-cup serving
Calories 256, Total fat 8.1 g, Saturated fat .2 g, Carbohydrates 21 g, Protein 24.2 g

Vegetable Dishes, Grain Dishes, and Quick Light Meals

The true essentials of a feast are only fun and feed.

OLIVER WENDELL HOLMES

Side dishes provide a great complement to any meal. They play an important role in rounding out the nutritional value and tastes of a meal. Several side dishes can constitute a meal in themselves. Mix and match several smaller dishes to make a simple, nutritious meal. Be creative.

As a light meal, mix and match a soup or stew with a side dish. For example: try Tortilla Soup with Avocado and Cilantro along with Spicy Mexican Rice, or try Eggplant and Yam Curry with Green Quinoa Pilaf. See more suggestions in the 30-Day Nutritional Plan menus.

The side dishes can be used in many creative ways. Combine a grain dish such as Indian Rice on a bed of greens, with Cucumber Raita, or use Greek Goddess Salad as a stuffing for a squash dish. Enjoy!

Vegetable Dishes, Grain Dishes, and Quick Light Meals Recipes

Wraps
    Vegetable Hummus Wrap*
    Black Bean and Rice Wrap
    Marinated Tofu Thai Wrap with Nutty
       Dipping Sauce*
    Lettuce Wrap
Cauliflower and Braised Tomato
Chinese Five-Spice Garden Pilaf
Curried Potatoes
Dilled Asparagus
Dilled Lemon Zucchini
Greek Goddess Salad*
Green Quinoa Pilaf
Egg-less Tofu Salad or Sandwich
Indian Rice
Nutty Spinach Greens
Oat Groat Pilaf with Spinach
Salad Greens
    Garden Salad
    Organic Mixed Field Greens Salad*
Savory Swiss Chard
Spanish Pilaf
Spicy Mexican Rice
Tuscany Bulgur Pilaf

*Quick meals with optional chicken or fish additions.

Wraps

A wrap is a great quick lunch-on-the-run, and a healthy alternative to fast food. Be creative. Use 8- to 10-inch whole wheat tortillas for your wraps. Use the extra salad, stew, grains, sauces, vegetables, or condiments from your daily meals in your wraps. When making a wrap, layer the filling ingredients in the center of the tortilla and use enough sauce so the wrap will stay rolled up. Roll up the tortilla to enclose the filling, and wrap in plastic wrap or place in a container.

In addition to the wrap recipes that follow, try wrapping up some of the other recipes in this book.

Wrap Suggestions

Eggless Tofu

Indian Rice and Cucumber Raita

Tofu Fajitas with Tomato Salsa

Spanish Pilaf and Cajun Bean Stew

Thai Tofu Vegetable Stew with Spicy Lime and Red Pepper Sauce

Curried Chickpea Stew and Indian Rice

Curried Potato and Cucumber Raita

Vegetable Hummus Wrap

SERVES 1

1 8- or 10-inch whole wheat tortilla
2 tablespoons Hummus (see page 236)
3 tablespoons grated carrot
3 tablespoons grated zucchini
¼ cup sprouts
1 leaf red-leaf or romaine lettuce

Spread the hummus in the middle and up to the edge of the tortilla; add the grated carrots, zucchini, sprouts and lettuce mix. Add any additional vegetable, grain, sauce, or condiment you like. Roll up tightly into a 2- to 3-inch-wide wrap.

VARIATION: CHICKEN OR TURKEY WRAP

Place 3 ounces of sliced cooked chicken or turkey breast on top of the hummus and roll up as directed.

NUTRITIONAL FACTS | *Per wrap*
For the vegetarian wrap
Calories 320, Total fat 7.6 g, Saturated fat 1.5 g, Carbohydrates 51.3 g, Protein 11.5 g

Black Bean and Rice Wrap

SERVES 1

1 8- to 10-inch whole wheat tortilla
½ cup Black Bean and Vegetable Stew (see page 176)
¼ cup cooked rice
2 tablespoons tomato salsa
¼ cup sprouts
2 tablespoons grated carrots
1 lettuce leaf

Place the black bean and vegetable stew in the center of the tortilla. Add the rice, salsa, sprouts, grated carrots, and lettuce leaf. Roll up tightly into a 2- to 3-inch-wide wrap.

NUTRITIONAL
FACTS

Per wrap
Calories 444, Total fat 6.6 g, Saturated fat 2.3 g, Carbohydrates 82.7 g, Protein 13.5 g

Marinated Tofu
Thai Wrap with
Nutty Dipping Sauce

SERVES 1

1 8- to 10-inch whole wheat tortilla
¼ cup thinly sliced marinated tofu
1 to 2 tablespoons Nutty Dipping Sauce (see page 241)
1 tablespoon grated carrot
1 tablespoon grated zucchini
1 tablespoon thinly sliced red cabbage
1 tablespoon chopped cilantro
¼ cup sprouts
1 leaf red-leaf or romaine lettuce

Place the tofu strips in the middle of the tortilla, and spread about 1 tablespoon of the nutty dipping sauce over them. Top with carrots, zucchini, cabbage, cilantro, sprouts, and lettuce leaf. Drizzle some additional nutty dipping sauce over the vegetables, then roll up into a 2- to 3-inch-wide wrap.

CHICKEN OR FISH VARIATION

Replace tofu with 3 ounces of grilled chicken or fish, add the nutty dipping sauce, and roll up as directed.

NUTRITIONAL
FACTS

Per wrap
For the vegetarian wrap
Calories 395, Total fat 15.8 g, Saturated fat 2.3 g,
Carbohydrates 43.4 g, Protein 19.4 g

Lettuce Wrap

SERVES 4
(2 WRAPS
PER PERSON)

4 ounces marinated tofu (see page 57)
10 large butter lettuce leaves
1 cup Hummus (see page 236)
2 medium carrots, thinly sliced like matchsticks
1 cup sunflower sprouts

Cut the tofu into long, thin strips. Wash the lettuce leaves, pat dry, and set aside.

Lay all the lettuce leaves flat on the counter. Spread the hummus in the middle of each leaf. Lay the tofu strips, carrot sticks, and sunflower sprouts together on top of the hummus, leaving some sprouts to hang over the edge of the lettuce about 1 inch. Fold up the bottom of the lettuce over the filling and then gently roll up from one side to the other to enclose all the ingredients. Serve with nutty dipping sauce (page 241) and spicy lime and red pepper dipping sauce (page 247) as an appetizer.

NUTRITIONAL
FACTS

Per 2 wraps
Using the two sauces
Calories 331, Total fat 14.6 g, Saturated fat 2.1 g,
Carbohydrates 37.5 g, Protein 12 g

Cauliflower and Braised Tomato

SERVES 4

1 large cauliflower, cut into florets
1 teaspoon ghee or olive oil
1 teaspoon mustard seeds
1 teaspoon cumin seeds
1 cup chopped leeks, onions, or shallots
1 inch gingerroot, minced
1 small jalapeno pepper, stem and seeds removed
1 tablespoon ground coriander
½ teaspoon turmeric
1 tablespoon Bragg Liquid Aminos or tamari
3 medium tomatoes, diced
1½ cups vegetable stock
1 tablespoon tomato paste
2 tablespoons garam masala

In a large soup pot, bring 4 quarts of water to a boil. Add the cauliflower and blanch for 5 minutes. Drain the cauliflower and set aside. Heat the oil in a large saucepan over medium heat; add the mustard and cumin seeds. As they begin to pop, add the leeks, ginger, and whole jalapeno pepper. Sauté for 3 minutes. Add the coriander, turmeric, and aminos and continue to sauté for another 2 minutes. Add the tomatoes and simmer for 5 minutes or until the tomatoes begin to break down. Add the stock and tomato paste. Simmer the sauce for another 3 to 4 minutes or until the sauce begins to thicken. Add more stock if necessary to maintain a smooth texture. Add the cauliflower and the garam masala. Continue to simmer until heated through. Remove the jalapeno before serving.

NUTRITIONAL FACTS

Per 1-cup serving
Calories 116, Total fat 2.8 g, Saturated fat 1.1 g, Carbohydrates 16.6 g, Protein 6.2 g

Chinese Five-Spice Garden Pilaf

SERVES 4

3 cups water or vegetable stock
1 teaspoon Bragg Liquid Aminos or tamari
1 stick cinnamon
1½ cups organic basmati rice, rinsed in a strainer
½ cup green peas, fresh or frozen
½ cup shredded carrots
½ cup corn, fresh or frozen
1 teaspoon Chinese five-spice powder
1 teaspoon ground ginger
2 tablespoons freshly chopped cilantro

Bring the stock, aminos, cinnamon, and rice to a boil in a small saucepan with a tight-fitting lid. Reduce the heat to the lowest possible and keep it at that temperature. Let the rice simmer for 20 minutes. Resist lifting the lid, as the rice will cook better without interruption. Meanwhile, combine in a bowl the peas, carrots, and corn. Mixing with a fork, add the Chinese five-spice powder and the ginger. When the rice has cooked for 20 minutes, remove the lid and fluff the rice with a fork. Put the lid back on and let the rice rest for 5 minutes. Then, using a fork, add the rice to the vegetable mixture and combine well. Garnish with the cilantro. Serve with a stir-fry.

NUTRITIONAL FACTS

Per ¾-cup serving
Calories 225, Total fat 1 g, Saturated fat .1 g, Carbohydrates 49.1 g, Protein 5.1 g

Curried Potatoes

SERVES 4

4 medium russet potatoes, peeled, cubed, set in water
1 teaspoon ghee or olive oil
1 teaspoon cumin seeds
1 teaspoon brown mustard seeds
1 teaspoon fenugreek seeds
1 cup chopped leeks or onions
2 teaspoons minced fresh gingerroot
¼ cup fruit chutney or apricot jam
½ teaspoon turmeric
1 tablespoon Bragg Liquid Aminos or tamari
1 pinch cayenne
2 teaspoons coriander
1 cup vegetable stock
2 teaspoons lemon juice
1 cup low-fat coconut milk
1 cup low-fat vanilla or plain soymilk
1 cup frozen peas
¼ cup freshly chopped cilantro

Bring 4 quarts of water to a boil, add the potatoes, and blanch them for 5 minutes or until just about soft. Drain the potatoes and set aside. Heat the same pot again and add the oil. Add the cumin seeds, mustard seeds, and fenugreek seeds. Allow the seeds to pop and then add the leeks and the ginger. Sauté for 2 minutes, then add the fruit chutney and sauté for another 1 to 2 minutes. Add the turmeric, aminos, cayenne, and coriander. Add the vegetable stock and sauté for 3 to 4 minutes. Add the potatoes and stir to coat well. Add the lemon juice, coconut milk, soymilk, peas, and cilantro. Bring the mixture to a boil, stirring frequently. Reduce to low heat and simmer for another 3 to 4 minutes or until the frozen peas are cooked. Be careful not to overcook this dish.

NUTRITIONAL FACTS | *Per 1-cup serving*
Calories 399, Total fat 11.2 g, Saturated fat 6.1 g, Carbohydrates 64.4 g, Protein 10.3 g

Dilled Asparagus

SERVES 4

1 pound fresh asparagus
½ cup vegetable stock
½ teaspoon black pepper
1 teaspoon dried dill plus fresh dill
1 tablespoon Bragg Liquid Aminos or tamari
1 teaspoon balsamic vinegar

Wash the asparagus. Cut 1 inch from the bottom of each stalk and discard. In a large sauté pan with a lid, heat the stock with the pepper, dill, and aminos. Lay the asparagus flat in the pan. The liquid should barely cover the asparagus. Cover the pan and bring to a boil. Reduce to medium heat and simmer the asparagus for 5 minutes or until tender. Move them in the pan once in a while for even cooking. Remove the asparagus from the heat, sprinkle the vinegar on top, cover, and let the asparagus rest for up to 10 minutes. Garnish with fresh dill.

NUTRITIONAL
FACTS

Per serving (6 to 8 spears)
Calories 49, Total fat .4 g, Saturated fat .1 g,
Carbohydrates 6.1 g, Protein 5.2 g

Dilled Lemon Zucchini

SERVES 4

1 teaspoon olive oil
4 large zucchini, cut into ¼-inch rounds
2 tablespoons lemon juice
2 teaspoons spicy Dijon or stone-ground mustard
2 tablespoons vegetable stock
1 pinch black pepper
1 tablespoon dried dill

Heat a sauté pan over medium heat and add the oil. Add the sliced zucchini and sauté for 3 to 4 minutes, stirring frequently. Add the lemon juice and mustard. Sauté another 2 minutes, then add the stock. Sprinkle the pepper and dill on the zucchini as it continues to sauté. Cook for approximately 4 to 5 more minutes until the zucchini is browned.

NUTRITIONAL FACTS

Per 1-cup serving
Calories 42, Total fat 1.3 g, Saturated fat .2 g,
Carbohydrates 5.3 g, Protein 2.3 g

Greek Goddess
Salad

SERVES 4

1 cup couscous
2 tablespoons toasted pine nuts
½ cup shredded carrots
½ cup chopped red bell pepper
3 stalks celery, chopped
1 cup chopped parsley
¼ cup kalamata olives, pitted and cut in half

Dressing

2 tablespoons lemon juice
2 tablespoons Bragg Liquid Aminos or tamari
1 teaspoon dried oregano
½ teaspoon black pepper
½ teaspoon salt
1 tablespoon dried basil
¼ cup olive oil
1 to 2 cups cubed grilled chicken or fish,
   optional

Bring 1½ cups of water to a boil in a small saucepan. Remove from the heat and add the couscous. Combine with a fork, cover the pan, and let stand for 7 minutes or until the couscous has absorbed the water. Fluff with a fork and place in a large bowl. Add the pine nuts, carrots, bell pepper, celery, parsley, and olives. Toss together with your hands or a large spoon.

In a small bowl, whisk together the lemon juice, aminos, oregano, black pepper, salt, and basil. As you whisk, slowly add the olive oil. Pour the dressing over the salad and toss together with your hands or a large spoon until well incorporated. Serve on a bed of lettuce or in a wrap.

If desired, garnish the salad with 1 to 2 cups of grilled chicken or fish for added protein. Slice or cube the chicken or fish and toss in with the other ingredients.

| NUTRITIONAL FACTS | *Per 1-cup serving*
For the salad and dressing only
Calories 262, Total fat 6.1 g, Saturated fat .9 g,
Carbohydrates 42.8 g, Protein 9.5 g |

Green Quinoa Pilaf

SERVES 4

1 cup quinoa, cleaned and rinsed
2 cups vegetable stock or water
1 teaspoon ghee or olive oil
1 pinch red chili flakes
½ teaspoon black pepper
1 cup chopped leeks or onions
1 teaspoon ground cumin
1 tablespoon Bragg Liquid Aminos or tamari
2 medium zucchini, halved lengthwise, then sliced
1 medium yellow squash, halved lengthwise, then sliced
2 handfuls mixed cooking greens (Swiss chard, spinach, mustard greens), washed and torn into pieces
3 tablespoons chopped fresh cilantro
1 teaspoon oregano
1 teaspoon paprika or chili powder
1 large tomato, diced

After rinsing, toast the quinoa in a dry skillet for about 2 minutes or until golden brown. Stir frequently. Bring 2 cups of the stock to a boil. Add the quinoa and simmer for 15 to 20 minutes or until the liquid is absorbed. Place the quinoa into a bowl and fluff with a fork. Cool.

In a sauté pan, heat the oil over medium heat; add the chili flakes, pepper, leeks, cumin, and aminos. Sauté until the leeks are browned. Add a little more stock if the mixture begins to dry. Add the zucchini and yellow squash and simmer for 3 or 4 minutes. Add the greens and continue to sauté until the greens are just wilted. Remove from the heat, drain any excess liquid, and set aside. Add the cilantro, oregano, paprika, and tomato to the quinoa. Stir together, then add the vegetable mixture. Toss together until well combined. This dish can be a hot pilaf side dish or a wonderful cold salad on a bed of greens.

NUTRITIONAL FACTS

Per 1-cup serving
Calories 287, Total fat 5.8 g, Saturated fat .9 g, Carbohydrates 40.6 g, Protein 18.1 g

Eggless Tofu Salad or Sandwich

SERVES 4

16 ounces fresh, low-fat tofu, firm or extra firm
¼ cup chopped green onions
2 tablespoons chopped cilantro
2 tablespoons chopped parsley
2 celery stalks, chopped
¼ cup grated carrots
1 teaspoon Bragg Liquid Aminos or tamari
1 pinch black pepper
½ teaspoon turmeric
1 teaspoon dried dill
1 teaspoon curry powder
2 tablespoons Dijon mustard
¼ cup plain yogurt or soy mayonnaise

Crumble the tofu into a medium-size bowl. Add the green onions, cilantro, parsley, celery, carrots, and aminos. Mix with your hands until the mixture is well combined. In a small bowl, combine the pepper, turmeric, dill, curry powder, mustard, and yogurt. Add to the tofu mixture and mix with a fork until a smooth consistency is achieved. Serve on a bed of field greens or as a filling for a wrap or sandwich between 2 pieces of homemade simple great whole grain bread (see page 52).

NUTRITIONAL
FACTS

Per ½-cup serving
For the salad only, without bread or wrap
Calories 149, Total fat 5.5 g, Saturated fat .2 g,
Carbohydrates 9.7 g, Protein 15.1 g

Indian Rice

SERVES 4

3 cups vegetable stock or water
1 stick cinnamon
3 whole cardamom pods
1½ cups organic basmati rice, rinsed in a strainer
1 teaspoon ghee or olive oil
1 cup chopped leeks or onion
1 cup diced green bell pepper
½ teaspoon turmeric
1 teaspoon garam masala
1 teaspoon coriander
½ cup grated carrots
¼ cup chopped roasted red bell pepper
2 tablespoons golden raisins
¼ cup chopped fresh cilantro

In a saucepan, bring the stock, cinnamon stick, cardamom pods, and rice to a boil. Reduce the heat to the lowest possible and keep it at that temperature. Simmer for 20 to 25 minutes. Resist lifting the lid; the rice will cook better without interruption. When the rice has cooked, fluff it with a fork, cover, and set aside.

Heat the oil in a sauté pan over medium heat. Add the leeks and bell pepper and sauté for 2 minutes. Add the turmeric, garam masala, and coriander and sauté for another 2 minutes, stirring frequently. Remove from the heat and let cool, then add the cooked rice. In a separate bowl, combine the grated carrots, roasted red pepper, raisins, and cilantro. Using a spoon, combine the vegetables and the rice mixture. Remove the cinnamon stick and cardamom pods just before serving. Serve as a hot side dish or as a cold salad on a bed of greens.

NUTRITIONAL FACTS

Per 1-cup serving
Calories 343, Total fat 2.8 g, Saturated fat 1 g, Carbohydrates 72.4 g, Protein 7 g

Nutty Spinach Greens

SERVES 4

1 teaspoon ghee or olive oil
½ cup chopped leeks or onions
1 teaspoon Bragg Liquid Aminos or tamari
½ teaspoon cumin seeds
½ teaspoon black pepper
2 bunches fresh spinach, washed, drained, and torn into pieces (about 10 cups)
¼ cup vegetable stock
2 tablespoons apple juice
¼ cup almonds, sliced and toasted

Heat the oil in a large sauté pan over medium heat. Add the leeks, aminos, cumin, and pepper. Sauté until the leeks are translucent, about 2 minutes. Add the spinach, stirring often to enable even cooking. Add the vegetable stock if the spinach begins to dry out. The spinach will be cooked when it is just wilted, or slightly limp, but still maintains a vibrant color. Add the apple juice and simmer for 1 minute to incorporate the flavors. Add the almonds just before serving.

NUTRITIONAL FACTS

Per 1-cup serving
Calories 80, Total fat 4.6 g, Saturated fat 1.1 g, Carbohydrates 6.1 g, Protein 3.4 g

Oat Groat Pilaf with Spinach

SERVES 4

1 cup oat groats, steel cut oats, or buckwheat groats
2 cups vegetable stock or water
1 teaspoon ghee or olive oil
1 cup chopped leeks or onions
1 teaspoon Bragg Liquid Aminos or tamari
4 cups spinach, washed, drained, and torn into pieces
¼ cup apple juice
2 tablespoons lemon juice
1 teaspoon dried dill
½ teaspoon black pepper
½ teaspoon garam masala
½ cup chopped fresh parsley

In a medium saucepan, combine the groats and the stock and bring to a boil. Reduce the heat to a simmer and cook, uncovered, until the groats are tender. Watch for sticking. Most of the water will be absorbed. Rinse the groats with cold water and place in a bowl.

Heat the oil in a large sauté pan over medium heat; add the leeks and the aminos, and sauté until the leeks are translucent. Add the spinach and cook until just wilted. Remove the pan from the heat. In a small bowl, whisk together the apple juice, lemon juice, dill, pepper, and garam masala. Pour over the groats and add the spinach mixture. Add the parsley and toss gently until combined. Taste for saltiness; you may need to add a little more aminos to taste.

NUTRITIONAL FACTS

Per 1½-cup serving
Using ghee
Calories 218, Total fat 3.1 g, Saturated fat 1 g,
Carbohydrates 40.6 g, Protein 7 g

Salad Greens

Keep some salad greens on hand in your refrigerator. Spinach, mixed field greens, romaine, and butter lettuce are good choices. A cold salad as a side dish can be as simple as tossing some olive oil and a splash of balsamic vinaigrette on a mixture of organic field greens. Don't add the olive oil to the salad if you are having a dressing.

Grilled chicken or fish can be added to any salad for additional taste and protein. Slice the chicken or fish into long thin pieces and lay on top of the salad. Here are two of our favorite salads.

Garden Salad

SERVES 1

3 leaves romaine lettuce, torn
2 tablespoons grated carrots
2 tablespoons grated zucchini
2 tomato wedges
½ cup alfalfa or sunflower sprouts
4 slices cucumber
1 teaspoon toasted sunflower seeds
1 teaspoon olive oil
1½ teaspoons balsamic vinegar
1 cup sliced cooked chicken or fish, optional

NUTRITIONAL
FACTS

Per 2-cup serving
For the salad only, no chicken or fish
Calories 92, Total fat 6.4 g, Saturated fat .8 g,
Carbohydrates 6.4 g, Protein 2.3 g

Organic Mixed Field Greens Salad

SERVES 1

2 leaves romaine or butter leaf lettuce, torn
6 leaves arugula, torn
1 cup spinach, torn
¼ cup watercress
2 cherry tomatoes
1 teaspoon walnuts, roasted
2 slices boiled and peeled beets
1 teaspoon olive oil
1½ teaspoons balsamic vinegar
1 cup sliced cooked chicken or fish, optional

NUTRITIONAL
FACTS

Per 2-cup serving
For the salad only, no chicken or fish
Calories 88, Total fat 6.2 g, Saturated fat .7 g,
Carbohydrates 5.5 g, Protein 2.4 g

Savory Swiss Chard

SERVES 4

1 teaspoon ghee or olive oil
¼ teaspoon brown mustard seeds
1 pinch black pepper
½ cup chopped leeks or onions
1 teaspoon Bragg Liquid Aminos or tamari
8 cups red or white Swiss chard, washed, drained, and torn
1 teaspoon balsamic vinegar
1 teaspoon garam masala

Heat the oil in a large sauté pan. Add the mustard seeds and pepper. When the seeds have popped, add the leeks and the aminos. Add the chard, stirring often to enable even cooking, and cook until they begin to look slightly limp but maintain a vibrant color. Add the balsamic vinegar and garam masala and simmer for 2 minutes before serving. Add a little more aminos if the chard tastes bitter.

NUTRITIONAL FACTS

Per 1-cup serving
Using ghee
Calories 42, Total fat 1.5 g, Saturated fat .9 g, Carbohydrates 5.1 g, Protein 1.9 g

Spanish Pilaf

SERVES 4

1 cup organic basmati rice
½ cup quinoa
3 cups plus 2 tablespoons vegetable stock or water
1 teaspoon ghee or olive oil
½ cup chopped leeks or onions
½ teaspoon black pepper
1 teaspoon Bragg Liquid Aminos or tamari
1 teaspoon paprika
1 teaspoon chili powder
1 teaspoon cinnamon
1 teaspoon cumin
½ cup corn, fresh or frozen
½ cup peas, fresh or frozen

Place the rice and quinoa in a strainer and rinse. In a saucepan, bring 3 cups vegetable stock to a boil with the rice and quinoa. Reduce the heat to the lowest possible and keep it there. Simmer the grains for 20 to 25 minutes. Resist lifting the lid; the grains will cook better without interruption. Fluff with a fork, cover, and set aside.

Heat the oil in a large sauté pan, then add the leeks, pepper, and aminos. Brown the leeks slightly. Add the paprika, chili powder, cinnamon, and cumin. Add the remaining 2 tablespoons stock when the mixture looks dry. Add the corn and the peas and continue to sauté for 2 minutes. Add the rice and quinoa and combine well.

NUTRITIONAL
FACTS

Per 1-cup serving
Using olive oil
Calories 360, Total fat 3.4 g, Saturated fat .1 g,
Carbohydrates 62.5 g, Protein 9.1 g

Spicy Mexican Rice

SERVES 4

3 cups plus ¼ cup vegetable stock or water
1½ cups organic basmati rice, rinsed in a strainer
1 teaspoon ghee or olive oil
½ cup chopped leeks or onions
1 tablespoon Bragg Liquid Aminos or tamari
½ cup diced green bell pepper
½ cup black beans, cooked or canned, rinsed
½ cup corn, fresh or frozen
½ teaspoon black pepper
1 teaspoon oregano
1 teaspoon cumin
1 teaspoon coriander
1 pinch cayenne
1 teaspoon chili powder
¼ cup chopped fresh cilantro
½ cup diced tomatoes

In a saucepan, bring 3 cups vegetable stock and rice to a boil. Reduce the heat to the lowest possible and keep it there. Simmer for 20 to 25 minutes. Resist lifting the lid; the rice will cook better without interruption. Fluff with a fork, cover, and set aside.

Heat the oil in a sauté pan over medium heat. Add the leeks, aminos, bell pepper, beans, and corn. Sauté for 3 minutes. In a small bowl, combine the black pepper, oregano, cumin, coriander, cayenne, and chili powder with a fork. Add the spice mixture to the pan and continue to sauté for another 1 minute. Be prepared to add the remaining ¼ cup stock if necessary if the mixture dries out. Using a rubber spatula, place the vegetable sauté in a bowl and add the rice. Combine well. Garnish with the cilantro and the tomatoes.

NUTRITIONAL
FACTS

Per 1-cup serving
Using ghee
Calories 485, Total fat 4.5 g, Saturated fat 1.3 g,
Carbohydrates 86.7 g, Protein 24.6 g

Tuscany Bulgur Pilaf

This pilaf can be served hot with an entrée or used as a stuffing for vegetables such as artichokes, zucchini, or squash. It will also make a great cold salad.

SERVES 4

1½ cups plus ¼ cup vegetable stock or water
1 cup bulgur wheat (cracked wheat)
1 teaspoon ghee or olive oil
½ cup chopped leeks or onions
¼ cup chopped roasted red peppers
1 cup cubed zucchini
½ cup Great Northern beans, cooked or canned and rinsed
1 cup diced tomatoes
½ cup chopped Italian parsley
2 tablespoons finely sliced fresh basil
2 tablespoons chopped fresh mint
2 tablespoons kalamata olives, pitted and sliced

Dressing

2 tablespoons lemon juice
1 tablespoon apple juice
1 tablespoon Bragg Liquid Aminos or tamari
1 teaspoon dried dill
½ teaspoon salt
½ teaspoon pepper
2 cloves garlic, pressed, or ½ teaspoon garlic powder
2 teaspoons olive oil

Bring 1½ cups vegetable stock to a boil in a small saucepan with a lid. Add the bulgur, stir with a fork, remove from the heat, and cover with a tight-fitting lid. Allow the bulgur to soak for 15 minutes. Fluff with a fork and place in a large, flat mixing bowl, and let cool. Meanwhile, heat the oil in a sauté pan over medium heat; add the leeks and sauté briefly. Add the red pepper and the zucchini and sauté for 2 minutes. Add the cooked beans and sauté for another 2 minutes. Add the remaining ¼ cup stock as the mixture begins to dry out. Remove from the heat and cool. Add the tomatoes, parsley, basil, mint, and olives to the cooled bulgur. Add the sauté and combine gently.

In a small bowl, combine the lemon juice, apple juice, aminos, dill, salt, pepper, and garlic. Continue to whisk together as you slowly add the olive oil. Pour the dressing over the bulgur mixture.

NUTRITIONAL FACTS	*Per 1-cup serving* Calories 304, Total fat 6 g, Saturated fat 1.3 g, Carbohydrates 49.8 g, Protein 12.6 g

Sauces, Condiments, and Finishing Touches

A good meal ought to begin with hunger.

FRENCH PROVERB

Sauces, dressings, chutneys, condiments, and salsas bring the components of a meal together. A touch of sauce to a sandwich adds moistness and flavor. A salsa on top of tofu adds a Latin flair. Greens tossed with a dressing create a delicious salad. Condiments provide flavor, color, spiciness, texture, excitement, and richness to any meal.

Be creative. Experiment with different tastes, colors, and textures. Tofu alone can be bland, but serve it with a savory sauce or a spicy chutney and it assumes a completely new personality. You will notice that some of the recipes make enough for 8 servings. Most of the condiments can be stored in the refrigerator for 4 to 5 days to provide a variety of tastes in different meals.

Sauces and Condiments Recipes

Apple Leek Chutney

Apricot Salsa

Basic Asian-Style Sauce

Basil and Friends Pesto

Cilantro Mint Sauce

Cilantro Pecan Sauce

Cucumber Raita

Eggplant Tapenade

Homemade Chili Sauce

Hummus

Kim Chi Chutney

Krazy Ketchup

Leek Sauce

Mandarin Tomato Salsa

Nutty Dipping Sauce

Orange Pear Chutney

Pesto-Tomato Pasta Sauce

Roasted Tomato Sauce

Russian Borscht Chutney

Spicy Lime and Red Pepper Dipping Sauce

Sweet Mixed Fruit Chutney

Tomato Salsa

Walnut Yogurt Sauce

Apple Leek Chutney

SERVES 8

2 large apples
1 teaspoon plus 1 teaspoon lemon juice
1 teaspoon ghee or olive oil
2 teaspoons chopped fresh ginger
4 whole cloves
2 cinnamon sticks
½ teaspoon mustard seeds
½ teaspoon fenugreek seeds
1 cup chopped leeks, onions, or shallots
1 pinch chili powder
1 pinch salt
1 teaspoon ground coriander
1 teaspoon cinnamon
½ teaspoon ginger powder
2 tablespoons apple cider vinegar
12 ounces frozen apple juice concentrate
¼ cup currants or raisins
2 tablespoons turbinado sugar or maple syrup

Core and chop the apples; place in a small bowl of water with 1 teaspoon lemon juice. Heat the oil in a sauté pan over medium heat. Add the fresh ginger, cloves, cinnamon sticks, mustard seeds; and fenugreek seeds. Sauté for 1 minute, then add the leeks. Sauté for 2 or 3 minutes. Drain the apples and add along with the chili powder, salt, coriander, cinnamon, and ginger powder. Sauté for another 4 or 5 minutes, until the apples begin to soften. Add vinegar, apple juice concentrate, and the remaining teaspoon lemon juice to cover the apples. Bring to a boil, then reduce the heat and simmer for up to 1 hour. Add the currants and sugar about halfway into the cooking process. Add additional apple juice, as needed, if the chutney becomes too dry. The chutney should have a thick consistency. Remove the cinnamon sticks and serve chilled or warm.

NUTRITIONAL
FACTS

Per ½-cup serving
Calories 170, Total fat 1.3 g, Saturated fat .5 g,
Carbohydrates 38.3 g, Protein .9 g

Apricot Salsa

SERVES 4

2 cups diced apricots, fresh or dried (soaked)
½ cup finely chopped leeks, onions, or green onions
1 cup chopped tomato
½ teaspoon garam masala
2 tablespoons chopped fresh mint
1 teaspoon chopped dill, dried or fresh
1 teaspoon ground cardamom
1 teaspoon lemon juice
1 teaspoon Bragg Liquid Aminos or tamari

If using dried apricots, soak in 2 cups of boiled hot water for 15 minutes. Drain and set aside. If you are using leeks or onions, lightly sauté them first in 1 teaspoon ghee or olive oil over medium heat. Green onions will not need to be sautéed. In a mixing bowl, place the apricots, tomato, and cooked leeks. Add the garam masala, mint, dill, and cardamom. Add the lemon juice and the aminos. Toss gently, then taste for seasonings.

NUTRITIONAL FACTS | *Per ½-cup serving*
Calories 64, Total fat .5 g, Saturated fat 0 g,
Carbohydrates 12.8 g, Protein 2 g

Basic Asian-Style Sauce

MAKES
ABOUT
1/3 CUP

1 teaspoon sesame oil
2 tablespoons Bragg Liquid Aminos or tamari
2 tablespoons maple syrup
2 tablespoons rice vinegar
1 tablespoon balsamic vinegar
1 pinch red chili flakes
½ teaspoon Chinese five-spice powder
1 teaspoon ginger powder
1 teaspoon ground coriander

Whisk all ingredients together in a bowl. Use as a marinade or as a stir-fry sauce.

NUTRITIONAL
FACTS

Per 2 tablespoons
Calories 62, Total fat 1.2 g, Saturated fat .2 g,
Carbohydrates 12 g, Protein 1 g

Basil and Friends
Pesto

1 cup raw shelled walnuts, whole or pieces
1 cup fresh basil
1 cup arugula
1 cup fresh spinach
2 tablespoons lemon juice
2 teaspoons Bragg Liquid Aminos or tamari
2 teaspoons olive oil
2 teaspoons apple juice

Preheat the oven to 350 degrees. Place the walnuts on a baking sheet and roast for 20 minutes. Remove from the oven and cool. In a food processor, place the basil, arugula, and spinach. Pulse to break down. Add the roasted walnuts, lemon juice, and aminos. Continue to pulse into a smooth consistency. Slowly drizzle the olive oil and apple juice into the food processor as it continues to run, blending until the pesto is very smooth.

NUTRITIONAL
FACTS

Per 1-ounce serving
Calories 65, Total fat 5.3 g, Saturated fat .5 g,
Carbohydrates 2.4 g, Protein 1.8 g

Cilantro Mint Sauce

SERVES 4

2 cups fresh cilantro
1 cup fresh mint
1 tablespoon lemon juice
½ teaspoon ground cardamom
1 tablespoon Bragg Liquid Aminos or tamari
1 tablespoon apple juice or vegetable stock
6 ounces silken tofu, optional

Place the cilantro, mint, and lemon juice in a blender. Pulse to combine. Add the cardamom, aminos, and apple juice. Blend together, adding more liquid if necessary to create a smooth sauce. Serve with spicy foods to cool down the meal. For a creamy texture, blend in 6 ounces of silken tofu.

NUTRITIONAL FACTS

Per ¼-cup serving
Without tofu
Calories 20, Total fat .2 g, Saturated fat 0 g,
Carbohydrates 3.2 g, Protein 1.2 g

Cilantro Pecan Sauce

SERVES 4

¼ cup raw pecans, whole or pieces
6 ounces low-fat silken tofu, firm or extra firm
½ bunch fresh cilantro
1 tablespoon lemon juice
2 tablespoons vegetable stock
1 clove garlic or ½ teaspoon garlic powder
1 teaspoon cumin
1 tablespoon Bragg Liquid Aminos or tamari
1 pinch black pepper

Place the pecans in a dry sauté pan and roast over high heat until they become golden brown. Place the tofu, cilantro, pecans, and lemon juice in a blender or food processor. Blend or pulse until the tofu begins to break down. Add the vegetable stock, garlic, cumin, and aminos. Continue to blend until smooth. Add the black pepper and continue to blend until well incorporated. Serve on steamed vegetables, as a sandwich spread, or thin with ¼ cup apple juice and ¼ cup rice vinegar for a salad dressing.

NUTRITIONAL FACTS

Per ¼-cup serving
Calories 80, Total fat 5.4 g, Saturated fat .4 g,
Carbohydrates 3.2 g, Protein 4.8 g

Cucumber Raita

SERVES 4

3 small cucumbers, peeled, seeded, and diced
2 tablespoons lemon juice
1 teaspoon cumin
½ teaspoon dried dill
1 pinch salt
2 teaspoons chopped fresh cilantro
1 cup low-fat plain yogurt

Place the cucumbers in a small bowl. Add the lemon juice, cumin, dill, salt, and cilantro and toss gently. Add the yogurt and combine with a fork. Serve as a condiment with curry or as a dressing for salads or wraps.

NUTRITIONAL
FACTS

Per ⅓-cup serving
Calories 59, Total fat 1.1 g, Saturated fat .6 g,
Carbohydrates 8 g, Protein 3.9 g

Eggplant Tapenade

SERVES 8

1 medium eggplant
1 tablespoon olive oil
2 teaspoons balsamic vinegar
1 tablespoon dried basil
1 teaspoon dried sage
1 teaspoon black pepper
½ cup kalamata olives
½ cup artichoke hearts, drained and rinsed
¼ cup roasted red peppers, canned or freshly roasted
1 tablespoon lemon juice
1 tablespoon apple juice or vegetable stock
2 tablespoons capers, drained
½ cup finely chopped fresh parsley

Preheat the oven to 350 degrees. Cut the eggplant into 1-inch cubes. Combine the olive oil, balsamic vinegar, basil, sage, and black pepper in a large bowl. Whisk together. Add the eggplant cubes and toss. Place the eggplant on an oiled baking sheet and roast for 30 minutes. Remove from the oven and cool.

In a food processor, place the roasted eggplant, olives, artichoke hearts, and roasted red peppers. Pulse into a coarse mixture, then add the lemon juice and apple juice. Remove from the food processor and place in a mixing bowl. Add the capers and chopped parsley and combine. Use the tapenade as a condiment, sandwich spread, or pizza topping.

NUTRITIONAL FACTS | *per ¼-cup serving*
Calories 70, Total fat 4.8 g, Saturated fat .2 g,
Carbohydrates 5.6 g, Protein 1.0 g

Homemade Chili Sauce

SERVES 8

1 teaspoon ghee or olive oil
½ cup chopped leeks or onions
½ teaspoon celery seeds
1 teaspoon black pepper
4 whole cloves
4 large tomatoes, chopped
4 stalks celery, diced
1 large bell pepper, chopped
¼ cup rice vinegar or apple cider vinegar
¼ cup vegetable stock
¼ cup turbinado sugar
½ teaspoon salt
1½ teaspoons mustard powder
1 teaspoon allspice
½ teaspoon ginger powder
½ teaspoon cinnamon
½ teaspoon nutmeg

Heat the oil in a saucepan over medium heat. Add the leeks, celery seeds, black pepper, and cloves. Sauté for 1 minute, then add the tomatoes, celery, and bell pepper. Sauté another 1 to 2 minutes, then add the vinegar and stock. Simmer for 2 minutes, then add the sugar and salt. In a small bowl, combine the mustard powder, allspice, ginger, cinnamon, and nutmeg. Add the spice mixture to the sauce and simmer on low heat for up to 30 minutes. Purée into a smooth sauce with a hand blender, blender, or food processor. Cool and store in the refrigerator in a glass jar with a tight-fitting lid. Use as a base in soups, marinades, and sauces. Use the sauce in chicken and fish preparations.

NUTRITIONAL FACTS

Per ¼-cup serving
Calories 87.5, Total fat 1.4 g, Saturated fat .5 g,
Carbohydrates 16.6 g, Protein 2 g

Hummus

1 cup garbanzo beans (chickpeas), rinsed and soaked overnight in water, or 1 14-ounce can cooked garbanzos, drained and rinsed

2 tablespoons tahini (sesame seed paste)

¼ cup chopped parsley

1 large green onion, chopped, or 1 tablespoon chopped leek

2 teaspoons minced garlic, or 1 teaspoon garlic powder

1 teaspoon cumin

1 pinch cayenne

1 teaspoon dried dill

2 tablespoons lemon juice

2 teaspoons Bragg Liquid Aminos or tamari

If using dried beans, drain and place in 4 quarts of water. Bring to a boil and cook the beans for 1 hour or until they are soft. Skim any foam and discard as the beans cook. Drain off the excess water and set aside.

In a food processor, place the cooked or canned beans, tahini, parsley, onion, cumin, cayenne, and dill. Pulse to combine. Slowly begin to add the lemon juice and aminos. Continue to pulse until a smooth consistency is achieved. Add more liquid or spices as necessary.

NUTRITIONAL
FACTS

Per ¼-cup serving
Calories 125, Total fat 3.6 g, Saturated fat .5 g, Carbohydrates 17.2 g, Protein 5.9 g

Kim Chi Chutney

SERVES 4

1 teaspoon sesame oil
1 cup leeks or onions, cut into large pieces
2 tablespoons minced fresh gingerroot
1 tablespoon Bragg Liquid Aminos or tamari
1 pinch red chili flakes
½ head cabbage, cut into 1-inch pieces
2 carrots, thinly sliced
1 large bell pepper, cut into 1-inch pieces
¼ cup rice vinegar
½ cup vegetable stock
1 teaspoon paprika

In a saucepan, heat the oil over medium heat. Add the leeks, ginger, aminos, and red chili flakes. Sauté for 2 minutes. Add the cabbage, carrots, and bell pepper. Sauté for 5 minutes, stirring frequently. Add the vinegar, vegetable stock, and paprika and simmer for up to 30 minutes. Cool and store in a glass jar. Serve as a spicy condiment with Buddha's delight vegetable stir-fry (page 114), Thai-style noodles with tofu (page 132), or cashew tempeh (page 116).

NUTRITIONAL FACTS

Per 1-cup serving
Calories 111, Total fat 1.9 g, Saturated fat .2 g, Carbohydrates 20.9 g, Protein 3.2 g

Krazy Ketchup

SERVES 8

1 teaspoon ghee or olive oil
1 cup chopped leeks or onions
1 stalk celery, diced
½ teaspoon black pepper
1 tablespoon Bragg Liquid Aminos or tamari
1 pinch cayenne (omit if you will be serving the ketchup to children)
1 teaspoon coriander
1 teaspoon ground rosemary
3 tablespoons apple cider vinegar
1 tablespoon lemon juice
¼ cup vegetable stock
1 cup tomato paste
2 tablespoons chopped fresh cilantro
2 tablespoons maple syrup

Heat the oil in a saucepan and add the leeks, celery, and black pepper. Sauté until the leeks are translucent, then add the aminos, cayenne, coriander, and rosemary. Continue to sauté for 1 to 2 minutes. Add the vinegar and lemon juice and simmer over medium heat for 4 to 5 minutes. Add the vegetable stock and tomato paste, combining well. Continue to simmer for another 5 minutes. Add the cilantro and maple syrup. If the mixture is too thin, continue to simmer until the liquid is absorbed. In a blender or with a hand blender, purée into a smooth consistency. If the ketchup is too thick, add vegetable stock before puréeing. Cool and store in the refrigerator in a glass jar with a tight-fitting lid. Serve with country potatoes (page 86), Masala potatoes (page 90), or tempeh and potato hash (page 100).

NUTRITIONAL FACTS

Per ¼-cup serving
Calories 34, Total fat .5 g, Saturated fat .3 g,
Carbohydrates 6.3 g, Protein 1 g

Leek Sauce

SERVES 4

1 teaspoon ghee or olive oil
1 cup chopped leeks
½ teaspoon black pepper
1 tablespoon Bragg Liquid Aminos or tamari
1 teaspoon thyme
½ teaspoon cumin
¼ to ½ cup vegetable stock

In a sauté pan, heat the oil and add the leeks, black pepper, aminos, thyme, and cumin. Brown the leeks well to create the best flavor. Add ¼ cup vegetable stock and simmer over medium heat. Add more stock if you want a juicy consistency. Simmer for 4 to 5 minutes or until reduced to the desired consistency. You can add some basic roux (see page 58) to the leek sauce to create creamy consistency. Serve on tofu burgers (page 134) or as a sauce on sautéed vegetables.

NUTRITIONAL
FACTS

Per 2-tablespoon serving
Using ghee
Calories 43, Total fat 1.7 g, Saturated fat .9 g,
Carbohydrates 4.1 g, Protein 2.8 g

Mandarin Tomato Salsa

SERVES 4

1 teaspoon ghee

½ cup chopped leeks, onions, or green onions

1 cup mandarin orange or satsuma tangerine, peeled and cubed, seeds removed

4 medium tomatoes, cubed

1 tablespoon mild Anaheim chili, roasted, peeled, and chopped, or 1 tablespoon canned mild Ortega green chilies

1 tablespoon Bragg Liquid Aminos or tamari

1 tablespoon apple juice

1 tablespoon lime juice

¼ cup chopped cilantro

1 teaspoon ground cumin

½ teaspoon ground coriander

Heat the ghee in a sauté pan over medium heat. Sauté the leeks. Green onions do not need to be sautéed. Remove from the heat and cool slightly. In a mixing bowl, place the oranges, tomatoes, chilies, sautéed leeks, and the aminos. Combine well. Add the apple juice, lime juice, cilantro, cumin, and coriander. Combine with a spoon. Cover and chill for 1 hour before serving.

NUTRITIONAL FACTS

Per ½-cup serving
Calories 66, Total fat .4 g, Saturated fat 0 g, Carbohydrates 13.6 g, Protein 1.8 g

Nutty Dipping Sauce

SERVES 8

1 teaspoon ghee or sesame oil
4 cloves garlic, minced
1 pinch red chili flakes
½ to 1 cup vegetable stock
2 tablespoons Bragg Liquid Aminos or tamari
¼ cup peanut butter or almond butter
1 tablespoon maple syrup
1 tablespoon sesame seeds
1 tablespoon chopped mint or cilantro

Heat the oil in a saucepan over medium heat. Briefly sauté the garlic and red chili flakes. Add ½ cup vegetable stock, aminos, peanut butter, and maple syrup. Simmer until heated through. Add the sesame seeds and mint. Cool. For a smooth texture, purée the ingredients in a blender. Add more stock if necessary to thin the sauce. Serve with lettuce wraps (page 203) or Szechwan baked egg rolls (page 130).

NUTRITIONAL
FACTS

Per 2-tablespoon serving
Using ghee
Calories 47, Total fat 3 g, Saturated fat .5 g,
Carbohydrates 2.5 g, Protein 2.4 g

Orange Pear Chutney

SERVES 8

1 orange, peeled and cubed
2 pears, cubed and placed in a bowl with lemon water
1 teaspoon ghee or olive oil
1 teaspoon mustard seeds
1 pinch chili powder (not cayenne)
½ cup chopped leeks or onions
1 inch gingerroot, finely chopped
1 teaspoon Bragg Liquid Aminos or tamari
1 teaspoon ground coriander
1 teaspoon cinnamon
4 whole cloves
¼ cup raisins
¼ cup apple cider vinegar
12 ounces frozen apple juice concentrate, undiluted
¼ cup maple syrup

Prepare the orange and the pears and set aside. Heat the oil in a sauté pan over medium heat and add the mustard seeds. After the seeds pop, add the chili powder, leeks, ginger, and aminos. Sauté for 1 to 2 minutes. Drain the pears and add to the pan. Sauté for another 2 to 3 minutes. Add the coriander, cinnamon, and cloves. Continue to sauté, then add the raisins, orange pieces, vinegar, and apple juice concentrate. Simmer over low heat up to 1 hour. Add the maple syrup about halfway through the cooking process. Serve as a complement to spicy vegetable dishes, Asian dishes, and in whole wheat crepes (page 103).

NUTRITIONAL FACTS

Per ¼-cup serving
Using ghee
Calories 74, Total fat .6 g, Saturated fat .2 g,
Carbohydrates 16.7 g, Protein .4 g

Pesto-Tomato Pasta Sauce

SERVES 8 2 tablespoons Basil and Friends Pesto (see page 230)
     1 cup chopped fresh tomatoes
     2 tablespoons balsamic vinegar
     ¼ cup vegetable stock
     ½ cup apple juice
     ¼ cup olive oil

In a blender, place the pesto, tomatoes, and the vinegar. Blend to combine, then add the vegetable stock and apple juice and continue to blend into a smooth consistency. Slowly drizzle the olive oil into the blender as it continues to run. Serve over your favorite hot or cold pasta dish or steamed vegetables.

NUTRITIONAL FACTS

Per ¼-cup serving
Using olive oil
Calories 92, Total fat 8 g, Saturated fat 1 g,
Carbohydrates 4.1 g, Protein .7 g

Roasted
Tomato Sauce

MAKES 4 CUPS

Roast
Tomatoes

5	or 6 large tomatoes
1	tablespoon olive oil
1	tablespoon balsamic vinegar
1	teaspoon black pepper
4	sprigs fresh rosemary, stems removed
1	tablespoon dried basil
1	teaspoon dried thyme

Sauce

1	teaspoon ghee or olive oil
2	cups chopped leeks or shallots
1	pinch red chili flakes
1	teaspoon black pepper
1	tablespoon Bragg Liquid Aminos and tamari
2	teaspoons balsamic vinegar
1	batch roasted tomatoes or 2 12- to 16-ounce cans tomatoes
¼	cup chopped fresh parsley
½	cup thinly sliced fresh basil leaves

Preheat the oven to 350 degrees. Cut the vine end off the tomatoes and cut an **X** with a paring knife on the smooth bottom end of each tomato. Place the tomatoes in a shallow roasting pan and drizzle with the olive oil and balsamic vinegar. Sprinkle the pepper, rosemary, basil, and thyme evenly over the tomatoes. Bake for 30 minutes or until the tomatoes are soft and the skin is easily removed. Remove from the oven and cool. Working over a bowl, break up the tomatoes with your hands, removing the skin as you go. Set aside the bowl of tomato pieces and juice.

Over medium heat, heat the oil in a 4-quart saucepan. Add the leeks, red chili flakes, black pepper, and aminos. Sauté until the leeks are translucent, 2 to 3 minutes. Add the tomatoes with their juice and the vinegar. Bring to a boil, then reduce the heat and simmer for 1 hour or more until thickened. Add the parsley and the basil 15 minutes before completion. To create a smooth texture, purée in a blender if desired.

NUTRITIONAL FACTS | *Per ½-cup serving*
Using olive oil
Calories 147, Total fat 5.5 g, Saturated fat 1.5 g, Carbohydrates 20.8 g, Protein 3.6 g

Russian Borscht Chutney

SERVES 8

1 teaspoon ghee or olive oil
½ cup chopped leeks or onions
1 pinch red chili flakes
1 teaspoon caraway seeds
1 teaspoon mustard seeds
1 teaspoon cinnamon
1 tablespoon vegetable stock
1 cup shredded red beets
1 cup shredded carrots
1 cup thinly sliced red cabbage
½ cup thinly sliced red or green bell pepper
½ cup rice vinegar

Heat the oil in a 4-quart saucepan over medium heat. Add the leeks, red chili flakes, caraway seeds, and mustard seeds. When the seeds have popped and the leeks are translucent, add the cinnamon and stock. Sauté for 1 minute. Add the beets, carrots, cabbage, bell pepper, and rice vinegar. Reduce the heat to a medium simmer and cook for 15 to 20 minutes. Stir frequently. Cool and store in a glass jar with a tight-fitting lid. Use as a condiment.

NUTRITIONAL FACTS

Per ½-cup serving
Using ghee
Calories 33, Total fat .5 g, Saturated fat .2 g,
Carbohydrates 7 g, Protein .5 g

Spicy Lime and Red Pepper Dipping Sauce

SERVES 4

¼ cup roasted red pepper, fresh or canned (drained)
¼ cup fresh lime juice
2 tablespoons rice vinegar
2 tablespoons maple syrup
1 tablespoon Bragg Liquid Aminos or tamari
1 pinch salt
1 pinch cayenne
2 tablespoons thinly sliced fresh basil leaves

In a blender, combine the pepper, lime juice, vinegar, maple syrup, aminos, salt, and cayenne and purée until smooth. Add the basil and pulse briefly. Use as a dipping sauce for lettuce wraps (page 203).

NUTRITIONAL FACTS

Per 2-tablespoon serving
Calories 54, Total fat 0 g, Saturated fat 0 g, Carbohydrates 12.8 g, Protein .7 g

Sweet Mixed Fruit Chutney

SERVES 4

1 teaspoon ghee
1 stick cinnamon
5 whole cloves
2 cups cubed apples or pears
¼ cup currants, raisins, or dried cranberries
2 teaspoons cinnamon
1 pinch ground cloves
1 pinch cardamom
1 fresh mango, cut into cubes
2 tablespoons toasted coconut
12 ounces frozen apple juice concentrate, undiluted
2 teaspoons lemon juice
3 tablespoons maple syrup

Heat the ghee in a saucepan over medium heat. Add the cinnamon stick and cloves. Sauté for 1 minute then add the apple cubes. Add the currants, cinnamon, ground cloves, and cardamom. Sauté for another 2 minutes. Add the mango, coconut, apple juice concentrate, lemon juice, and maple syrup. Simmer until the apples or pears are soft and the juice is absorbed. Use this chutney in whole wheat crepes (page 103), as a complement to a spicy dish, or as a simple dessert.

NUTRITIONAL
FACTS

Per ¾-cup serving
Calories 182, Total fat 2.5 g, Saturated fat 1.5 g,
Carbohydrates 38.8 g, Protein 1 g

Tomato Salsa

SERVES 4

1 teaspoon ghee or olive oil
¼ cup chopped leeks or onions
2 cups diced tomato
¼ cup cilantro
1 teaspoon coriander
½ teaspoon garlic powder
½ teaspoon cumin
½ teaspoon black pepper
1 tablespoon lemon juice

Heat the oil in a sauté pan over medium heat. Add the leeks and sauté until translucent. Cool. In a small bowl, place the diced tomato, sautéed leeks, cilantro, coriander, garlic powder, cumin, black pepper, and lemon juice. Combine well with a spoon. Cover and chill before serving.

NUTRITIONAL FACTS

Per ½-cup serving
Using ghee
Calories 39, Total fat 1.6 g, Saturated fat .9 g, Carbohydrates 5.3 g, Protein .9 g

Walnut Yogurt Sauce

SERVES 4

2 tablespoons walnut pieces
½ teaspoon grated nutmeg
1 cup low-fat yogurt
½ teaspoon salt
1 tablespoon apple juice
1 teaspoon honey, optional

Place the walnut pieces in a heated sauté pan and roast until the walnuts are slightly brown. Remove from the heat and cool. In a blender, grind the walnuts into a coarse meal. Add the nutmeg, yogurt, salt, and apple juice. Blend until smooth. If a sweeter taste is desired, add 1 teaspoon honey. Use this sauce with curry filo tarts (page 111).

NUTRITIONAL FACTS

Per ¼-cup serving
Calories 68, Total fat 3.2 g, Saturated fat .8 g,
Carbohydrates 5.4 g, Protein 4.2 g

Desserts

A house is beautiful not because of its walls,
but because of its cakes.

OLD RUSSIAN PROVERB

Including dessert in every meal is one way of incorporating the sweet taste into each meal. Some of our dessert recipes are wheat-free, dairy-free, egg-free, and gluten-free. Some are protein-enhanced with tofu and nuts and sweetened with mango purée and applesauce. Admittedly, some of our traditional dessert recipes cannot be considered low-fat, as butter, cream, and sugar are used—we believe that an *occasional* indulgence is good for the body, mind, and soul. Balance your decadent desserts with lighter meals.

The quality of ingredients is the most important aspect of good baking. Favor organic dairy products. Use organically raised eggs from free-range chickens, and raw, unbleached sugar. Purchase high-quality organic whole wheat pastry flour, which works well in most applications, for your baking.

The recipes for Apricot Pecan Cookies, Double Almond Cookies, Linzertorte Cookies, and Walnut Chocolate Chip Cookies are all variations on a theme. These power-packed cookies make great midday snacks and will satisfy your craving for sweets. You can make all of them in less than 30 minutes. The cookie recipes can be made without wheat by using alternative flour products such as soy, rice, spelt, or barley flour. The dough also works well as the base of a baked fruit tart. Press the dough into a tart pan, arrange some sliced fruit, such as apples or apricots, on top, and bake for 30 to 40 minutes. Glaze by brushing the fruit with melted jam. This makes a very simple, healthy, and elegant dessert.

The Blueberry Orange Cake recipe can be used in a variety of different ways by following the basic cake recipe and changing the fruit and/or the spices to your taste.

Helpful Pointers

- Careful measuring is important in baking.
- Always blend or combine the ingredients very gently, a method referred to in baking as folding in. Use a rubber spatula or a spoon.
- Use a whisk to blend together both wet and dry ingredients. The dry ingredients will sift together well without the use of extra tools.
- A good assortment of whisks, spoons, spatulas, and stainless steel bowls is essential for baking. Our favorite tool is the 1-ounce ice-cream scoop for quick cookies.

Dessert Recipes

Almond Tart

Apple Cobbler

Apple Custard Pie

Apricot Pecan Cookies

Banana-Cocoa-Tofu Frozen Mousse

Blueberry Orange Cake

Berry Tofu Sorbet

Cardamom Butter Cookies

Chocolate Tofu Mousse with Walnut Coconut
Praline

Coconut Cookies

Cranberry Bliss Balls

Double Almond Cookies

Double Delight Cookies

Kabocha Squash or Pumpkin Pie

Lemon Birthday Cake

Ginger Cookies

Lemon Poppy Seed Cake

Mother Earth's Apple Pie

Linzertorte Cookies

Oatmeal Power Cookies

Peanut Butter Cookies

Traditional Awesome Brownies

Traditional Chocolate Chip Cookies

Unbelievable Double Chocolate Cake

Walnut Chocolate Chip Cookies

Almond Tart

SERVES 12

¼ cup whole almonds
1¼ cups whole wheat pastry flour
¼ cup turbinado sugar
1 pinch salt
½ cup butter, cut into ½-inch pieces
½ teaspoon nutmeg
1 egg yolk or 2 teaspoons mango purée
1 teaspoon vanilla extract
4 cups fresh or sautéed thinly sliced fruit of your choice

Topping

½ cup turbinado sugar
1 teaspoon arrowroot powder
2 tablespoons butter, cut into small pieces
½ cup apricot jam, melted

Preheat the oven to 425 degrees. Oil a 10-inch tart pan and set aside. In a food processor, pulse the almonds into a coarse meal. Remove from the processor and set aside in a bowl. Measure out ¼ cup of ground almonds. In the food processor, place the flour, ¼ cup ground almonds, sugar, and salt. Pulse together, then, piece-by-piece, add the butter, pulsing to create a coarse mixture. Sprinkle in the nutmeg as the processor continues to combine. Add the egg yolk and the vanilla. Pulse until the mixture looks smooth and begins to ball up. Press into the oiled tart pan. Create a ½-inch lip around the pan. Place any combination of fresh or sautéed fruit on the dough in a circular design.

Combine the sugar and the arrowroot and sprinkle on top of the tart. Dot the fruit with the small pieces of butter. Cover with foil and bake for 15 minutes, then turn down the oven to 350 degrees and bake for another 30 to 40 minutes, until golden brown. Cool for 10 minutes and glaze the tart with the melted jam, using a small pastry brush.

NUTRITIONAL FACTS | *Per 2-inch slice*
Using 1 egg yolk with no fruit
Calories 239, Total fat 11.4 g, Saturated fat 6.3 g, Carbohydrates 31.6 g, Protein 2.3 g

Apple Cobbler

You can decrease the fat in this recipe by using less oil and nuts.

Crust
- 3 cups whole wheat pastry flour, rice flour, or spelt flour
- ¾ cup turbinado sugar
- ½ teaspoon nutmeg
- ¾ cup low-fat vanilla soymilk or rice milk
- ¼ cup ghee or canola oil

Filling
- 3 large apples, peeled, cubed, and placed in water with lemon juice
- ¼ cup maple syrup
- ½ teaspoon cinnamon
- 1 tablespoon turbinado sugar
- ¼ teaspoon cardamom
- 2 tablespoons apple juice
- 2 teaspoons arrowroot powder

Topping
- 1 cup whole rolled oats
- ½ cup whole wheat pastry flour, rice flour, or spelt flour
- 1 teaspoon cinnamon
- ½ cup chopped walnuts
- 2 tablespoons ghee or melted butter
- 2 tablespoons turbinado sugar
- 2 tablespoons maple syrup

Preheat the oven to 350 degrees. Oil an 8-inch square or 9-by-13-inch baking pan. In a large bowl, whisk together the flour, sugar, and nutmeg. Combine the soymilk and oil; slowly pour into the flour mixture to create a soft dough. Knead the dough until well combined and press into the bottom of the prepared baking pan. Bake for 10 to 15 minutes or until golden brown. Remove from the oven and set aside. Leave the oven on.

Drain the apples and combine in a bowl with the maple syrup, cinnamon, sugar, cardamom, apple juice, and arrowroot powder. Place the apple mixture evenly on the baked crust.

Combine the oats, flour, cinnamon, walnuts, ghee, sugar, and maple syrup, mixing with a fork or using your hands. Sprinkle the mixture evenly over the apples and cover with foil. Bake for 30 to 45 minutes or until golden brown.

NUTRITIONAL FACTS | *Per 2-inch square*
Calories 386, Total fat 11.2 g, Saturated fat 1.5 g, Carbohydrates 64.7 g, Protein 6.8 g

Apple Custard Pie

SERVES 10

Sweet Pie Crust

1¼ cup whole wheat pastry flour
¼ cup turbinado sugar
¼ teaspoon cinnamon
1 pinch salt
½ cup cold butter, cut into ½-inch pieces

Apple Filling

5 whole apples, unpeeled, sliced thinly, and placed in water with lemon juice
1 teaspoon ghee
1 teaspoon cinnamon
1 teaspoon nutmeg
1 teaspoon cardamom
½ cup coconut flakes
½ cup currants or raisins
½ cup turbinado sugar

Custard

3 whole eggs
½ cup milk or cream
1 teaspoon cinnamon
¼ teaspoon cardamom

Preheat the oven to 350 degrees. Oil an 8- or 9-inch springform pan. In a food processor, place the flour, sugar, cinnamon, and salt. Pulse until well combined. With the processor running, begin to drop the pieces of butter into the flour mix. Continue to pulse until a soft dough forms. Press the dough into the prepared pan in a smooth pattern around the edge about 1 inch up the side of the pan. Bake for 20 to 30 minutes or until golden brown. Remove from the oven and cool. Leave the oven on.

Drain the apples. Heat the ghee in a sauté pan. Add the apples, cinnamon, nutmeg, and cardamom. Sauté for 3 to 5 minutes. Add the coconut, currants, and sugar. Sauté another 2 to 3 minutes. Arrange the apple slices along the bottom of the dough-lined pan, then layer in a circular pattern.

Whisk together the eggs, milk, cinnamon, and cardamom. Pour the custard evenly over the apples. Bake for 20 to 30 minutes or until golden brown. An inserted toothpick should come out clean. Cool. Serve warm or at room temperature.

NUTRITIONAL FACTS | *Per 2-inch serving*
Calories 336, Total fat 13.1 g, Saturated fat 7.8 g, Carbohydrates 49.9 g, Protein 4.5 g

Apricot Pecan Cookies

MAKES
24 SMALL
COOKIES

1 cup rolled oats
1 cup pecans, whole or pieces
¼ cup chopped dried apricots
1 cup whole wheat pastry flour, rice flour, or spelt flour
½ teaspoon cinnamon
½ teaspoon salt
¼ cup maple syrup
2 tablespoons canola oil
½ cup mango purée, applesauce, or mashed ripe bananas
1 cup organic apricot jam

Preheat the oven to 350 degrees. Oil a baking sheet and set aside. Using a food processor, grind the oats, pecans, and apricots together into a coarse mixture. Place in a bowl, add the flour, cinnamon, and salt and combine well. In a separate bowl, whisk together the maple syrup, oil, and fruit purée. Add the wet mixture to the dry mixture. Combine with a spatula or place plastic bags on your hands to mix. Using a small 1- or 2-ounce scoop or a tablespoon, scoop the dough onto the baking sheet. Make a small depression on each cookie with your thumb and spoon in a small amount of apricot jam. Bake for 15 to 20 minutes or until golden brown.

NUTRITIONAL
FACTS

Per cookie
Calories 125, Total fat 3.7 g, Saturated fat .4 g,
Carbohydrates 20.1 g, Protein 2.7 g

Banana-Cocoa-Tofu Frozen Mousse

SERVES 8

4 whole very ripe bananas, cut into 1-inch pieces and frozen

12 ounces low-fat silken tofu, firm or extra firm, cut into cubes

2 tablespoons organic chocolate syrup, sweetened with natural sugar

2 tablespoons maple syrup

1 teaspoon vanilla extract

1 pinch ground cloves

Toasted coconut flakes

Sliced almonds

Place the bananas in a food processor or blender and pulse until almost smooth. Add the tofu and chocolate syrup. Pulse until combined; add the maple syrup, vanilla, and cloves. Continue to process until the mousse is smooth, without any lumps. Remove from the machine and place in a freezer container. Let the mousse firm up for 1 hour. Take out of the freezer 15 minutes before you plan on serving. Scoop out into small bowls and garnish with toasted coconut flakes and sliced almonds. Store any unused mousse tightly covered in the freezer.

NUTRITIONAL FACTS

Per ½-cup serving
Calories 159, Total fat .9 g, Saturated fat .2 g, Carbohydrates 33.5 g, Protein 4.3 g

Blueberry Orange Cake

For a smaller cake, cut the recipe in half and use an 8-inch square cake pan.

SERVES 16

- 4 cups whole wheat pastry flour
- 1 cup turbinado sugar
- 3 teaspoons baking powder
- 1 teaspoon baking soda
- ½ teaspoon salt
- 2 teaspoons cinnamon
- ½ teaspoon cloves
- 1 teaspoon nutmeg
- ¼ cup canola oil
- 1 cup mango purée or other fruit purée such as applesauce or mashed banana
- 1 cup orange juice
- 2 tablespoons grated orange rind
- 1 cup low-fat vanilla soymilk or vanilla rice milk
- ½ cup maple syrup
- 2 cups fresh or frozen blueberries, defrosted if frozen

Preheat the oven to 350 degrees and oil a 12-cup bundt pan or other baking pan. In a bowl, whisk together the flour, sugar, baking powder, baking soda, salt, cinnamon, cloves, and nutmeg. In a separate bowl, whisk together the oil, fruit purée, orange juice and zest, soymilk, and maple syrup. Pour the dry ingredients into the wet ingredients and gently combine with a rubber spatula. Add the blueberries and combine briefly. Pour the batter into the prepared pan and bake for 30 to 40 minutes or until an inserted toothpick comes out clean. Cool and slice into thin pieces.

VARIATION

Try adding any of these combinations to the basic cake batter.

- ½ cup coconut, ½ cup unsweetened cocoa powder, ½ cup chopped almonds
- ½ cup cranberries, ½ cup chopped almonds, ½ cup pine nuts
- ½ cup unsweetened cocoa powder, ½ cup chocolate chips, ½ cup chopped walnuts
- 1 cup blueberries, 1 cup chopped almonds
- 1 cup grated carrots, ½ cup currants
- 1 cup grated zucchini, ½ cup chopped walnuts
- 1 cup raspberries
- 1 cup sautéed apples, ½ cup currants
- 2 tablespoons lemon zest, ¼ cup poppy seeds, ¼ cup chopped almonds

NUTRITIONAL FACTS	*Per 1-inch slice* Calories 252, Total fat 4 g, Saturated fat .2 g, Carbohydrates 50.4 g, Protein 3.6 g

Berry Tofu Sorbet

SERVES 8

1 10 ounce package frozen raspberries
1 10-ounce package frozen blackberries or strawberries
12 ounces low-fat silken tofu, firm or extra firm, cut into cubes
¼ cup maple syrup
1 teaspoon vanilla extract
1 pinch ground cloves
Toasted coconut flakes
Toasted sliced almonds

In a food processor, pulse berries until almost smooth. Add the tofu as you continue to purée the fruit. Add the maple syrup, vanilla, and cloves. Continue to purée until a smooth texture is achieved. Taste for sweetness, adding more maple syrup if necessary. Remove from the food processor and scoop out into small bowls and serve immediately. Garnish with toasted coconut flakes and toasted sliced almonds. Store unused sorbet tightly covered in the freezer.

NUTRITIONAL FACTS

Per ½-cup serving
Calories 83, Total fat .6 g, Saturated fat 0 g, Carbohydrates 15.8 g, Protein 3.6 g

Cardamom Butter Cookies

MAKES 12
COOKIES

½ cup cold butter, cubed
½ cup turbinado sugar
1¾ cups whole wheat pastry flour
½ teaspoon salt
½ teaspoon nutmeg
½ teaspoon cardamom
2 tablespoons lemon juice

Preheat the oven to 350 degrees. Oil a cookie sheet and set aside. In a mixer, combine the butter and sugar until creamy. In a separate bowl, combine the pastry flour, salt, nutmeg, and cardamom. Slowly add the flour mixture to the butter mixture ½ cup at a time. Continue mixing at a low speed and slowly add the lemon juice until a stiff dough forms. Using a 1-ounce scoop or a tablespoon, place the cookie dough on the cookie sheet. Leave 2 inches between cookies. Flatten lightly with the palm of your hand. Bake for 10 to 15 minutes or until light golden brown.

NUTRITIONAL
FACTS

Per cookie
Calories 171, Total fat 5.9 g, Saturated fat 3.8 g, Carbohydrates 20.2 g, Protein 2.3 g

Chocolate Tofu Mousse with Walnut Coconut Praline

SERVES 6

2 tablespoons butter or ghee (or canola oil for a vegan dessert)
2 tablespoons apple juice
1 cup semisweet chocolate chips
12 ounces low-fat silken tofu, firm or extra firm, cut into cubes
¼ cup maple syrup
2 teaspoons vanilla extract
½ recipe Walnut Coconut Praline (recipe follows)

In a small saucepan over low heat, heat the butter, apple juice, and chocolate chips. Stir frequently to avoid burning. When the chips are melted, remove from the heat and stir to a creamy consistency. Set aside.

In a blender or food processor, place the tofu, maple syrup, and vanilla. Combine for 1 minute at high speed. Scrape the sides down with a spatula, then continue to blend to a smooth consistency. Add the melted chips to the tofu mixture. Continue to blend together until smooth and well incorporated. Spoon the mousse into small dessert bowls or refrigerate in a container with a tight-fitting lid until ready to serve. Sprinkle with walnut coconut praline.

NUTRITIONAL FACTS | *Per ½-cup serving*
Calories 169, Total fat 8.7 g, Saturated fat 5.5 g, Carbohydrates 19.1 g, Protein 3.9 g

Walnut Coconut Praline

MAKES 1½
CUPS, 12
SERVINGS

1 tablespoon butter, ghee, or canola oil
2 tablespoons maple syrup
1 cup walnut pieces
¼ cup coconut flakes

In a sauté pan, heat the butter and maple syrup over medium-high heat. Add the walnuts and stir to coat well with the syrup mixture. Allow the walnuts to brown slightly, then stir in the coconut, continuing to brown the mixture in the syrup. When the walnuts and coconut are well-coated and golden brown, remove from the heat and spread the mixture onto a lightly oiled sheet pan to cool. When hard, crumble on top of chocolate tofu mousse or use as a dessert topping in other recipes. Store the remainder of the praline in a resealable plastic bag.

NUTRITIONAL
FACTS

Per 2 tablespoons
Using butter
Calories 94, Total fat 7.7 g, Saturated fat 1.6 g,
Carbohydrates 4.7 g, Protein 1.5 g

Coconut Cookies

MAKES 24
SMALL
COOKIES

½ cup butter, softened
¾ cup turbinado sugar
2 tablespoons lemon juice
2 eggs
1½ cup whole wheat pastry flour
2 teaspoons baking powder
½ teaspoon ground cloves
1 teaspoon nutmeg
1 cup plus 1 cup coconut flakes

Preheat the oven to 350 degrees. Oil a cookie sheet and set aside. In a mixer or food processor, cream together the butter and sugar. Add the lemon juice and the eggs, one at a time. In a separate bowl, combine the flour, baking powder, cloves, nutmeg, and 1 cup coconut flakes. With the mixer running, slowly add the flour mixture to the butter mixture. Combine together into a soft dough. Remove the dough from the mixer and knead slightly. Place the remaining cup of coconut flakes in a flat bowl. With a 1-ounce scoop, form the dough into balls. Roll each ball of dough in the coconut flakes and place on the prepared pan, 2 inches apart. Flatten the cookies slightly with the palm of your hand. Bake for 15 to 20 minutes or until golden brown.

NUTRITIONAL
FACTS

Per cookie
Calories 126, Total fat 6.3 g, Saturated fat 4.3 g, Carbohydrates 15.5 g, Protein 1.5 g

Cranberry Bliss Balls

These make a great quick energy snack.

MAKES
20 BALLS

1 cup pine nuts
1 cup sunflower seeds
1 cup whole almonds
2 cups dried cranberries, or use dried fruit of your choice
2 tablespoons maple syrup
1 teaspoon vanilla extract
1 teaspoon nutmeg
½ cup coconut flakes

Place the pine nuts, sunflower seeds, and almonds in a food processor and pulse until coarsely ground. Add the dried fruit and pulse 3 or 4 times, then add the maple syrup, vanilla, and nutmeg. Continue to pulse until the mixture begins to stick together. Taste for sweetness. Add more maple syrup if necessary. Place the coconut flakes in a flat bowl. Roll the nut and fruit mixture into 1-inch balls and roll them in the coconut flakes to coat. Store in an airtight container.

NUTRITIONAL
FACTS

Per ball
Calories 232, Total fat 14.4 g, Saturated fat 2.3 g,
Carbohydrates 21.5 g, Protein 4.1 g

Double Almond
Cookies

MAKES 18
SMALL
COOKIES

1 cup almonds
1 cup rolled oats
1 cup whole wheat pastry flour, rice flour, or spelt flour
½ teaspoon cinnamon
½ teaspoon salt
½ cup maple syrup
2 tablespoons canola oil
½ cup mango purée, applesauce, or mashed bananas
12 to 15 whole almonds

Preheat the oven to 350 degrees. Oil a cookie sheet. In a food processor, grind the almonds and oats together into a coarse mixture. Place in a bowl.

Add the flour, cinnamon, and salt and whisk together. In a separate bowl, whisk together the maple syrup, oil, and fruit purée. Add the dry mixture to the wet mixture. Combine with a spatula or place plastic bags on your hands to mix. Using a 1- or 2-ounce scoop or a tablespoon, scoop the dough onto the prepared pan. Make a small depression in each cookie with your thumb and place a whole almond into the center. Bake for 15 to 20 minutes or until golden brown.

NUTRITIONAL
FACTS

Per cookie
Calories 140, Total fat 7.4 g, Saturated fat .7 g,
Carbohydrates 15.3 g, Protein 3.3 g

Double Delight Cookies

MAKES 24
SMALL
COOKIES

1 cup plus 1 cup semisweet chocolate chips
½ cup butter (1 stick)
1 cup turbinado sugar
2 teaspoons vanilla extract
1 egg
2 cups whole wheat pastry flour
½ teaspoon salt
1 teaspoon baking soda
1 cup walnuts or macadamia nuts, chopped coarsely

Preheat the oven to 350 degrees. Lightly oil a cookie sheet and set aside. In a double boiler or small saucepan, melt 1 cup of chocolate chips until smooth, stirring often as the chips melt. Remove from the heat and cool slightly. With a mixer, cream the butter and sugar together until fluffy. Add the vanilla and egg. Combine briefly, then add the melted chocolate. In a separate bowl, combine the flour, salt, and baking soda. With the mixer on low, begin to add the flour mixture a little at a time. Once combined, add the nuts and the remaining cup of chocolate chips and briefly mix. Using a 1-ounce scoop or a tablespoon, place the cookie dough onto the sheet pan, 2 inches apart. Bake for 15 to 20 minutes or until golden brown.

NUTRITIONAL
FACTS

Per cookie
Calories 203, Total fat 10.3 g, Saturated fat 4.7 g,
Carbohydrates 24.6 g, Protein 2.7 g

Kabocha Squash or Pumpkin Pie

SERVES 8

Crust	1¼ cups whole wheat pastry flour
	1 pinch salt
	½ cup cold butter, cut into ½-inch pieces
	1 tablespoon apple cider vinegar or white vinegar
	4 to 6 tablespoons ice water
Filling	1 3-pound kabocha squash or pumpkin
	Apple juice
	1 cup low-fat vanilla soymilk, milk, or cream
	½ cup turbinado sugar
	2 tablespoons maple syrup
	2 eggs or ¼ cup applesauce or mango purée plus ¼ cup canola oil
	1 teaspoon cinnamon
	1 teaspoon ground ginger
	½ teaspoon ground cloves
	1 pinch salt

Place the flour and salt in a food processor and pulse to combine. With the machine running, begin to add the butter, one piece at a time. Continue to pulse until the mixture looks like coarse meal. Add the vinegar. With the machine still running, begin to slowly add the ice water, 1 tablespoon at a time, waiting a moment or two before each addition, until the dough begins to form into a ball in the bowl of the processor. Remove the dough and place on an oil-sprayed surface and roll out into a circle that is 1 inch larger around than the pie pan. Lightly oil the pie pan and place the dough in it, leaving a 1-inch edge around the perimeter of the pan. Create a nice border around the pie pan, trimming off any excess dough. Place the piecrust in the refrigerator while you make the pumpkin filling.

Preheat the oven to 350 degrees. Wash and cut the kabocha squash in half and remove the seeds. Place cutside down in a baking dish with about ½ inch of apple juice, cover with parchment paper and foil, and bake for 45 minutes or until an inserted knife comes out easily. Leave the oven on. When the squash is cool enough to handle, scoop out the pulp with a large spoon. Reserve the pulp in a bowl and discard the skin. In a blender or food processor, combine 3 cups of pulp, soymilk, sugar, maple syrup, eggs, cinnamon, ginger, cloves, and salt. Mix well. Remove the piecrust from the refrigerator; pour the batter up to the rim of the dough. Bake for approximately 45 minutes. If the pie begins to brown too much, place some foil over it. Bake until an inserted toothpick comes out clean. The pie should be golden brown.

NUTRITIONAL FACTS | *Per 2½-inch piece*
Using eggs and pumpkin
Calories 291, Total fat 13.4 g, Saturated fat 7.7 g,
Carbohydrates 37.5 g, Protein 4.9 g

Lemon Birthday Cake

SERVES
12 TO 16

2 cups whole wheat pastry flour
2 cups unbleached organic white flour
2 teaspoons baking powder
2 teaspoons baking soda
1 teaspoon cinnamon
1 teaspoon nutmeg
2 teaspoons salt
2 teaspoons lemon zest
⅓ cup canola oil
1½ cups maple syrup
1⅔ cups low-fat vanilla soymilk
½ cup lemon juice (juice of about 6 lemons)
⅔ cup apple juice
2 teaspoons vanilla extract
2 teaspoons lemon extract

Preheat the oven to 350 degrees. Spray two round 8-inch cake pans or one 9-by-13-inch pan with oil, then lightly dust with flour, shaking off any excess. In a large bowl, sift together the two flours, baking powder, baking soda, salt, cinnamon, nutmeg, and lemon zest. In a separate mixing bowl, whisk together the oil, maple syrup, soymilk, lemon juice, apple juice, and vanilla and lemon extracts. Pour the dry ingredients into the wet ingredients and mix together. Avoid overmixing. Pour the batter into the prepared baking pan(s) and bake for 20 to 30 minutes for two 8-inch round cakes or 30 to 40 minutes for one 9-by-13-inch cake. The cake should look lightly browned and spring back when touched. An inserted toothpick should come out clean. Cool on a rack for 5 minutes before removing from the pan.

Serve the cake with fresh berries or sprinkle on walnut coconut praline (page 267) or simple frozen fruit syrup using raspberries (page 50).

NUTRITIONAL FACTS	*Per 1 2-by-2-inch slice* *Cake only* Calories 288, Total fat 6.1 g, Saturated fat .5 g, Carbohydrates 54.2 g, Protein 4.1 g

Ginger Cookies

MAKES 22
COOKIES

¼ cup ghee or canola oil
1 cup applesauce
½ cup molasses
¾ cup plus ¼ cup turbinado sugar
3 cups whole wheat pastry flour
2 teaspoons ground ginger
2 teaspoons allspice
1 teaspoon cinnamon
2 teaspoons baking soda
1 teaspoon salt

Preheat the oven to 350 degrees. Lightly oil a cookie sheet and set aside. In a large bowl, whisk together the oil, applesauce, molasses, and ¾ cup sugar. In a separate bowl, whisk together the flour, ginger, allspice, cinnamon, baking soda, and salt. Add the dry mixture to the wet mixture. The dough will get thick, so use your hands wrapped in plastic bags to mix if necessary. Using a 1-ounce scoop or a tablespoon, place the dough 2 inches apart on the oiled cookie sheet. Sprinkle the remaining ¼ cup of sugar evenly over the cookie dough. Bake for 10 to 12 minutes.

NUTRITIONAL
FACTS

Per cookie
Calories 149, Total fat 2.9 g, Saturated fat 1.9 g,
Carbohydrates 28.8 g, Protein 1.8 g

Lemon Poppy Seed Cake

SERVES 12

2¼ cups whole wheat pastry flour
1½ teaspoons baking powder
1 teaspoon baking soda
½ teaspoon salt
¼ cup poppy seeds
1 tablespoon lemon zest
¼ cup low-fat silken tofu, firm or extra firm, crumbled
¼ cup canola oil
1 cup turbinado sugar
¼ cup applesauce or mango purée
¼ cup lemon juice
1 teaspoon vanilla extract
1 teaspoon lemon extract
1 cup low-fat vanilla or lemon yogurt

Preheat the oven to 350 degrees. Spray a 12-inch bundt pan or a 9-by-13-inch baking pan with oil and lightly flour, shaking off any excess. In a large bowl, whisk together the flour, baking powder, baking soda, salt, poppy seeds, and lemon zest. In a food processor or blender, combine the tofu, oil, sugar, applesauce, lemon juice, and vanilla and lemon extracts. Pulse until just combined. Pour the wet mixture into the dry mixture. Using a rubber spatula, gently fold in the yogurt and combine until just blended. Be careful not to overmix. Bake for 30 to 45 minutes, depending on the size of the pan used, or until golden brown and an inserted toothpick comes out clean. Cool before serving.

NUTRITIONAL FACTS

Per 2-inch slice
Calories 199, Total fat 5.1 g, Saturated fat .5 g, Carbohydrates 34.5 g, Protein 3.6 g

Mother Earth's Apple Pie

SERVES 8

Double Crust

3   cups whole wheat pastry flour
1   pinch salt
½   cup cold butter, cut into ½-inch pieces
1   tablespoon apple cider vinegar
4   to 6 tablespoons ice water

Filling

1   teaspoon ghee
5   large green apples, unpeeled, thinly sliced and placed in water with lemon juice
1   tablespoon apple juice
1   teaspoon cinnamon
½   teaspoon nutmeg
½   cup turbinado sugar
2   teaspoons arrowroot powder
2   tablespoons maple syrup
1   tablespoon cold butter, cut into ½-inch pieces
1   tablespoon milk or soymilk
1   tablespoon sugar
1   teaspoon cinnamon

Place the flour and salt in a food processor and pulse to combine. With the machine running, begin to add the butter, one piece at a time. Continue to pulse until the mixture looks like coarse meal. Add the vinegar. With the machine still running, begin to slowly add the water, 1 tablespoon at a time, waiting a moment or two before each addition, until the dough begins to form a ball in the bowl of the processor. Remove the dough and divide in half. Wrap one half in plastic wrap and place in the refrigerator. On an oil-sprayed surface, roll out the other half to the size of the pie pan, plus 1 inch around. Lightly oil the pie pan and place the dough in it, leaving a 1-inch edge around the perimeter of the pan. Place the piecrust in the refrigerator while you prepare the apple filling.

Preheat the oven to 425 degrees.

In a large sauté pan over medium heat, place the ghee, apples, apple juice, cinnamon, nutmeg, and sugar. Sauté for 3 to 5 minutes or until the apples are well coated with the spices. Add the arrowroot and the maple syrup and sauté another 2 minutes. Remove from the heat and set aside.

Take the piecrust and the extra dough from the refrigerator. Roll out the unrolled dough into a round piece larger than the piecrust. Arrange the apples in the piecrust evenly, mounding them above the level of the piecrust. Dot the apples with the little pieces of butter. Place the other piece of dough on top of the apples. Using your fingers, press the dough into the apples. Trim the dough to match the bottom layer then press together. To create a finished look, pinch the dough along the edge by placing the dough between your pointer finger on one hand and your thumb and pointer finger on the other hand. Vent the pie by making small diagonal slashes in the crust in an attractive design. Bake for 10 minutes, then lower the oven to 350 degrees and bake for 40 minutes. Brush the pie with milk or soymilk just as it comes out of the oven. Mix the sugar and cinnamon and sprinkle on top of the milk. Let the pie sit for 20 to 30 minutes before serving.

NUTRITIONAL FACTS	*Per 3-inch slice* Calories 343, Total fat 13.8 g, Saturated fat 8.6 g, Carbohydrates 34.3 g, Protein 2.7 g

Linzertorte Cookies

MAKES 24
SMALL
COOKIES

1 cup rolled oats
1 cup almonds, whole or pieces
1 cup whole wheat pastry flour, rice flour, or spelt flour
½ teaspoon cinnamon
½ teaspoon salt
½ cup maple syrup
2 tablespoons canola oil
½ cup mango purée, applesauce, or mashed banana
1 cup organic raspberry jam

Preheat the oven to 350 degrees. Oil a cookie sheet and set aside. Using a food processor, grind the oats and the almonds together into a coarse mixture. Place in a bowl and add the flour, cinnamon, and salt. In a separate bowl, whisk together the maple syrup, oil, and the fruit purée. Add the dry ingredients to the wet ingredients. Combine with a spatula or place plastic bags on your hands to mix. Using a 1-ounce scoop or a tablespoon, scoop out onto the prepared pan. Make a small depression with your thumb in each cookie and spoon in a small amount of raspberry jam. Bake for 15 to 20 minutes or until golden brown.

NUTRITIONAL
FACTS

Per cookie
Calories 125, Total fat 3.7 g, Saturated fat .4 g,
Carbohydrates 20.1 g, Protein 2.7 g

Oatmeal Power Cookies

When you need a high-energy snack, try one of these.

MAKES 24
COOKIES

1 cup whole wheat pastry flour or spelt flour
1 cup rolled oats
1 cup chopped dried fruit or fresh apples
1 cup raisins or currants
1 cup coconut flakes
½ teaspoon baking soda
1 teaspoon cinnamon
1 teaspoon allspice
½ cup mango purée
¾ cup turbinado sugar
½ cup maple syrup
1 teaspoon vanilla extract

Preheat the oven to 350 degrees. Oil a cookie sheet and set aside. In a mixing bowl, place the flour, oats, fruit, raisins, coconut, baking soda, cinnamon, and allspice. Combine with a wire whisk. In a separate bowl, whisk together the mango purée, sugar, maple syrup, and vanilla. Pour the dry ingredients into the wet ingredients. Using plastic bags on your hands or a spatula, combine until well mixed. Using a 1-ounce scoop, place the cookies on the oiled baking sheet and bake for 15 minutes or until golden brown.

NUTRITIONAL
FACTS

Per cookie
Calories 145, Total fat 1.5 g, Saturated fat 1 g,
Carbohydrates 30.9 g, Protein 2 g

Peanut Butter Cookies

MAKES 18
COOKIES

¼ cup ghee or canola oil
¾ cup turbinado sugar
¼ cup applesauce
¼ cup maple syrup
½ cup peanut butter or almond butter
½ cup low-fat vanilla soymilk or rice milk
1 teaspoon vanilla extract
1¾ cup whole wheat pastry flour
1 teaspoon baking soda
½ teaspoon baking powder
½ teaspoon salt

Preheat the oven to 350 degrees. Oil a cookie sheet and set aside. Using a mixer or food processor, cream together the oil and sugar. Add the applesauce, maple syrup, peanut butter, soymilk, and vanilla. Process to a smooth consistency. In a separate bowl, whisk together the flour, baking soda, baking powder, and salt. Add the dry mixture to the wet mixture. Mix by hand until smooth. Using a 1-ounce scoop or a tablespoon, scoop the mixture out onto the oiled cookie sheet. Flatten each cookie slightly with a fork, then press the fork in the opposite direction, to create a cross-hatched design. Bake for 12 to 15 minutes or until golden brown. Cool on a rack before eating.

NUTRITIONAL
FACTS

Per cookie
Calories 136, Total fat 7.2 g, Saturated fat 2.8 g,
Carbohydrates 14.3 g, Protein 3.5 g

Traditional Awesome Brownies

MAKES 16
SERVINGS

½ cup cold butter, cut into ½-inch cubes
1 cup turbinado sugar
½ cup applesauce
1 teaspoon vanilla extract
½ cup low-fat milk, or vanilla soymilk
2 eggs
1½ cups whole wheat pastry flour
½ teaspoon salt
¾ cup unsweetened cocoa powder
1 teaspoon baking powder
½ cup walnuts, macadamia nuts, or almonds, chopped and toasted
½ cup chocolate chips

Preheat the oven to 350 degrees. Spray an 8-inch square baking pan with oil and set aside. With an electric mixer, cream together the butter, sugar, and applesauce. Add the vanilla and milk, then add the eggs, one at a time, mixing between each addition. Mix only briefly after adding the last egg. In a separate mixing bowl, whisk together the flour, salt, cocoa, and baking powder. Turn the mixer on low and slowly add the flour mixture, 1 cup at a time. Scrape down the sides of the mixing bowl with a spatula to incorporate all the ingredients. Be careful not to overmix. Add the nuts and chocolate chips and mix again, very briefly. Pour into the prepared pan and bake for 30 minutes or until an inserted toothpick comes out clean. Cool the brownies before eating. Warning: These brownies are really good, so control yourself and eat only a little at a time.

NUTRITIONAL
FACTS

Per 1 2-inch square
Calories 265, Total fat 12.4 g, Saturated fat 5.8 g,
Carbohydrates 32.8 g, Protein 5.3 g

Traditional Chocolate Chip Cookies

MAKES 28
COOKIES

1 cup turbinado sugar
1 cup butter, softened
1 teaspoon vanilla extract
2 eggs
2¼ cups whole wheat pastry flour
1½ teaspoons baking powder
½ teaspoon salt
2 cups chocolate chips
½ cup chopped almonds or walnuts, optional

Preheat the oven to 350 degrees. Lightly oil a cookie sheet and set aside. In a mixer or food processor, cream the sugar and butter together. Add the vanilla and the eggs, one at a time. In a separate bowl, whisk together the flour, baking powder, and salt. Gently fold the dry ingredients into the butter mixture. Fold in the chocolate chips. If desired, add almonds. Drop the cookie dough onto the baking sheet using a tablespoon or a 1-ounce scoop. Bake for 8 to 10 minutes or until golden brown.

NUTRITIONAL
FACTS

Per cookie
Does not include nuts
Calories 180, Total fat 9.3 g, Saturated fat 5.7 g,
Carbohydrates 22.1 g, Protein 1.8 g

Unbelievable Double Chocolate Cake

SERVES 12

1 cup whole wheat pastry flour
¾ cup unsweetened cocoa powder
2 teaspoons baking powder
1 teaspoon baking soda
12 ounces low-fat silken tofu, firm or extra firm
¼ cup ghee or canola oil
¾ cup applesauce
1 cup maple syrup
2 teaspoons vanilla extract
1 cup nondairy chocolate chips

Preheat the oven to 350 degrees. Oil a 9-by-13-inch baking pan and set aside. Using a whisk, combine the flour, cocoa, baking powder, and baking soda in a large mixing bowl. Place the tofu, oil, applesauce, maple syrup, and vanilla in a food processor or blender, and purée until smooth. Pour the wet ingredients into the dry ingredients, combine, then gently fold in the chocolate chips. Be careful not to overmix. Pour the batter into the prepared baking pan and bake for 30 to 40 minutes or until an inserted toothpick comes out clean.

NUTRITIONAL FACTS

Per 2-inch square
Calories 286, Total fat 10.6 g, Saturated fat 3.7 g, Carbohydrates 42.1 g, Protein 5.5 g

Walnut Chocolate Chip Cookies

MAKES 24
SMALL
COOKIES

1 cup organic rolled oats
1 cup walnuts
1 cup whole wheat pastry flour, rice flour, or spelt flour
½ teaspoon cinnamon
½ teaspoon salt
½ cup maple syrup
2 tablespoons canola oil
½ cup mango purée, applesauce, or mashed bananas
1 cup nondairy chocolate chips

Preheat the oven to 350 degrees. Oil a cookie sheet and set aside. Using a food processor, grind the oats and the walnuts together into a coarse mixture. Place in a bowl.

Add the flour, cinnamon, and salt and mix well. In a separate bowl, whisk together the maple syrup, oil, and the fruit purée. Add the dry mixture to the wet mixture and add the chocolate chips. Combine with a spatula or place plastic bags on your hands to mix. Using a 1-ounce scoop or a tablespoon, scoop out the dough onto the prepared cookie sheet. Bake for 15 to 20 minutes or until golden brown.

NUTRITIONAL
FACTS

Per cookie
Calories 148, Total fat 6.9 g, Saturated fat 1.9 g,
Carbohydrates 17.3 g, Protein 3.6 g

The Chopra Center
30-Day Nutritional Plan

Nutritional Information

The following nutritional information is based upon a projected daily intake of about 2,200 calories. If you are a moderately active person, this diet would stabilize your weight at about 138 pounds.

You can calculate your ideal daily caloric intake by multiplying your desired weight in pounds by 16. For example, if your desired weight is 120 pounds, your daily caloric intake should be 1,920.

If your desired weight is 160 pounds, your daily intake should be 2,560 calories ($160 \times 16 = 2,560$).

Adjust your serving size to reflect your caloric needs. If you want to sustain your weight of 124 pounds with an intake of 1,980 calories daily, you will need to reduce your serving size by 10 percent. If you want to sustain your weight of 151 pounds with a daily intake of 2,420 calories, you should increase your serving size by 10 percent.

Remember that listening to your body's cues of hunger and satiety is more important than counting calories. Honoring the wisdom of your body is the most direct path to health and renewal of body and soul.

	Calories	Total Fat (g)	Sat. Fat (g)	Carbs (g)	Protein (g)
Per serving: target	**2250**	**50–60**	**<20**	**325–375**	**90–100**
Percent of Calories Daily Totals		20–24%	5–9%	59–68%	16–18%

Day 1
Breakfast

	Calories	Total Fat (g)	Sat. Fat (g)	Carbs (g)	Protein (g)
Morning Bliss Shake	424	6.8	2.8	61.3	29.8
Breakfast Bar	339	11.4	3	50.9	8.2
Totals	763	18.2	5.8	112.2	38

Main Meal

	Calories	Total Fat (g)	Sat. Fat (g)	Carbs (g)	Protein (g)
Tomato Florentine Soup	223	4.1	0.4	24.8	22
Rainbow Risotto	328	2.8	0.4	55.8	19.7
Nutty Spinach Greens	80	4.6	1.1	6.1	3.4
Almond Tart	319	11.9	6.3	55.5	3.5
Totals	950	23.4	8.2	142.2	48.6

Light Meal

	Calories	Total Fat (g)	Sat. Fat (g)	Carbs (g)	Protein (g)
Vegetable Hummus Wrap	320	7.6	1.5	51.3	11.5
Ginger Cookie	149	2.9	1.9	28.8	1.8
Totals	469	10.5	3.4	80.1	13.3
Daily Totals	2182	52.1	17.4	334.5	99.9
Percent of Calories Daily Totals		21%	7%	61%	18%

Day 2
Breakfast

	Calories	Total Fat (g)	Sat. Fat (g)	Carbs (g)	Protein (g)
Vegetable Tofu Scramble	160	6.7	0.8	9.5	15.2
Cilantro Mint Sauce	20	0.2	0	3.2	1.2
Apple Raisin Muffin	234	5	0.5	42	4.9
Totals	414	11.9	1.3	54.7	21.3

Main Meal

	Calories	Total Fat (g)	Sat. Fat (g)	Carbs (g)	Protein (g)
Tofu Fajitas	282	8	0.2	34.1	18.4
Mandarin Tomato Salsa	66	0.4	0	13.6	1.8
Spanish Pilaf	360	3.4	0.1	62.5	9.1
sautéed carrots and cauliflower	68	1.5	0.9	10.7	2.7
Apple Custard Pie	336	13.1	7.8	49.9	4.5
Totals	1112	26.4	9	170.8	36.5

Light Meal

	Calories	Total Fat (g)	Sat. Fat (g)	Carbs (g)	Protein (g)
Italian White Bean Stew	349	5.2	1	59	16.8
Oatmeal Power Cookie	145	1.5	1	30.9	2
Totals	494	6.7	2	89.9	18.8
Daily Totals	2020	45	12.3	315.4	76.6
Percent of Calories Daily Totals		20%	5%	62%	15%

	Calories	Total Fat (g)	Sat. Fat (g)	Carbs (g)	Protein (g)
Day 3					
Breakfast					
Rolled Oats Hot Cereal	208	3.3	1	37.3	7.5
Blueberry Banana Syrup	123	1.9	1.1	25.9	0.8
Zucchini Pecan Bread	269	10.1	1.1	39	5.5
Totals	600	15.3	3.2	102.2	13.8
Main Meal					
Spinach Soup	112	2.9	1.1	15.2	6.3
Vegetable Paella	348	10.4	1.6	51.7	11.8
Eggplant Tapenade	70	4.8	0.2	5.6	1
Dilled Asparagus	49	0.4	0.1	6.1	5.2
sautéed strawberries	167	3.3	1.9	33.2	1.3
Totals	746	21.8	4.9	111.8	25.6
Light Meal					
Vegetable White Bean Chili	364	4.2	0.5	53.2	28
Simple Great Whole Grain Bread	156	1.4	0.3	30.4	5.8
Peanut Butter Cookie	136	7.2	2.8	14.3	3.5
Totals	656	12.8	3.6	97.9	37.3
Daily Totals	2002	49.9	11.7	311.9	76.7
Percent of Calories Daily Totals		22%	5%	62%	15%
Day 4					
Breakfast					
Coffee Bliss Shake	194	1	0.6	44.2	2.1
Nutty French Toast	360	15.3	4	43	12.5
sautéed apples	99	1.4	0.8	21.1	0.3
Totals	653	17.7	5.4	108.3	14.9
Main Meal					
Summertime Tomato Basil Soup	257	4.2	0.5	37.5	17.1
Spinach Polenta	172	1.9	0.2	28	10.8
Ratatouille Stew	215	6.8	3.4	27.1	11.5
sautéed swiss chard	32	1.3	0.2	3.7	1.4
Walnut Chocolate Chip Cookie	148	6.9	1.9	17.3	3.6
Totals	824	21.1	6.2	113.6	44.4
Light Meal					
Eggless Tofu Salad or Sandwich	301	7.7	0.6	37.9	20.1
Lemon Poppy Seed Cake	199	5.1	0.5	34.5	3.6
Totals	500	12.8	1.1	72.4	23.7
Daily Totals	1977	51.6	12.7	294.3	83
Percent of Calories Daily Totals		23%	6%	60%	17%

	Calories	Total Fat (g)	Sat. Fat (g)	Carbs (g)	Protein (g)
Day 5					
Breakfast					
Chai Bliss Shake	289	1.2	0.7	43.6	26
Chopra Granola	353	15.6	4.4	43.8	9.8
fresh blueberries and sliced bananas	80	0.4	0.1	18.4	0.8
Totals	722	17.2	5.2	105.8	36.6
Main Meal					
Vegetable Hot and Sour Soup	148	4.8	0.2	16.1	10.1
Buddha's Delight Vegetable Stir-Fry	172	7.5	1	20	6.3
steamed rice	171	0.3	0.1	38.7	3.2
Kim Chi Chutney	111	1.9	0.2	20.9	3.2
Unbelievable Double Chocolate Cake	307	11	6.9	46.3	5.8
Totals	909	25.5	8.4	142	28.6
Light Meal					
Roasted Tofu and Yams	305	8.2	0.5	41.7	16.1
Garden Salad with Cilantro Pecan Sauce	126	7.3	0.6	8.1	7.1
sautéed apricots	178	3.2	1.9	35.4	2
Totals	609	18.7	3	85.2	25.2
Daily Total	2240	61.4	16.6	333	90.4
Percent of Calories Daily Totals		25%	7%	59%	16%
Day 6					
Breakfast					
Broccoli Tofu Scramble	181	6.9	0.2	13.9	15.6
Mandarin Tomato Salsa	66	0.4	0	13.6	1.8
Simple Great Whole Grain Bread with Almond Butter	231	5.1	1	31.6	7
Totals	478	12.4	1.2	59.1	24.4
Main Meal					
Potato Leek Soup	279	3.4	0.3	37.3	24.4
French Vegetable Stew	145	2.1	0.2	24.1	7.7
toasted millet	187	2.1	0.4	36.4	5.5
steamed carrots and green beans	80	0.4	0.1	18.4	0.8
Linzertorte Cookie	125	3.7	0.4	20.1	2.7
Totals	816	11.7	1.4	136.3	41.1
Light Meal					
split pea dahl	262	2.6	1.4	43.9	16
Indian Rice	343	2.8	1	72.4	7
Apple Leek Chutney	170	1.3	0.5	38.3	0.9
Cardamom Butter Cookie	171	5.9	3.8	20.2	2.3
Totals	946	12.6	6.7	174.8	26.2
Daily Totals	2240	36.7	9.3	370.2	91.7
Percent of Calories Daily Totals		15%	4%	66%	16%

	Calories	Total Fat (g)	Sat. Fat (g)	Carbs (g)	Protein (g)
Day 7					
Breakfast					
Almond Bliss Shake	487	12.4	3.3	61.1	32.9
Apple and Rice Hot Cereal	382	6.8	2	71.9	8.2
Totals	869	19.2	5.3	133	41.1
Main Meal					
Italian Vegetable Soup	268	2.1	0.4	46.3	15.9
Curry Filo Tarts	227	5.2	2.3	37.8	7.7
Walnut Yogurt Sauce	68	3.2	0.8	5.4	4.2
roasted sweet potatoes	164	1.7	1	34.2	3.1
Berry Tofu Sorbet	83	0.6	0	15.8	3.6
Totals	810	12.8	4.5	139.5	34.5
Light Meal					
Marinated Tofu Thai Wrap with Nutty Dipping Sauce	395	15.8	2.3	43.4	19.4
Cranberry Bliss Balls	232	14.4	2.3	21.5	4.1
Totals	627	30.2	4.6	64.9	23.5
Daily Totals	2306	62.2	14.4	337.4	99.1
Percent of Calories Daily Totals		24%	6%	59%	17%
Day 8					
Breakfast					
Mango Yogurt	178	1.5	0.8	36.4	5
Tempeh and Potato Hash	305	6.8	1.1	38.7	22.6
Orange Pear Chutney	73.5	0.6	0.2	16.7	0.4
Totals	556.5	8.9	2.1	91.8	28
Main Meal					
Butternut Squash Soup	123	2.9	1.1	20	4.3
Eggplant and Yam Curry	424	7.5	1.1	73.1	15.9
Curried Potatoes	399	11.2	6.1	64.4	10.3
Cucumber Raita	59	1.1	0.6	8	3.9
sautéed apples and blackberries	99	1.4	0.8	21.1	0.3
Totals	1104	24.1	9.7	186.6	34.7
Light Meal					
Asian Clear Broth	158	6.5	0.4	11.6	13.3
Thai Tofu Vegetable Stew	444	15.6	6.1	48.6	27.5
Coconut Cookie	126	6.3	4.3	15.5	1.5
Totals	728	28.4	10.8	75.7	42.3
Daily Totals	2388.5	61.4	22.6	354.1	105
Percent of Calories Daily Totals		23%	9%	59%	18%

	Calories	Total Fat (g)	Sat. Fat (g)	Carbs (g)	Protein (g)
Day 9					
Breakfast					
Chopra Granola	353	15.6	4.4	43.8	9.8
Very Berry Yogurt	173	3	1.8	30.4	6.3
Totals	526	18.6	6.2	74.2	16.1
Main Meal					
Italian Vegetable Soup	268	2.1	0.4	46.3	15.9
fresh spinach pasta	104	0.4	0.1	21.2	3.8
Tofu "Meat Balls" with Roasted Tomato Sauce	408	15.9	2.2	44.9	21.1
sautéed arugula and roasted eggplant	63	3	1.8	6.2	2.9
Lemon Birthday Cake	288	6.1	0.5	54.2	4.1
Totals	1131	27.5	5	172.8	47.8
Light Meal					
Potato Leek Soup	279	3.4	0.3	37.3	24.4
poached peaches and blueberries	147	2.9	1.9	29.3	0.9
Totals	426	6.3	2.2	66.6	25.3
Daily Totals	2083	52.4	13.4	313.6	89.2
Percent of Calories Daily Totals		23%	6%	60%	17%
Day 10					
Breakfast					
Mango Bliss Shake	281	4.1	2.6	47.5	13.4
Vegetable Tofu Scramble	160	6.7	0.8	9.5	15.2
Russian Borscht Chutney	33	0.5	0.2	6.8	0.5
Cinnamon Roll	149	3.9	1.5	24.8	3.6
Totals	623	15.2	5.1	88.6	32.7
Main Meal					
Vegetable Barley Soup	280	4	0.4	38.8	22.5
Tofu Burger with Leek Sauce	304	12.1	1.6	28.2	20.3
Steamed Broccoli	32	0.3	0	4.6	2.6
Berry Tofu Sorbet	83	0.6	0	15.8	3.6
Totals	699	17	2	87.4	49
Light Meal					
Roasted Tofu and Yams	305	8.2	0.5	41.7	16.1
steamed asparagus	39	0.3	0.1	6.1	3.1
Blueberry Lemon Cake	252	4	0.2	50.4	3.6
Totals	596	12.5	0.8	98.2	22.8
Daily Totals	1918	44.7	7.9	274.2	104.5
Percent of Calories Daily Totals		21%	4%	57%	22%

	Calories	Total Fat (g)	Sat. Fat (g)	Carbs (g)	Protein (g)
Day 11					
Breakfast					
Tofu and Potato Italiano	272	7	0.3	33.8	18.3
Homemade Chili Sauce	87.5	1.4	0.5	16.6	2
Zucchini Pecan Bread	269	10.1	1.1	39	5.5
Totals	628.5	18.5	1.9	89.4	25.8
Main Meal					
red lentil dahl	262	2.6	1.4	43.9	16
Eggplant Cauliflower Curry	237	4.1	2.2	44	6.2
steamed green beans	52	0.3	0.1	9.9	2.4
Orange Pear Chutney	74	0.6	0.2	16.7	0.4
sautéed pears with cardamom	175	3.5	1.9	34.9	1.1
Totals	800	11.1	5.8	149.4	26.1
Light Meal					
Black Bean and Vegetable Stew	442	4.4	1.1	70.2	30.5
Oat Groat Pilaf with Spinach	218	3.1	1	40.6	7
Apricot Pecan Cookie	125	3.7	0.4	20.1	2.7
Totals	785	11.2	2.5	130.9	40.2
Daily Totals	2213.5	40.8	10.2	369.7	92.1
Percent of Calories Daily Totals		17%	4%	67%	17%
Day 12					
Breakfast					
Chai Bliss Shake	289	1.2	0.7	43.6	26
Breakfast Burrito	213	8.6	4.3	25.8	8.2
whole apple	56	0.3	0	13	0.2
Totals	558	10.1	5	82.4	34.4
Main Meal					
Tortilla Soup with Avocado and Cilantro	347	14.7	1.8	32.6	21.1
Braised Tofu with Mango Tomato Salsa	309	8.2	0.4	40.7	18.4
sautéed corn, peppers, and broccoli	108	2.3	1	17.6	4.3
sautéed greens	28	1.4	0.9	2.2	1.5
Banana-Cocoa-Tofu Mousse	159	0.9	0.2	33.5	4.3
Totals	951	27.5	4.3	126.6	49.6
Light Meal					
Black Bean and Rice Wrap	444	6.6	2.3	82.7	13.5
simple carrot soup	72	1.5	0.3	11.6	2.9
Traditional Awesome Brownie	265	12.4	5.8	32.8	5.3
Totals	781	20.5	8.4	127.1	21.7
Daily Totals	2290	58.1	17.7	336.1	105.7
Percent of Calories Daily Totals		23%	7%	59%	18%

	Calories	Total Fat (g)	Sat. Fat (g)	Carbs (g)	Protein (g)
Day 13					
Breakfast					
Traditional French Toast	277	8	3	39.2	11.9
sautéed apples and blackberries	198	3.2	1.9	41.2	1
Totals	475	11.2	4.9	80.4	12.9
Main Meal					
Vegetable Barley Soup	280	4	0.4	38.8	22.5
Moroccan Vegetables	187	6.6	0.9	24.4	7.4
Dilled Lemon Zucchini	42	1.3	0.2	5.3	2.3
Hummus	125	3.6	0.5	17.2	5.9
Banana-Cocoa-Tofu Mousse	159	0.9	0.2	33.5	4.3
Totals	793	16.4	2.2	119.2	42.4
Light Meal					
Roasted Winter Vegetable Stew	368	7.1	2.1	61.3	14.5
Organic Mixed Field Greens					
Salad with olive oil	88	6.2	0.7	5.5	2.4
Kabocha Pumpkin Pie	291	13.4	7.7	37.5	4.9
Totals	747	26.7	10.5	104.3	21.8
Daily Totals	2015	54.3	17.6	303.9	77.1
Percent of Calories Daily Totals		24%	8%	60%	15%
Day 14					
Breakfast					
Masala Potatoes	372	6.2	2.5	67.7	11.2
Apple Leek Chutney	170	1.3	0.5	38.3	0.9
Mango Yogurt	178	1.5	0.8	36.4	5
Totals	720	9	3.8	142.4	17.1
Main Meal					
Tomato Florentine Soup	223	4.1	0.4	24.8	22
Mediterranean Pasta	269	4	0.9	47.8	10.3
Savory Swiss Chard	42	1.5	0.9	5.1	1.9
steamed asparagus	39	0.3	0.1	6.1	3.1
Ginger Cookie	149	2.9	1.9	28.8	1.8
Totals	722	12.8	4.2	112.6	39.1
Light Meal					
Tofu, Eggplant, and					
Yukon Gold Stew	318	8.6	0.7	40.1	19.8
Greek Goddess Salad	262	6.1	0.9	42.8	9.5
Blueberry Orange Cake	252	4	0.2	50.4	3.6
Totals	832	18.7	1.8	133.3	32.9
Daily Totals	2274	40.5	9.8	388.3	89.1
Percent of Calories Daily Totals		16%	4%	68%	16%

	Calories	Total Fat (g)	Sat Fat (g)	Carbs (g)	Protein (g)
Day 15					
Breakfast					
Broccoli Tofu Scramble	181	6.9	0.2	13.9	15.6
Russian Borscht Chutney	33	0.5	0.2	7	0.5
Blueberry Muffin	138	1.7	0.4	27.6	2.9
Totals	352	9.1	0.8	48.5	19
Main Meal					
Rosemary White Bean Soup	307	4	1.6	53	14.7
Vegetarian Paella	348	10.4	1.6	51.7	11.8
sautéed green beans					
and almonds	121	6	1.3	12.6	4.5
Raspberry Lemon Cake	246	4.2	0.5	47.4	4.7
Totals	1022	24.6	5	164.7	35.7
Light Meal					
Curried Chickpea Stew	498	12.6	5.1	64.9	31.4
steamed rice	145	0.4	0.1	32.5	3
Ginger Cookie	149	2.9	1.9	28.8	1.8
Totals	792	15.9	7.1	126.2	36.2
Daily Totals	2166	49.6	12.9	339.4	90.9
Percent of Calories Daily Totals		21%	5%	63%	17%
Day 16					
Breakfast					
Whole Wheat Crepes	248	11.1	2.2	26.8	10.2
Blueberry Banana Syrup	123	1.9	1.1	25.9	0.8
Country Potatoes	180	3.8	0.5	32.5	4
Totals	551	16.8	3.8	85.2	15
Main Meal					
Sweet Potato Ginger Soup	247	2.9	0.3	50.5	5
broccoli almond stir-fry and					
Basic Asian-Style Sauce	112	3	0.3	17.3	4.1
Szechwan Baked Egg Rolls	186	5.5	1.1	25.1	9.1
Spicy Lime and Red Pepper					
Dipping Sauce	54	0	0	12.8	0.7
Chinese Five-Spice Garden Pilaf	225	1	0.1	49.1	5.1
sautéed peaches with nutmeg	197	2.9	1.9	41.4	1.6
Totals	1021	15.3	3.7	196.2	25.6
Light Meal					
Mexican Tofu Stew	256	8.1	0.2	21	24.2
Garden Salad with no olive oil	46	1.9	0.2	4.9	2.3
Cilantro Pecan Sauce	80	5.4	0.4	3.2	4.8
Peanut Butter Cookie	136	7.2	2.8	14.3	3.5
Totals	518	22.6	3.6	43.4	34.8
Daily Totals	2090	53.7	16	300.5	95.3
Percent of Calories Daily Totals		23%	7%	58%	18%

	Calories	Total Fat (g)	Sat. Fat (g)	Carbs (g)	Protein (g)
Day 17					
Breakfast					
Coffee Bliss Shake	194	1	0.6	44.2	2.1
Hot Quinoa Breakfast Cereal	293	4.4	1	54.1	9.4
Pumpkin Muffin	200	3.7	0.6	37.7	3.7
Totals	687	9.1	2.2	136	15.2
Main Meal					
Nutty Broccoli Soup	187	8.9	1.5	18.6	8.1
Simple Whole Grain Pizza with Basil and Friends Pesto and zucchini	229	9	1	24	6.8
sautéed swiss chard	32	1.3	0.2	3.7	1.4
baked spaghetti squash	43	0.6	0.1	7.8	1.6
Almond Tart	338	12.8	7.1	52.7	2.6
Totals	829	32.6	9.9	106.8	20.5
Light Meal					
Thai Tofu Vegetable Stew	444	15.6	6.1	48.6	27.5
steamed rice	171	0.3	0.1	38.7	3.2
Oatmeal Power Cookie	145	1.5	1	30.9	2
Totals	760	17.4	7.2	118.2	32.7
Daily Totals	2276	59.1	19.3	361	68.4
Percent of Calories Daily Totals		23%	8%	63%	12%
Day 18					
Breakfast					
Chopra Granola	353	15.6	4.4	43.8	9.8
Apple Syrup	124	1.6	0.9	27.1	0.3
Strawberry Banana Yogurt	186	1.8	1.1	35.7	6.6
Totals	663	19	6.4	106.6	16.7
Main Meal					
Vegetable Hot and Sour Soup	148	4.8	0.2	16.1	10.1
Thai-Style Noodles with Tofu	414	9	0.5	64.3	18.9
Nutty Spinach Greens	80	4.6	1.1	6.1	3.4
Kim Chi Chutney	111	1.9	0.2	20.9	3.2
Double Almond Cookie	140	7.4	0.7	15.3	3.3
Totals	893	27.7	2.7	122.7	38.9
Light Meal					
Tofu, Eggplant, and Yukon Gold Stew	318	8.6	0.7	40.1	19.8
Green Quinoa Pilaf	287	5.8	0.9	40.6	18.1
sautéed pears with cardamom	175	3.5	1.9	34.9	1.1
Totals	780	17.9	3.5	115.6	39
Daily Totals	2336	64.6	12.6	344.9	94.6
Percent of Calories Daily Totals		25%	5%	59%	16%

	Calories	Total Fat (g)	Sat. Fat (g)	Carbs (g)	Protein (g)
Day 19					
Breakfast					
Simple Great Whole Grain					
Bread with Almond Butter	231	5.1	1	31.6	7
sautéed peaches and currants	144	2.9	1.9	28.2	1.6
Very Berry Yogurt	173	3	1.8	30.4	6.3
Totals	548	11	4.7	90.2	14.9
Main Meal					
Zucchini Tofu Bisque	142	3.5	1	17.9	9.8
Curry Filo Tarts	227	5.2	2.3	37.8	7.7
Cauliflower and Braised Tomato	116	2.8	1.1	16.6	6.2
Sweet Mixed Fruit Chutney	182	2.5	1.5	38.8	1
Mother Earth's Apple Pie	343	13.8	8.6	34.3	2.7
Totals	1010	27.8	14.5	145.4	27.4
Light Meal					
French lentil dahl	262	2.6	1.4	43.9	16
steamed rice	171	0.3	0.1	38.7	3.2
steamed carrots, broccoli,					
and zucchini	38	0.3	0	7	1.8
Cranberry Bliss Ball	232	14.4	2.3	21.5	4.1
Totals	703	17.6	3.8	111.1	25.1
Daily Totals	2261	56.4	23	346.7	67.4
Percent of Calories Daily Totals		22%	9%	61%	12%
Day 20					
Breakfast					
Toasted Millet Hot Cereal	424	4.9	1.3	83	12
Pear Syrup	166	3.2	1.9	34	0.5
Totals	590	8.1	3.2	117	12.5
Main Meal					
Spinach and Lentil Soup	319	3	1	55	17.7
Winter Vegetables with Couscous	352	14.6	3.8	43.9	11
zucchini, tomato, feta,					
and fresh dill	117	4.8	2.9	13	5.3
Walnut Chocolate Chip Cookie	148	6.9	1.9	17.3	3.6
Totals	936	29.3	9.6	129.2	37.6
Light Meal					
Curried Potatoes	399	11.2	6.1	64.4	10.3
Cucumber Raita	59	1.1	0.6	8	3.9
Organic Mixed Field Greens					
Salad with olive oil	88	6.2	0.7	5.5	2.4
Berry Tofu Sorbet	83	0.6	0	15.8	3.6
Totals	629	19.1	7.4	93.7	20.2
Daily Totals	2155	56.5	20.2	339.9	70.3
Percent of Calories Daily Totals		24%	8%	63%	13%

	Calories	Total Fat (g)	Sat. Fat (g)	Carbs (g)	Protein (g)
Day 21					
Breakfast					
Tempeh and Potato Hash	305	6.8	1.1	38.4	22.6
Tomato Salsa	39	1.6	0.9	5.3	0.9
Zucchini Pecan Bread	269	10.1	1.1	39	5.5
Totals	613	18.5	3.1	82.7	29
Main Meal					
Spinach Soup	112	2.9	1.1	15.2	6.3
Tuscany Bulgur Pilaf with stuffed acorn squash	326	6	1.3	55.1	13
Leek Sauce	43	1.7	0.9	4.1	2.8
braised carrots and fennel	55	1.4	0.9	8.8	1.6
Almond Tart	328	13	7.2	49.3	3.3
Totals	864	25	11.4	132.5	27
Light Meal					
Eggplant and Yam Curry	424	7.5	1.1	73.1	15.9
Greek Goddess Salad	262	6.1	0.9	42.8	9.5
Oatmeal Power Cookie	145	1.5	1	30.9	2
Totals	831	15.1	3	146.8	27.4
Daily Totals	2308	58.6	17.5	362	83.4
Percent of Calories Daily Totals		23%	7%	63%	14%
Day 22					
Breakfast					
Chai Bliss Shake	289	1.2	0.7	43.6	26
Seasonal Fruit Salad	142	0.8	0.2	32.4	1.1
Strawberry Banana Yogurt	186	1.8	1.1	35.7	6.6
Totals	617	3.8	2	111.7	33.7
Main Meal					
Very Simple Pumpkin Soup	172	3	0.4	23.8	12.2
Rainbow Risotto	328	2.8	0.4	55.8	19.7
sautéed spinach	28	1.4	0.9	2	1.7
steamed asparagus with lemon	44	0.3	0.1	7.4	3.2
Unbelievable Double Chocolate Cake	286	10.6	3.7	42.1	5.5
Totals	858	18.1	5.5	131.1	42.3
Light Meal					
Asian Clear Broth	158	6.5	0.4	11.6	13.3
Lettuce Wrap with two sauces	331	14.6	2.1	37.5	12
Peanut Butter Cookie	136	7.2	2.8	14.3	3.5
Totals	625	28.3	5.3	63.4	28.8
Daily Totals	2100	50.2	12.8	306.2	104.8
Percent of Calories Daily Totals		22%	5%	58%	20%

	Calories	Total Fat (g)	Sat. Fat (g)	Carbs (g)	Protein (g)
Day 23					
Breakfast					
Whole Wheat Crepes	248	11.1	2.2	26.8	10.2
Sweet Mixed Fruit Chutney	182	2.5	1.5	38.8	1
Strawberry Syrup	124	3.1	1.9	23.3	0.7
Totals	554	16.7	5.6	88.9	11.9
Main Meal					
Italian Vegetable Soup	268	2.1	0.4	46.3	15.9
Spinach Polenta	172	1.9	0.2	28	10.8
Roasted Tomato Sauce	147	5.5	1.5	20.8	3.6
Garden Salad with olive oil	92	6.4	0.8	6.4	2.3
Linzertorte Cookie	125	3.7	0.4	20.1	2.7
Totals	804	19.6	3.3	121.6	35.3
Light Meal					
Cajun Bean and Tempeh Stew	449	9.4	1.9	61.9	29.6
Steamed Rice	171	0.3	0.1	38.7	3.2
Steamed Broccoli	32	0.3	0	4.6	2.6
Apple Cinnamon Cake	351	5.5	1.2	71.2	3.9
Totals	1003	15.5	3.2	176.4	39.3
Daily Totals	2361	51.8	12.1	386.9	86.5
Percent of Calories Daily Totals		20%	5%	66%	15%
Day 24					
Breakfast					
Seasonal Fruit Salad	142	0.8	0.2	32.4	1.1
Apple Maple Yogurt	184	3.1	1.9	33	6.1
Totals	326	3.9	2.1	65.4	7.2
Main Meal					
Tortilla Soup with Avocado and Cilantro	347	14.7	1.8	32.6	21.1
Mexican Tofu Stew	256	8.1	0.2	21	24.2
Spicy Mexican Rice	485	4.5	1.3	86.7	24.6
steamed yellow and zucchini squash	28	0.3	0	4.8	1.6
Apricot Pecan Cookie	125	3.7	0.4	20.1	2.7
Totals	1241	31.3	3.7	165.2	74.2
Light Meal					
Vegetable Hummus Wrap	320	7.6	1.5	51.3	11.5
Apple Cobbler	386	11.2	1.5	64.7	6.8
Totals	706	18.8	3	116	18.3
Daily Totals	2273	54	8.8	346.6	99.7
Percent of Calories Daily Totals		21%	3%	61%	18%

	Calories	Total Fat (g)	Sat Fat (g)	Carbs (g)	Protein (g)
Day 25					
Breakfast					
Couscous Hot Cereal	289	1.1	0.7	60.4	9.3
sautéed apples and blackberries	149	1.6	0.3	30.8	2.7
Totals	438	2.7	1	91.2	12
Main Meal					
Cuban Black Bean and Sweet Potato Soup	294	2.6	0.1	53.7	14
French Vegetable Stew	145	2.1	0.2	24.1	7.7
Oat Groat Pilaf with Spinach	218	3.1	1	40.6	7
Dilled Asparagus	49	0.4	0.1	6.1	5.2
Chocolate Tofu Mousse with Walnut Coconut Praline	169	8.7	5.5	19.1	3.9
Totals	875	16.9	6.9	143.6	37.8
Light Meal					
Spinach and Lentil Soup	319	3	1	55	17.7
Cashew Tempeh	269	11.3	3	25.3	16.8
Coconut Cookie	126	6.3	4.3	15.5	1.5
Totals	714	20.6	8.3	95.8	36
Daily Total	2027	40.2	16.2	330.6	85.8
Percent of Calories Daily Totals		18%	7%	65%	17%
Day 26					
Breakfast					
Coffee Bliss Shake	194	1	0.6	44.2	2.1
Cardamom Whole Wheat Pancakes	333	10.4	5.8	50.7	9.1
fresh blueberries and sliced bananas	80	0.4	0.1	18.4	0.8
Totals	607	11.8	6.5	113.3	12
Main Meal					
Nutty Broccoli Soup	187	8.9	1.5	18.6	8.1
Tuscany Bulgur Pilaf	304	6	1.3	49.8	12.6
roasted sweet potatoes	93	1.5	0.9	18	2
steamed yellow and zucchini squash	28	0.3	0	4.8	1.6
Apple Custard Pie	336	13.1	7.8	49.9	4.5
Totals	948	29.8	11.5	141.1	28.8
Light Meal					
Vegetable White Bean Chili	364	4.2	0.5	53.2	28
sautéed spinach	28	1.4	0.9	2	1.7
Traditional Chocolate Chip Cookie	180	9.3	5.7	22.1	1.8
Totals	572	14.9	7.1	77.3	31.5
Daily Totals	2127	56.5	25.1	331.7	72.3
Percent of Calories Daily Totals		24%	11%	62%	14%

	Calories	Total Fat (g)	Sat. Fat (g)	Carbs (g)	Protein (g)
Day 27					
Breakfast					
Country Potatoes	180	3.8	0.5	32.5	4
Krazy Ketchup	134	1.9	1	25	4.2
Traditional French Toast	277	8	3	39.2	11.9
Strawberry Syrup	124	3.1	1.9	23.3	0.7
Totals	715	16.8	6.4	120	20.8
Main Meal					
Vegetable Barley Soup	280	4	0.4	38.8	22.5
Simple Whole Grain Pizza with roasted tomato and spinach	171	2.2	7	27.3	6
steamed carrots and green beans	55	0.6	0.1	10.8	1.7
Traditional Awesome Brownie	265	12.4	5.8	32.8	5.3
Totals	771	19.2	13.3	109.7	35.5
Light Meal					
Butternut Squash Soup	123	2.9	1.1	20	4.3
Eggless Tofu Salad on Simple Great Whole Grain Bread	461	8.3	0.8	70.5	26.7
Oatmeal Power Cookie	145	1.5	1	30.9	2
Totals	729	12.7	2.9	121.4	33
Daily Totals	2215	48.7	22.6	351.1	89.3
Percent of Calories Daily Totals		20%	9%	63%	16%
Day 28					
Breakfast					
Morning Bliss Shake	424	6.8	2.8	61.3	29.8
Pumpkin Muffin	200	3.7	0.6	37.7	3.7
Totals	624	10.5	3.4	99	33.5
Main Meal					
yellow split pea dahl	262	2.6	1.4	43.9	16
Tofu Burger with Leek Sauce	304	12.1	1.6	28.2	20.3
steamed rice	171	0.3	0.1	38.7	3.2
steamed broccoli, carrots, and zucchini	38	0.3	0	7	1.8
sautéed strawberries with cinnamon	114	3.3	1.9	20	1.3
Totals	889	18.6	5	137.8	42.6
Light Meal					
Thai Tofu Vegetable Stew	444	15.6	6.1	48.6	27.5
Kabocha Pumpkin Pie	291	13.4	7.7	37.5	4.9
Totals	735	29	13.8	86.1	32.4
Daily Totals	2248	58.1	22.2	322.9	108.5
Percent of Calories Daily Totals		23%	9%	57%	19%

	Calories	Total Fat (g)	Sat Fat (g)	Carbs (g)	Protein (g)
Day 29					
Breakfast					
Nutty French Toast	360	15.3	4	43	12.5
Nectarine and Blueberry Syrup	145	3.1	1.9	28.5	0.8
Totals	505	18.4	5.9	71.5	13.3
Main Meal					
Sweet Potato Ginger Soup	247	2.9	0.3	50.5	5
Buddha's Delight Vegetable Stir-Fry with Tofu Cubes	272	10.5	1	28	28.3
Chinese Five-Spice Garden Pilaf	225	1	0.1	49.1	5.5
Lemon Birthday Cake	288	6.1	0.5	54.2	4.1
Totals	1032	20.5	1.9	181.8	42.9
Light Meal					
Roasted Eggplant and Spinach Pasta with Beans	395	7.6	2.1	64.9	16.9
Organic Mixed Field Greens Salad with olive oil	88	6.2	0.7	5.5	2.4
sautéed mango and blueberries	223	3.5	2.1	45.9	2.1
Totals	706	17.3	4.9	116.3	21.4
Daily Totals	2243	56.2	12.7	369.6	77.6
Percent of Calories Daily Totals		23%	5%	66%	14%
Day 30					
Breakfast					
Polenta Hot Cereal	221	2.3	0.8	45.4	4.7
Apple Syrup	124	1.6	0.9	27.1	0.3
Cinnamon Roll	149	3.9	1.5	24.8	3.6
Totals	494	7.8	3.2	97.3	8.6
Main Meal					
Summertime Tomato Basil Soup	257	4.2	0.5	37.5	17.1
Mediterranean Pasta	269	4	0.9	47.8	10.3
roasted butternut squash rings	47	1.4	0.9	7	1.7
braised fennel, beans, and almonds	65	1.4	0.9	6.2	5.9
poached peaches with blackberry sauce	147	2.9	1.9	29.3	0.9
Totals	785	13.9	5.1	127.8	35.9
Light Meal					
Very Simple Pumpkin Soup	172	3	0.4	23.8	12.2
Marinated Tofu Thai Wrap with Nutty Dipping Sauce	395	15.8	2.3	43.4	19.4
Double Delight Cookie	203	10.3	4.7	24.6	2.7
Totals	770	29.1	7.4	91.8	34.3
Daily Totals	2049	50.8	15.7	316.9	78.8
Percent of Calories Daily Totals		22%	7%	62%	15%

Index

chutney
apple leek, 226–227
kim chi, 237
orange pear, 242
Russian borscht, 246
sweet mixed fruit, 248
cilantro
mint sauce, 231
pecan sauce, 232
tortilla soup with avocado and, 164–165
cinnamon rolls, 84–85
cobbler, apple, 256–257
coconut cookies, 268
condiments
basic, to keep on hand, 23–24
with pure ingredients, usage of, 23
sauces, and finishing touches, 224
cookies
apricot pecan, 260
cardamom butter, 265
chocolate chip, traditional, 284
coconut, 268
double almond, 270
double delight, 271
ginger, 276
linzertorte, 280
oatmeal power, 281
peanut butter, 282
walnut chocolate chip, 286
couscous with winter vegetables, 140–141
cranberry bliss balls, 269
crepes, sweet or savory whole wheat, 103
cucumber raita, 233
curry
chickpea stew, 175
eggplant and yam, 180–181
eggplant cauliflower, 118–119
filo tarts, 111
paste, 45
potatoes, 206–207

dahl, 44. See also soup; stock
desserts, 251–252
eating small portions of, 27
helpful pointers for, 252
detoxification, of kitchen, 19–20
diet
average Western, 6
Ayurvedic approach to, 25. See also
Ayurveda

health problems related to, 15–16
health value of vegetarian, 25
importance of fresh and natural foods
in, 24–25
negative aspects of crash, 12–13
promotion of renewal through, 12
recommendation for nutritional program, 24
digestion, 2
food that stimulates, 11
relationship of pungency to, 11. See also
pungency
dilled asparagus, 208
dilled lemon zucchini, 209

edamame (fresh soybeans), 56. See also
soy
eggplant
cauliflower curry, 118–119
roasted, and spinach pasta with beans,
124–125
tapenade, 234
tofu and Yukon gold stew, 192–193
and yam curry, 180–181
egg roll, Szechwan baked, 130–131
energy, vii–viii
component of food, 2
gleaning, from Mother Earth, 17
entrées, 107
general outline for a day's, 109
helpful pointers for, 108–109
environment
as component of nourishment, 16
creating a nurturing, 16–18
minimizing chaos in, 10
exercise, importance of, 13

fajitas, tofu, tempeh, or chicken, 136–137
filo tarts, curry, 111
fish
addition of, 25
with garden salad, 217
grilled, Greek goddess salad with,
210–211
marinated
braised with mango tomato salsa,
112–113
Thai wrap with nutty dipping sauce,
202

fish *(continued)*
    Mediterranean pasta sauce over, 117
    Moroccan vegetables with freshwater
      bass, 121
    ratatouille stew with marinated and
      grilled, 186–187
    roasted eggplant and spinach pasta
      with, 124–125
    in tortilla soup with avocado and
      cilantro, 164–165
    with vegetable hot and sour soup,
      168–169
flavonoids, 12, 14
flavors, viii, 14
food, 24
    association of comfort with, 7
    astringent, 12
    bitter, 11
    confusion regarding, 2–3
    eating wide variety of, 6–7
    energy component of, 2
    as energy of universe, viii
    favoring seasonal and local, 17
    flavors in. *See* flavors
    freshly prepared, 8–9, 20
    healing, ix
    hot. *See* food, pungent
    importance of healthy, 4, 5–6
    informational aspect of, 2
    natural and vital, 8–10
    nourishment of delicious, 8
    nurturing body and soul through, ix
    organic. *See* organic food
    preparing and eating delicious, 16
      healthful aspects of, 18
    pungent, 11
    relationship between spirit and, viii
    relationship of human body to, 1–2
    salty, 10
    seven simple precepts pertaining to, 6–10
    sour, 10
    sweet, 10
    that stimulates digestion, 11
    variety of choices regarding, 2–3
French toast
    nutty, 96
    traditional, 102
fruit
    about sautéeing, 48

astringent, 12
chutney, sweet mixed, 248
gaining visual and aromatic apprecia-
    tion of, 17
organic, 24. *See also* organic food
recommended servings of, 24, 28
sauté, simple, 49
syrup, simple frozen, 50
fruit salad, seasonal, 98

garden salad, 217
ghee, 38–39
ginger
    cookies, 276
    elixir, 41
    sweet potato soup, 161
    tea, 40
grains
    to keep in stock, 21–22
    purchasing, 21
granola, Chopra, 83
Greek goddess salad, 210–211
greens
    benefits and types of, 59
    salad, 217
      organic mixed field, 218
    simmered, 60
    spinach, nutty, 215

herbs, 9, 12
    growing indoor, 17
hummus, 236
    wrap, vegetable, 200
hunger, 7, 13, 27, 287. *See also* appetite;
    satiety

Indian rice, 214
isoflavones, 55
isothiocyanates, 12

kabocha squash pie, 272–273
ketchup, krazy, 238
kim chi chutney, 237
kitchen, detoxification of, 19–20

leek
    apple, chutney, 226–227
    sauce, 239
legumes
    list of staple, 22